# SUPERMAC

# SUPERMAC

## MY AUTOBIOGRAPHY

### MALCOLM MACDONALD

#### WITH COLIN MALAM

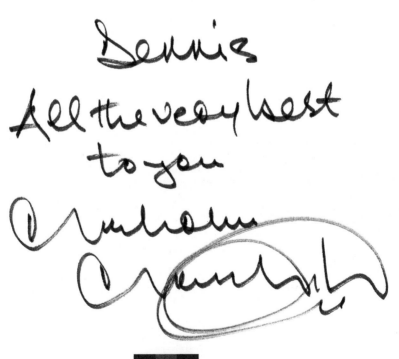

Dennis

All the very best
to you

Malcolm
Macdonald

highdown

## Dedication

To all the players I've played with and against who sought to make the
1970s a fabulous era in which to play football.


## Acknowledgments

I'd like to pay tribute to my mother, who, without a solitary moan, washed all my
dirty kit, sent me out spick and span and unceasingly continued that support
throughout. She also supplied a rare copy of my previous, 1983 autobiography,
written with the help of Jason Tomas, which provided a good starting point for this
one. Somebody else of great importance to me is my wife, Carol, who has stood by
me in turbulent times like a rock. Without her support, I don't know where I would
have been today. I want, too, to extend my gratitude to my collaborator this time,
Colin Malam. But for his perseverance, this book might never have been published.

I am also indebted to Highdown's Jonathan Taylor and Julian Brown for the
enthusiastic backing they have given the project. Finally, thanks are due to Eslyn Valles
for transcribing mountains of taped interviews at high speed and to Steve Preston for
his help in compiling most of the photographs that illustrate the book. Anyone
wishing to make use of the valuable service Steve can provide should contact him on
www.sportmemorabilia.co.uk.

Published in 2003 by Highdown,
an imprint of Raceform Ltd
Compton, Newbury, Berkshire, RG20 6NL
Raceform Ltd is a wholly-owned subsidiary of Trinity Mirror plc

A catalogue record for this book is available from the British Library.

ISBN 1-904317-34-0

Designed by Fiona Pike
Printed by CPD, Wales

# CONTENTS

# FOREWORD

I am delighted to have been given the opportunity to write this foreword for Malcolm.

Newcastle United and goal-scoring centre forwards have gone hand in hand from Jock Peddie in 1898, through the likes of Hughie Gallacher and Jackie Milburn to Alan Shearer in the present day; and Malcolm Macdonald emphatically belongs in that exalted company.

Strangely enough, I had a considerable part to play in Malcolm's rise to stardom. Back in 1968, when I was manager at Fulham, I paid the princely sum of £1,750 to non-league Tonbridge for Malcolm's services. He was a full back with Tonbridge but, together with my chief scout, Harry Haslam, we saw something in the bow-legged, brash, bustling youngster which led us to believe he could become a centre forward. And we weren't far wide of the mark were we!

With natural goalscoring instincts and a cannonball shot, he soon started banging in the goals – five in six games. It wasn't long before Harry, who had left his Craven Cottage post to join Luton Town as chief scout, persuaded Alec Stock to take Malcolm to Kenilworth Road, where his rich vein of form continued. Then, in the summer of 1971, Newcastle United manager Joe Harvey took the plunge whilst other managers dithered and paid big money for Malcolm. The rest, as they say, is history.

Malcolm's England career was perhaps somewhat unfulfilled, yielding only 14 caps and six goals. But who will forget that marvellous Wembley night in April 1975 when he led the line magnificently and banged in all five of England's goals against Cyprus?

In his younger days, Malcolm had boundless energy, oozed confidence and was blessed with an attribute essential to a striker wanting to make his mark in the game – pace. He had a one-track mindset – goals – and he would do anything he could to put the ball in the net. Excitement, rip-roaring action and pulsating football were certainly the name of the game when Malcolm was around and this book reflects that theme.

Sir Bobby Robson

# CHAPTER ONE
# PER ARDUA AD SUSSEX

I could not have had a better start in life. If belonging to a loving, caring family is the key to future happiness, my life ought to have been sunshine all the way. It did not work out quite like that, unfortunately, but the many downs I have experienced during more than half a century on this earth can certainly not be attributed to the early family life I enjoyed as a boy in Fulham and East Sussex. As I will explain in the ensuing pages, there were many reasons for the periods of unhappiness that have peppered my life and career; but the strength I found to get through them was undoubtedly attributable to the adversity that eventually overtook our happy family.

I was born in Fulham on 7 January 1950, the first of the four sons with whom the marriage of Charles Harold and Florence Kathleen Macdonald was to be blessed. My father was a Yorkshireman, born just outside Hull. He was an intelligent man, notable for a tremendously acute mathematical brain, and a bit of an oddity in those days because he went to a grammar school despite coming from a working-class background. My dad was also a keen sportsman. Short and stocky, he played both football and rugby and turned out for Hull City as an amateur at centre-half as well as centre-forward. He was a bit of a sprinter, too. In fact, he was so good at it that he ran in the Powderhall Sprint, the high-class event for professional athletes in Edinburgh, when there was still a distinction between amateurs and professionals in athletics. In other words, the Powderhall sprinters were openly running for prize money. There's no need, then, to wonder where I got my pace from, along with the broad shoulders and barrel chest that made me and my father so alike physically.

Unfortunately, he had to leave school at fifteen because his parents couldn't afford to keep him there, and he became an apprentice painter and decorator. Having completed his apprenticeship, he moved to Blyth in Northumberland, where his elder sister had married a policeman, and he got a job as a paint-sprayer in the local shipyards. While he was there, he kept up an active interest in football by playing for Blyth Spartans, one of the north-east's many famous amateur sides.

Incidentally, I've no idea how I came by my thoroughly Scottish name, Malcolm Ian Macdonald. I've often been asked about it, but can't give an answer. As I've said, my father was a Yorkshireman from the Hull area, and I haven't been able to trace the family tree back any further than him. I believe his family originated in Cumbria, just one step over the border from Scotland, but I don't know who he was descended from, never mind whether it was the mainland Macdonalds or those from the Isle of Skye.

When the Second World War started, my father joined the RAF. He wanted to be a fighter pilot, but they turned him down because his eyesight, though good, was not good enough. He became a wireless operator on a Catalina flying boat instead and spent most of the war years out in Ceylon with Canadians and New Zealanders. As a kid, I used to love listening to his war stories, although I had to work hard to get him to tell them because, like a lot of servicemen who were directly involved in the action, he was reluctant to talk about the dangerous situations he'd been in and the harrowing things he'd seen. He preferred to natter on about Ceylon and the friendships he'd formed with Canadians and New Zealanders. However, one melancholic evening when we were all sitting around the fire, I do remember him recounting a time when an American troop carrier was under attack by Japanese submarines and the Catalina set off in search of survivors. They arrived some time after the attack to find a sub on the surface, its deck completely covered with American soldiers. Relieved, the Catalina's crew sent back a report that all the survivors had been picked up, but then the sub dived below the surface with the soldiers still chained to the deck. On another occasion, Dad told me, quite matter-of-factly, about the day his Catalina was shot down over the Burmese jungle and they crash-landed right in the middle of swampland. Thankfully, he was with a Canadian crew, all of them six foot plus, West Atlantic hero types, and they saved him from drowning. Of course, to kids, war is glamorous; it's difficult for them to conceive of death because it doesn't happen in the comics. It's only now that I look back and think that I could so easily not have been here at all.

Dad's wartime experiences were not all doom and gloom though. I remember him telling me that he was told once at short notice to get his football boots out because there was a game to be played for the RAF. He played on the wing, I think, and playing at centre-forward in the same team was none other than Stan Mortensen, the bustling striker who starred for Blackpool and England alongside Stanley Matthews after the war. Dad then rattled off a whole list of players who were in the side and went on to make great names for themselves in the game.

My mother was born in Chelsea, one of nine children. Her Irish father died soon after the birth of the last child, and her mother had a hard time bringing them all up. She had to slave away all hours of the day, taking in other people's laundry and what have you, to keep the family together. When my mother left school at fourteen, she became an apprentice seamstress with one of the major dressmakers in Kensington. Then, when war broke out, she joined the Land Army. She was stationed at Wollaston in the southern part of Northamptonshire, and it was there that she met my father when he came back from the Far East. On his return, he had been stationed at a place in Northamptonshire that became the Santa Pod hot-rod racing track. They got married after the war, in 1946, at All Saints Church by Putney Bridge. He was 31, she was 25, and they were entirely different as people. There were no similarities of any kind between them, and strangely enough, I think it was that as much as anything that brought them so closely together.

Dad was a very outgoing type. He'd walk into a strange pub and within half an hour everyone would know his name. Mum was much more reserved. She had a very strict Roman Catholic upbringing, and was subject to all the restrictions the Catholic religion in those days tended to instil in people's minds. For example, my mother has since told me that it wasn't until she went into the Land Army that she began to acquire knowledge about sex, and she was seventeen by then. Dad, on the other hand, had no truck with religion at all, although he did send us to Sunday school for Mum's sake. Mum began to change a great deal when she started going out with Dad, to the point where she eventually turned her back on Catholicism and became much more broad-minded. Dad did much to widen her outlook on life, as did the Land Army. She met a couple of right old East End cockneys in there, and she has often said, 'I used to sit there with my knees tight together, as I had been taught by the nuns at school, listening to them effing and blinding!' I get the impression that during her first few months in the Land Army she went through utter mental shock. She couldn't believe that females like that existed. They would talk about their nights out with the soldiers from the camp, and what have you, and she was absolutely horrified by it all. So she went through this sudden mind-broadening process, and became close with the manager of the farm, and the farm workers' families, where she was based.

One Boxing Day, about 25 years ago, I arranged for her to visit all of them. She didn't know I'd done it. I just said, 'Come on, Mum, let's go for a drive.' I started driving up Wollaston way, and she said, 'Good Lord, do you realise where we are? That's where we used to go on Saturday nights for the dance... we used to cycle along here...' The memories were tumbling out of her. I asked her where she used to stay, and she started to mention all the names of the people we were going to see. They were all there to greet her when we arrived. We had a glass of sherry with them. I just sat in a corner, watching my mother being taken back 35 years or so to the turning-point of her life, to the stage where she reached maturity. It was fascinating to learn so much about a part of her life that had been only fragmentary in my mind, and to get a much fuller knowledge of her life before I was born. From there, we went to another house to see somebody who was in the Land Army with her. It was one of those East End girls – Rose, her name was – who had married a local lad and settled in the area. She was about 60, I suppose, and she was an absolute scream. She still managed to shock my mother with some of the things she said! But she had me in fits – so much so that afterwards my stomach ached from laughing.

When my parents got married, Dad took Mum back to Hull, but she couldn't settle there at all. Being a Londoner, she couldn't understand what people were saying, for a start. Nor could she understand their way of life. I don't know if it's changed over the years, but up there all the blokes used to go out to the social club, or somewhere like that, on a Saturday night. Then they would repeat the exercise at Sunday lunchtime, and on Sunday night. That wasn't for my mother at all. Dad's was an exceptionally close family too, and she felt something of an outsider, although she realised afterwards that she hadn't really worked hard enough to become part of it. All in all, she experienced quite a few problems. Yorkshire people look upon Londoners as being cold, but I know some of them to be shy and backward, believe it or not, in coming forward. My mother was of that type, and I would think she was a great disappointment to all of my Dad's family in Yorkshire.

Although my mother is a strong-willed character who will dig her heels in over anything she feels strongly about, it was my father who actually instigated the move back to London after about two years in Hull. I don't think he really wanted to leave, but he could see how unhappy my mother was, and being much the more adaptable of the two he wasn't a man to make a big issue of things like that. He found a job as a painter with Fulham Borough Council, and they lived on the Fulham Palace Road, above a newsagent's. Within three years they had moved to 33 Finlay Street, which is just a stone's throw from Craven Cottage, Fulham FC's famous old ground. Initially, they went into part ownership with one of my mother's older sisters, Gladys, and her husband, Jack. But then those two had to move to the coast, to Lancing in Sussex, because their son, John, had terrible asthma problems. My father bought the rest of the house from them, but as he couldn't afford it on the money he was getting from the council, he started his own painting and decorating business. He did a lot of exhibition stand work, and at one point employed about twelve people. He'd have to go away now and again, and I remember that he was forever up the road at Earls Court. Companies would suddenly phone him up and say they'd been let down and needed an exhibition stand ready in three days. Then, when he got there, he'd find it was about six days' work to do it! He also decorated a lot of the 'blue-blood' houses in Kensington and Chelsea.

For me, it was great to be brought up in the 1950s and 1960s. In the 1950s you could still sense the camaraderie that had existed during the war. I can just about remember rationing, particularly of sugar and sweets, and the atmosphere was one of people rebuilding not only houses and towns, but their own lives. Not only that, but I was fortunate enough to have two parents who always had time for their children, time to sit down with them and communicate with them. That's the clearest memory I have of my childhood. My mother and father were devoted to each other and would sit talking for hours and hours. As I got older, I also started to take part in all this. I think I was about ten when we got our first television, and for a fortnight it was quite a novelty. But then it wore off, and the TV would never go on. I know it must be hard to imagine now, but most evenings we would all just settle down in front of the fire together and discuss anything – religion, politics, you name it.

By then, I had two brothers, David and Neil. David, the second son, is two and a half years younger than me. He's married with four daughters and lives in Forest Row, the same Sussex village as my mother and the one we eventually moved to as a family from Fulham. David has worked in the construction industry all his life and is hugely talented. Unfortunately, he's never put that talent to best use. His forte was swimming, and he swims like a fish, but he never persevered with that. Instead, he preferred to seek to emulate me on the football field, and that was never on. I think it all goes back to childhood, when little brothers want to do what their big brothers do. That said, David, who was a defender, carried on playing longer than any of us. He was 44 or 45 when he finally hung up his boots.

Neil, who is six years younger than David, is a solicitor and lives in Essex. He went through school, college and university in London to get his law degree and helped to fund himself by playing as a part-time pro, as a midfielder, for Hornchurch and Romford. After Neil had graduated, I introduced him to Alan Hurd, Ian Botham's lawyer, and Alan invited him to join his firm. Neil made the licensed trade his field of expertise and now has his own practice specifically designed to cater for that section of the food and drink industry. Divorced and living with a partner, he has one daughter from his marriage and another from his current relationship.

Several more years after Neil's birth we were joined by James, the youngest son. Like Neil, James has inherited our mother's height. He stands six foot two inches in his stockinged feet and weighs eighteen stone. His weight varies because as a child he had breathing problems and was put on steroids. That played havoc with his weight, but it has hardly held him back. He is now the European sales manager for Lego, for one thing. After taking a business studies course at college, James joined Filofax and was pretty much responsible for making their business a big success. From there, he went to Loctite, the glue company, and then on to Lego, who have the licence to sell Harry Potter merchandise. In his spare time, James also referees at county league level in Sussex, where he lives. A centre-half in his playing days, he decided to retire early from the game to take the referees' course. A long time ago he became a grade two referee, and I think he was running the line in the London Combination. He thoroughly enjoys it. In fact, I think he gets more enjoyment out of being a referee than he ever did as a player. As you can imagine, at six foot two and eighteen stone, he gets no problems on the football field. But because he's an asthmatic, the last few seasons have seen him really struggle in the annual fitness tests referees must pass. Sometimes he's not made it first time, but got straight through at the second attempt.

My brothers are all strong lads. Put us together, and believe me, people behave themselves around us. We've even been known to come to blows with one another. I suppose I'm closer to Neil than to the others. We are very similar as people and get on exceptionally well. But that never stopped the fists flying between us. Neil has a habit, when he's had a few drinks, of poking people in the chest, and I can't stand that. He did it to me once while he was telling me something in Mum's kitchen, and I saw red. I just landed him one on the chin. He responded by saying, 'You've hit me!' and then sticking a right-hander on my nose.

Then we looked at each other, laughed and finished up joking about it over a large brandy.

My greatest thrill as a kid was playing football in Bishop's Park, next door to Craven Cottage. To this day, my mother says that during the school holidays I'd be out of the door first thing and she wouldn't see me until dark. Crazy about the game from the start, I was always up the park playing football. We were there so much that the park keepers could only grit their teeth and grin and bear it.

The hardest thing, as I recall, was just finding someone who had a ball that was good enough to play with. Whoever did have one, by God, he was king for the day. It would start off with maybe three or four a side, but as the day went on and more and more kids came along, it would always expand. And in those days we had a tremendous ability to organise ourselves. We had an imagination. Once we'd got a ball, we were off and running and the games would just grow and grow. In the end, there would be so many kids playing that you very quickly learnt valuable skills. You'd get the ball and you didn't dare lose it, otherwise you wouldn't see it again for heaven knows how long. It's where you learnt that your first touch was invaluable to you. Passing had to be spot-on too, and dribbling became an art. I was fortunate: Jackie Milburn used to talk of playing in back lanes in Ashington, but I had a park just 50 yards up the road, and if that one was closed there was a choice of about three others. David would tag along every now and again and try to persuade me to go to the swimming baths, and I would enjoy doing that once in a blue moon. But I was never, ever a water kid.

There used to be a great spirit then among kids. There was the usual troublemaking/hooligan element, but we used to ignore them. We were too great in numbers for them if they tried to have any effect on us, so we were pretty much left to get on with what we wanted to do. We had a huge sense of fairness about it all too. As the number of players grew, we would always chop and change the teams to keep them evenly matched and the game tight. If one side started to get too far ahead, the two captains would agree to swap two weaker players, say, for two stronger ones.

My father took me to see my first professional game when I was four. We went to watch Blackburn play Fulham at Craven Cottage.

There would have been the usual 26,000 there, because back in the 1950s it was boom time for football. People wanted the relaxation, the excitement and the entertainment of a football match after all the suffering and deprivation of the war years. I went regularly to Craven Cottage after that. I pestered my father to take me. I just wanted to keep going. I loved the buzz of it, the whole thing. I used to study players, and my father was a great one for talking to me about it. He would sit there and say, 'Come on, son, you tell me. What did you see in that game? Who were the good players, who had a good game?' It's amazing what you learn that way.

The first professional footballer to really make an impact on me was Blackburn's England international Bryan Douglas. I met him during the 2002/03 season for the first time, and it was a great honour for me. What a good little player he was. Just like Tom Finney, he could play outside-right, outside-left or go through the middle. But then, pretty soon afterwards, a young man came into the Fulham side and, wow, he was the best thing I've ever seen on a football field. His name was Johnny Haynes. He'd get the ball in the middle of the field and his left arm would go up. Then he would just spin around on the ball until he'd got the right angle and half a yard of space and he would ping it. He'd knock it 50 yards, and his pinpoint passes would see one of the two wingers through to cross the ball. It was all marvellous stuff. Haynes just fascinated me. He was quite phenomenal. He could run all day, he was so incredibly fit, and he still looks athletic today. People would talk of Bobby Charlton, who was another youngster emerging then, but for me it was Haynesie.

My father, having taken me to see Fulham when I was four, then introduced me to Chelsea FC. They were always home and away on the same day, of course, because they were the alternating clubs in west London. I would certainly go to watch my beloved Fulham every other Saturday, but I would also get to as many Chelsea games as I possibly could. I discovered every way to 'bunk' into the two grounds. As a result, when I became Fulham manager about twenty years later I blocked up all the 'bunking-in' holes because, to my amazement, they were still there. I took the stadium manager around the ground and said, 'I'll show you where all the kids get in for free.' It was a bit of a mean-spirited thing to do, I suppose, but our attendances were down to three and a half thousand and we were absolutely desperate for money.

When I think back now to the risks we took as kids to bunk in at the two grounds, my blood runs cold. At Stamford Bridge, you had to go over the railway lines, the London Underground lines, and hop over about six live electric rails. There'd be four or five of us and we'd just go hopping happily over all the rails. After that, there was one particular bar in the railings that you could pull out. The gap was just wide enough for a kid to squeeze through, and you were in. It was not a lot easier to get in for nothing at Craven Cottage, either. You might have risked electrocution at Chelsea, but drowning was the threat at Fulham because you had to go along the bank of the Thames to find a way in.

Risk-taking of that kind was all part of the fun back then, of course, but my semi-idyllic existence, and that of my family, was rudely shattered when my father, at only 48, had a massive coronary, followed two weeks later by a cardiac arrest. I remember it all vividly. Dad, having come in late from work, had gone to get washed and changed. He then went out to the toilet – we had an outside loo – and he must have been in there for more than half an hour before any of us realised something might be wrong. It was a good thing I was there to help my mother and my Aunt Connie, who had come round to see her, because he was just slumped in the toilet and we had to break down the door.

That was the beginning of one of the most difficult but most character-building periods of my life. Dad was in hospital for months and months, and it was quite a struggle for us to survive. His business collapsed because obviously he couldn't give his men any work, and we had to live on the sickness benefit my mother received. So I did paper rounds, weekend jobs, greengrocery deliveries, butchery deliveries – anything to help out financially. I started working for WHSmith at Putney Bridge station, and had to be there at five o'clock in the morning to do the marking-up of newspapers to be delivered by their eight paper boys. That usually took me two hours, and then I had a paper round to do myself after that. Each lad had one day off a week, so after doing my round I'd come back and do the relief round; then, if somebody failed to show up, I'd do their round as well. I also did the evening rounds, by the way!

The trouble was, I was then in my second year at Sloane Grammar School, opposite the Chelsea ground, and I was always late for school. It meant I was forever in detention on a Friday because the school authorities were rather unsympathetic towards family problems, and the fact that I had worked for a number of hours before going to school didn't really matter to them. As far as they were concerned, I was required by law to be at school by nine a.m., and that was that. So I got punished every week. It became part of my life, so much so that after a while I took it for granted that my name had been put down for detention and didn't even bother checking.

One job they couldn't punish me for doing was during the weekend. All day Saturday and all day Sunday I worked in Bishop's Park for an ice-cream seller called Marie. She had a wagon, a kind of hand-pulled cart like an old milk float, and I used to travel back and forth to the factory on my bike to get ice-cream for her. I'd actually started working for her from the age of eleven. Then, when I was twelve and my father became ill, things got progressively worse and it was a question of having to go out and do it. I think we coped very well in the circumstances, actually. Having experienced the war years, my mother had already become an expert at making something out of nothing, especially when it came to cooking.

When my father eventually came out of hospital, he was a semi-invalid for a long time. He tried to go back to painting and decorating, but it was too much for him, so he was forced to take an office job at the Pitman School of English in Goodge Street. That meant travelling into the West End, the centre of the city, every day standing on a crowded Tube train, and we could see him just slowly wasting away. He had five heart attacks during this period and was forever in and out of hospital.

The situation certainly brought us all very much closer together. We were a close unit to begin with, but we became even closer now. In particular, I'll never forget the closeness I had with my mother at this time. The lovely thing for Mum was that here she was with her first son and she was able to give him the instructions about life – the advice, the knowledge, the comfort – that she had never had herself because of her family's Catholicism. She would talk quite openly about her pre- and post-marital relationship with Dad; it was a very natural, uninhibited mother–son relationship. We could talk about anything, sex included. There was no silly giggling or anything like that. It was all very matter of fact.

Prior to Dad's final, fatal deterioration, he'd realised there was no way he could work to support the family, so he decided to put his business acumen to work. His body was pretty useless, he reasoned, but he still had his brain. 'Even if I'm going to spend my life in a wheelchair, I can still make myself useful,' he said. 'What we will do is get a little tobacconist and confectioner's shop. I can handle all the book-work, I can do all the ordering and I can serve, too. I can do a lot in a wheelchair.' So the house was put on the market – it was sold for £6,750 – and he went in search of the kind of business he could cope with. He and Mum looked at a number of shops in and around London, but eventually came to the conclusion that it might be better to get out into the country, where everybody worked at a slower pace and where his physical limitations might be more acceptable. He was a realist right to the end, my dad; he had no dreams about life at all. Oh yes, a very practical man my dad was. They finally decided on a small shop in the Sussex village of Forest Row, near East Grinstead, on a parade just opposite the village church. Cars could be parked in front of the shop, and Dad reasoned that if people could park, they'd pop in. In addition, it was situated on the main A22 road between London and Eastbourne, so there was bound to be a considerable flow of traffic, especially at weekends.

I had left school by then. I had been due to take O-levels, but I went out to work instead, partly because I wanted to become a professional footballer (of which more later) and partly to help the family out financially. I started with Alec Brooke Ltd, a sports shop and clothing place at King's Cross. I was putting hardly any money into the home, but at least I was paying my way. When the plans for our move to Sussex were being finalised, I finished working there and spent a few months helping out a plumber who lived in Finlay Street whose wife had become friendly with my mother. It was hard work. He was self-employed and worked all the hours God sent, just as my Dad had done over the years, but I thoroughly enjoyed working with him. He was a

Communist, which made for some very interesting discussions. I just couldn't understand how a self-employed man, a man with his own business, could be a Communist. 'You're only holding yourself back,' I'd say. 'You've got to have democracy.' We used to go into a café for lunch, and while all the other workmen there would be discussing what had happened in the pub the previous night, or boasting about their latest sortie on the female front, we'd talk politics! Although I had a certain sympathy with his views, he did as much as anyone to form my own political opinions, which were in direct opposition to his.

Towards the end of 1966 it was becoming increasingly obvious that Dad didn't have long to live. It was four years since the initial coronary, but now he went into hospital for another spell suffering from a steady deterioration of a great number of other organs. The doctor took my mother aside and said, 'You obviously realise that this will be his last Christmas. There's not a lot of damage he can do to himself, so we are going to let him spend it at home.' The ambulance brought him back on Christmas Eve, and he was literally stretchered into the house and laid on the settee in our living-room, just a shadow of his former self.

That night he struggled for breath, and we got up on Christmas Day to find him in a coma. We called for an ambulance, and it took him back to the hospital, where he died later that morning. My mother had gone in the ambulance with my father, so I organised my three brothers, locked the house up and took them round to my Aunt Connie's. She'd never had kids of her own, but she and her husband, Dennis, had been superb to us, especially over the years Dad had been ill. I remember that Uncle Dennis once took us off to a pub, the Telegraph on Putney Common, and we stood outside, chatting over a drink. Dennis was a tremendously kind-hearted man. Although very much an introvert, he kept us all talking and thinking about anything but what was going on at the hospital.

We had Christmas lunch, and then, at about three p.m., my mother came in. She was so cheerful we thought things were not as bad as they had appeared. It was ten o'clock when we got home, and after getting the two younger lads, Neil and James, to bed, Mum called David and me into the sitting-room. 'Your father died late this morning,' she told us, quite calmly. 'I know you are going to be upset, but he went very peacefully – he didn't suffer. I'm not going to tell the younger ones and spoil their Christmas, and I would expect you to do the same.' It wasn't until about three days later that we told them. We couldn't keep it from them any longer because the funeral was scheduled for the next day.

The strength my mother showed that Christmas Day was amazing. She fought back every kind of emotion so as not to spoil the festivities, and she kept it going even up to the moment we arrived at the crematorium. When we got into the chapel, I put my arm around her and said, 'Come on, Mum, let it out.' And she did. Nor shall I ever forget what happened later that day, when we had a few relatives and friends back to the house for a sherry. She took me aside and said, 'I now realise that you are old enough and man enough to do what we've got ahead of us, and that has given me a great deal of confidence.' I didn't really understand at the time what she was saying. All I was thinking was, 'What else is a son for if he can't comfort his mother in times of stress?' What I'd done was just a natural reaction on my part, but she'd read much more into it.

It was from that point on that she became a very resolute woman and I became a very resolute young man. We certainly needed all the determination we could muster because we were due to move out of the Finlay Street house at the end of January 1967, and here we were in a situation where my mother had sons of seventeen (just), fourteen, eight and four to bring up, plus a business to run for the first time in her life. All the house and shop contracts had been signed and the solicitor made it clear to my mother when she enquired that there was no getting out of them.

The removal van was due to come on Monday, 29 January, but the shop stocktakers had advised us to take the shop over on the Sunday. My mother said she couldn't go because she had to empty the house and get ready for the removal people, so I arranged to meet the stocktakers at Kennington station at 7.30 on the Sunday morning and travelled down to Forest Row in their car. To be honest, I hadn't a clue what was going on. I didn't even know what a stocktaker was! But my father had always told me, 'If you don't know, son, ask.' So I sat in this car saying, 'What about this, what about that?' A thousand and one questions. The whole situation must have seemed ridiculous to them:

a young lad just turned seventeen, just about shaving only once a week, taking a business over. But the guy who had been running the shop was very good to me. He explained as much as he could, as simply as possible. He gave me a tremendous amount of advice, although I had been crammed with so much information I think I forgot half of it.

It was arranged that the previous owner would stay with me until Monday lunchtime. From then on, I'd be on my own. On the Sunday morning, I wrote down all the prices. There were thousands of small items, none of them marked with a price, and you had to memorise them all. Later, the guy told me about the weighing scales and pointed out that the Weights and Measures people would come round every quarter to check them. 'Always go a fraction over the amount,' he advised, 'just in case the scales are weighing a bit under.' Then he gave me a run-down on what sold well and what didn't, went through the list of reps, etc., etc.

That Sunday night, when I booked into a hotel in East Grinstead, my head was spinning. The next morning I opened the shop and had been working for two hours by the time the guy came in at about ten o'clock. I didn't know what I was doing either. I had people coming in and saying, 'Twenty Park Drive, please,' and I'd say, 'Do you know where they are and how much they cost?' Still, we had a bit of a laugh and I got to know the customers that way. It's always surprising how people can appreciate your difficulties and club together to help you out. And a lot of people helped us out that day.

The lives of my mother and her children could not have changed more dramatically. Previously, the family had gathered around the dining table or in the living-room in Finlay Street, where we would play Monopoly or Scrabble, or listen to the radio or talk. Now it was the shop, the business, that our lives revolved around. It was two people, mother and eldest son, who didn't know what the hell they were doing, rolling up their sleeves and saying, 'We've got a family to keep together, and we are going to do it.' That was the spirit I saw beginning to emanate from my mother that fateful Christmas Day.

You'd do anything sometimes to be able to turn back the clock and change things, but they happen and you get on with it. Rather than be disaffected, you allow it only to affect you for the good. Then, I think, as time goes on, life gets an awful lot easier. Modern society certainly shows a lack of discipline. I suppose I've become more old-fashioned in my way of thinking – I'll be accused of being an old fogey, I'm sure – but there was a discipline created then by what our family went through. You either knuckled down or things went bust.

I would open up the shop in the morning, then my mother would come in later so that I could go and check the stock and work out orders for whichever reps were coming in that particular day. It was all a big headache to begin with, the books especially. I had never seen a business accounts book before in my life and I made a lot of mistakes, but eventually we got it together and I became quite a good book-keeper in the end, even if I do say so myself.

All these experiences made me think about how ridiculous our schooling is. At the age of seventeen, I was having to deal with solicitors, bank managers, accountants, the Inland Revenue, all the professional people we need in our lives. The only people I wasn't dealing with was the building society, because the property was rented. At school they never teach you – at least, not when I was at school – how these people function and what they can do for you.

Provided the shop turned over the same amount of money as before, we knew our family could live on the income from the business. What we didn't know was that the previous owner had got out just before a rent review was due. As a result of it the rent was doubled, then the rates started to go up (along with all the other expenses), and all of a sudden we had to start doubling the trade. I'd spend days trying to dress up the window so it would attract people into the shop. We added new lines to our stock, opened all day Sunday for the passing trade, and did everything in our power to make a go of it. But without any great success. The shop kept the family alive, but that was about it. My mother was never able to put a penny away in savings, and it was just one big battle to stay solvent. I used to take out a fiver a week for myself and my mother would take £40 to cover food and everything else. That was what we slogged away for from 7.30 in the morning to nine at night, £45 a week. My mother struggled with that business for years without ever being able to say she'd achieved anything other than the survival of her family.

The shop had been bought in 1966 for £3,200, I believe, and it was sold in 1974 for only £3,500. The last straw for my mother had come when the landlord decided to alter the whole structure of the premises. This involved extensive rebuilding of the living accommodation and meant that my mother had to live in terrible conditions for months while all the work was going on. Finally, after she'd suffered all this discomfort, he doubled the rent again. 'That's it,' she said. 'There's no way I can afford to live here any more.' By that time I was playing for Newcastle and earning some decent money as a professional footballer, so I suggested she start working for me, which she did until I ceased to be manager of Fulham ten years later. I suppose you could have called her my personal assistant. She kept tabs on all the things that come along in football, such as fan mail, sponsorships, media interviews, diary engagements and so on. Mum used the money she got for the shop to pay off various debts – VAT, income tax, etc. – and had just enough left for a deposit on a house, but she needed to pay the mortgage, rates and household bills, and that's where the weekly wage I paid her came in. I suppose you could say I bought her the house that way. At no time did she like it, because she was always one to stand on her own two feet, but it was a victory for common sense. It was necessary for her to have some income, and her time was still very much tied up in looking after Neil and James, who were still at school and whose education was vitally important. As I have already mentioned, both went on to get very good jobs, so I feel the financial arrangement my mother and I came to proved to be fully justified. It certainly enabled her to take an enormous amount of pressure off the two boys.

In the end, then, it was something of a success story for Mum. This might sound a rather callous thing to say, but I sometimes wonder whether things would have turned out so well for us lads if my father had remained alive. To some extent, we all found a certain strength and self-confidence in the adversity we experienced, and I feel that has stood us in good stead in our adult lives. I definitely think that's true in my case.

I would add just one other thing. For most of my adult life, my father's death has been a shadow hanging over me. Because he suffered from such serious heart trouble, whenever I've tried to get life insurance

I've either been turned down or the policy has been loaded to such a degree that it was unaffordable. I'm not one to get paranoid about things, but the insurance companies' implication that heart problems could run in the family created a large, nagging doubt in the back of my mind. I was sixteen when my dad died, and for 37 years the cause of his death has been quite a bugbear for me. He was 52 when he passed away, so I felt I had reached quite a significant milestone when I turned 53 in January 2003.

# CHAPTER TWO
# FULHAM: PARADISE LOST

Sadly, my father never saw me make it as a professional footballer, but nobody did more to push me in that direction. As I have said, Dad took me to my first professional football match and helped me develop my knowledge of the game by watching the players at Fulham and Chelsea carefully. And it was he who took the decision to let me leave school at sixteen to pursue a career in football. It wasn't an easy step for him to take either because, having been forced to leave grammar school early himself owing to his parents' difficult financial circumstances, he was a great believer in the importance of a good education. However, events forced his hand.

At Sloane Grammar, between the ages of thirteen and sixteen, I had established myself as the best player and had represented London Grammar Schools. But my early steps along the road towards a professional career were fraught with problems. That was partly because of the upheaval caused at home by my father's ill health, and partly because I neglected my lessons in my all-consuming enthusiasm for the game. Right from the start, I had made up my mind I wanted to be a professional footballer, and nothing else mattered as far as I was concerned.

It all came to a head when I was invited to go for a trial with Barnet FC by Terry Casey, one of the coaches of the London Grammar Schools XI. Terry, who later became the Welsh FA's national coach, was then captain of Barnet. They wanted to put me in their reserve team in the Metropolitan League (which no longer exists) so that they could assess me, and applied to Sloane Grammar for permission to do so. But not only did the school refuse, they banned me from playing in the school team because I was not concentrating enough on my academic work, which I have to admit was correct. I had been playing for the school first team since the fourth year, and one Wednesday we had quite an important match against another school. I was really keyed up for it, but when I got to the ground the sports master, Mr Alford, told me I wasn't playing.

'I beg your pardon?' I said.

'You're not playing,' he repeated. 'I've had instructions from the headmaster that you're not to play until you start concentrating more on your school work.'

Needless to say, I went absolutely berserk, so much so that I think the teacher was afraid I was going to put one on him. In the end, he allowed me to play for the second team, which won 6–1 with me scoring four of the goals.

When, later, I told my father what had happened, he asked, 'Well, what do you want to do?'

'I want to be a professional footballer,' I replied, 'and all the school work in the world isn't going to help me achieve it. I'd be better off leaving.'

I knew that in his heart of hearts Dad would have loved me to become a professional footballer; but, as I've said, he did have this strong belief in the importance of a good education. So he came along with me to discuss the situation with the headmaster, in the hope of persuading him – and me – to listen to reason and come to some sort of compromise. After five minutes in the headmaster's study, however, my father had completely changed his mind. Finding it impossible to establish a rapport with the guy, who was a bit of a pompous so-and-so to put it mildly, he finished up having a full-scale row with him. 'You are the most pompous, ignorant man I have ever met!' he yelled. Then, having turned angrily on his heel and opened the door to walk out of the room, his parting shot was, 'My son is leaving this school to find a career for himself.'

So I left school.

Barnet was not the first club I'd been associated with. Even before I played for London Grammar Schools I'd been writing around asking for trials. As a result, I'd been training with Fulham in the evenings and I'd also had a spell at Queens Park Rangers. Back in the 1960s, though, youth schemes did not quite measure up to the sophistication of today's academies and centres of excellence. At Fulham, the facilities were basic, to say the least. As most football followers will know, their ground gets its name from the two-storey cottage that actually sits in one corner and was used as offices. Well, to the left of the cottage are very big exit gates, and our practice pitch was the huge slope of concrete down to the gates. There was one security light shining down on the area, and that's where we used to play. Not that we always saw a ball. There were so many kids there – between 40 and 60 usually – that some would be told to get changed and run twelve laps of the track instead. Fulham just couldn't cope with so many youngsters.

I was always small for my age and didn't really fill out until I reached my late teens, so when I was only thirteen or fourteen I found it a bit difficult playing against fifteen-, sixteen- and seventeen-year-olds at QPR. I wasn't really matching them on the physical side of the game. I was continually brushed aside all too easily, but it just made me all the more determined to succeed. Determination was not enough, though. I thought I stood out a mile as a teenage footballer at Sloane Grammar School, but it seemed people in the profession were looking for things they couldn't see in me. At any rate, I didn't feel I was getting anywhere at either club.

I have to admit I didn't help myself by turning up late, or not at all, for training sessions. That, of course, was because I was doing so many part-time jobs to help keep the family afloat financially. I learnt to get by with very little sleep. I'd be up at five o'clock in the morning in an effort to cram as much into my day as was humanly possible. Some days, though, it was just physically impossible to go to school, do my jobs and get to training. So perhaps Fulham and QPR might have interpreted that as me not being totally reliable. But I did try hard to fit it all in. My mother and I would sit down and organise a schedule. When does my mum need to go and see my dad in hospital? Can we work it around the fact that I need to go and train here at Fulham or there at QPR? We always got it organised some way or another.

Barnet's interest in me, then, was a godsend. I joined them as a left-back, which was the position I had opted for when I went for the London Grammar Schools trials, and the position in which I began my professional career. At school, I'd play at centre-half, centre-forward or maybe in midfield. It would depend on where I was needed to play most of all because I was their star and had become a sort of utility player. When Mr Alford, who was my history teacher as well as the games master, told me he was nominating me for the London Grammar Schools team, he asked me what position I wanted to put myself down as.

I thought about it, and said, 'Left-back.'

He looked at me in surprise, and said, 'Why left-back? You don't play left-back.'

'Because I'm not the biggest lad in the world, but I'm very quick and I've got a good left foot, which is rare. So a lack of inches isn't going to matter.'

London Grammar Schools was an under-19 team, and here I was, just turned fifteen. I'd played for the school first team, but in a wider position than I had at my own age level. I knew I would get into the side as a left-back, so that's what I opted for. Mr Alford accepted the logic of my argument. I went for a couple of trials and, sure enough, got into the side at left-back.

It was in that position that Barnet's Terry Casey saw some potential in me. He saw me when I was playing for London Grammar Schools at a national county knockout tournament which took place in the Easter holidays, if I remember rightly, at Butlin's Holiday Camp in Bognor. Terry, an amateur who had played for the Republic of Ireland, was one of the organisers of the matches. A jovial man, Terry liked me a lot and said, 'I'm going to recommend you to the football club I'm at. Why don't you come along?'

Dexter Adams was manager of Barnet at the time, and I became a regular fixture with them as a kid. They had a hell of a side then, too –

Terry Casey, Roger Stiggins, Les Barnett, Reg Finch. Dennis Roach, now one of the most powerful football agents in the world, was at centre-half. I was training with these guys, and they'd got experience with West Ham and other League clubs. I was only fifteen, and they were seasoned old hands who'd been around a bit. Les Eason, for instance, had got something like sixteen England amateur caps.

After I'd been there a bit, Adams said to me, 'All right, son, you're getting very close to playing, so I'm going to contact your headmaster.' He wanted to try me out in the Metropolitan League for a couple of games with a view to playing me in the first team. The rest you know.

When I left school, I continued with Barnet, but then I found I'd arrived at that dodgy age when, all of a sudden, you start to fill out. All your strength goes into growing, and I was struggling to cope with the game physically. I never did get to play for Barnet's first team because 1966 was the year my father became really ill, and events surrounding him took me over. Next thing I knew, he was dead and we were moving to Sussex.

But I'd learnt a lot of the tricks of the trade at Barnet. We used to play practice matches all the time and the old, experienced pros were constantly feeding me information. I was like a sponge, just soaking it all in. 'If it's on to knock it short, make yourself available, create an angle. If it tightens up, then it's got to go ping down the line' – that sort of thing. I have to say they taught me basics which, when I look at the game now, I'm not so sure have been taught to today's players as well as they were taught to me. I'm talking about the golden rules that are just flagrantly broken week in, week out by modern-day players. One of the things I remember being taught at Barnet was that when you, as a full-back, go on an overlap in a crossing position, you have to beat the near-post man with your cross. So when I got the ball in a crossing position during one of those practice matches, everybody would just queue at the far post. They knew I'd stick it there.

Anyway, we went to Sussex, and for a while I was just working in the shop. There was the local village side, Forest Row, and I did play for them three or four times. They wanted me to play more, but the standard wasn't good enough, so I wasn't really all that bothered. All the time I could feel this urge building up in me to go and play at a much better level.

Working out how to achieve that was a bit difficult in completely new surroundings. You needed contacts, and I'd severed my ties with Barnet. I'd apologised to them, of course, but as my father had died there wasn't much they could say about it. Then, as luck would have it, I was taking driving lessons and I got talking to the instructor as we were driving along. To my surprise and delight, it turned out he'd played as an amateur with Leeds, and he responded helpfully when I told him I needed a challenge. 'Well,' he said, 'I know a guy by the name of George Piper and he runs a side in the Sevenoaks League called Knole Juniors. It's a fairly good standard over there, and I'd thoroughly recommend them. See how you go.'

This was in the spring of 1967, and I could hardly wait. It took me about three hours to get over to Kent by bus, but I was just bursting to play again. When they asked me what position I played, I again said left-back, and they welcomed me with open arms. As it turned out, I played only three or four times for Knole Juniors because George Piper, who obviously liked what he had seen, recommended me to Harry Haslam, the manager of Tonbridge, the Southern League club just down the road. Harry, who was to play a big part in my career, agreed with George's assessment and signed me just before the end of the 1966/67 season.

I was seventeen now, and I'd played three or four times for the reserves when Tonbridge got to a cup final at the end of that season. It was to be played on a Sunday, and Harry phoned me up to say he wanted me to play in it. They were travelling to Ashford, or somewhere like that, for the game and Harry was going to give me my first-team debut. Unfortunately, there was no public transport from our Sussex village on a Sunday and I hadn't passed my test yet, so there was no way I could get there. I had to ring Harry and say, 'I'm awfully sorry, but I just can't get out of this damned village!' In those days, not everybody had a car, and Tonbridge was a hell of a trek anyway. These days it would be twenty minutes down the road, but everything was so different back then. There was a taxi service, but they wanted double fare on a Sunday, and that was so exorbitant I couldn't afford it.

Thankfully, Harry didn't hold my non-appearance against me. I passed my driving test, got a little car and was a regular in the Tonbridge first team by the start of the following season. But they already had a very good left-back called Vicky Akers. You'll see him now if you look at the Arsenal bench on television. Vicky, who doubles as the Gunners' kitman and manager of the Arsenal Ladies team, usually sits in the row behind Arsène Wenger and Pat Rice. Anyway, Vic was left-back at Tonbridge, so Harry said to me, 'Right, you'll play right-back. That's your spot for the season, son. If you don't like it, tough shit. Get on with it. But look at it this way – I'm teaching you to kick with your right foot!'

I was also starting to earn money from the game. The part-time contract Harry had offered me was for £10 a week, plus £2 for a win and £1 for a draw. I also got the pre-decimal equivalent of 50p per game for travelling expenses, too. And most weeks we used to play three times – Monday or Tuesday, Thursday and Saturday. Apart from being in the First Division of the Southern League, Tonbridge were in several other competitions. We entered all the cups in Kent, plus the Southern League Trophy, the FA Vase, all sorts of things. The club was doing well at the time, so it was no surprise if we won a couple of times in the week and the money went up from the basic £10 to £14. Add the travelling expenses, and I was earning a grand total of £15.50 most weeks, £17.50 at the end of a really good one. My first wage packet was about £11, after tax. I remember showing it to my mother and saying, 'Great news – I don't need to take any money out of the shop now!'

I celebrated by taking Mum out for a meal. Unfortunately, I'd never eaten out in my life and didn't realise you had to book a table at some restaurants. So you can just imagine how I, my wage packet burning a hole in my pocket, felt when we arrived at the Felbridge Hotel in East Grinstead on the Saturday night and couldn't get in. We went to a Chinese restaurant instead, but neither of us had ever eaten Chinese food before and that led to some fun and games. The waiter was trying to help us out by recommending things on the menu, and I kept asking him whether it was for one person or two, but he misunderstood and thought we wanted two of everything! To my mother's embarrassment, we finished up with a table full of dishes and enough food to feed the whole of East Grinstead. It was still a super night, though.

I'm not exactly sure what the national average wage was in those days, but I think I, a kid who hadn't turned eighteen yet, was probably earning what some people were bringing up families and paying mortgages on. Apart from anything else, though, I thoroughly enjoyed playing for Tonbridge. I was improving rapidly as a footballer, and the guys were absolutely brilliant. John Barr, the goalkeeper, used to play for Dartford, and I think he'd been at West Ham as well. There was myself at right-back and Vicky Akers at left-back, and our centre-half was Geoff Truitt, an England amateur international with a huge number of caps. He was also, believe it or not, a director of Blue Circle, the cement company, and therefore not short of a few bob. Number six was a fellow called Dave Waters, a very good player. I think he went on to play some lower-level League football, but I always felt he was going to go a lot further than that. We also had a right-winger called Johnny Saunders, who went to Cambridge United. The inside-right was John Ripley, who'd played for West Ham and Dartford, and at outside-left, the problem position in the team, was Dave Foreman, who still lives in East Grinstead. But our outstanding player was centre-forward Joe Carolan, a Republic of Ireland international who had played for Manchester United, Tottenham Hotspur and Leyton Orient. Joe had appeared on the biggest football stages in the world, and here he was at the very end of his career providing experience that was invaluable for youngsters like me. Yet Joe's nerves were so bad before a game, he used to go and be sick in the bathroom. The other members of the side included Bobby Taylor, who was an English amateur international and later became a scout for me when I was manager of Fulham. He had a great eye for a player.

There was also a right-sided midfield player called Malcolm Pike, who had played for West Ham for many years. He had a huge stutter off the field but, remarkably, none at all on it. One day, Malcolm got sent off for swearing at a referee. Harry Haslam appealed, and they ended up before an FA disciplinary committee. Before the proceedings started, the wily Harry said, 'Gentlemen, to make this short, quick and easy for you, can I just cut across the protocol and put one question to the referee and one to my player?'

The chairman of the committee replied, 'It's highly unusual, Mr Haslam, but if you feel it's the best way to defend your player, go ahead.'

So Harry turned to the referee and said, 'Mr Referee, would you tell me exactly what my player is accused of calling you?'

To which the referee said, 'Well, he called me an effing bee.'

Quick as a flash, Harry turned to Malcolm Pike and said, 'Malcolm, call the referee a f★★★ing bastard!'

'F–, f–, f–, f–, f–,' Malcolm began.

Case dismissed – mistaken identity.

Harry, who was known as 'Happy' Harry because he was always laughing and joking, was quite a character. A Mancunian who was signed by Manchester United as a kid, Harry was one of those unfortunate youngsters, I have a feeling, who had their careers interrupted by the Second World War. Later, he went on to play for Leyton Orient. Harry was manager of Hastings before he took over at Tonbridge, he always made good use of his northern contacts, and he knew the game inside out. Harry was also at Fulham and Luton when I was there, and he became like a second father to me. My mother used to ring him up and ask how I was getting on, and he'd always be very open with her. 'Look, I think the boy's got something,' he would tell her. 'I'll try everything in my power to get him in as a full-time pro, and then we'll see how he goes. But I'm not making any promises beyond that.' Although I still had a burning ambition to be a professional footballer, I never had dreams. Like my father, I'm very realistic. So I just left it to Harry to sort out my future for me.

The first thing he did, in the early summer of 1968 at the end of my first full season with Tonbridge, was engineer an invitation for me to go to Holland with Crystal Palace's under-19 team to play in a tournament there. That team included Stevie Kember and some other really tasty lads, and we reached the final. It was played at the Feyenoord Stadium in Rotterdam, and we beat Ajax Amsterdam 1–0, the winning goal coming from my long throw-in. Afterwards, we were presented with a huge silver cup that was not dissimilar in proportions to the FA Cup. It was in a beautifully polished wooden case whose front would come down to show it off. But on our return to England – I think we were coming through Heathrow airport – customs stopped Bert Head, the Palace manager. They had him open this trophy and they questioned him for ages. He kept on saying, 'I'm the manager of Crystal Palace and this is the under-19 side who've just won this trophy. We beat Ajax in the Feyenoord Stadium 1–0 and I'm returning with the trophy.' Whether they found that an unlikely story, or whether you weren't allowed to transport silverware across borders, I'm not really too sure. But I'm sure Celtic, Liverpool, Nottingham Forest, Aston Villa or Manchester United never had that kind of trouble. In the end, of course, they finally allowed Bert to go on his way with our trophy.

Having seen me in action, Bert wanted to sign me for Palace. He actually agreed a fee with Tonbridge and offered me terms, but I had trained with Palace for a few days prior to going away to this tournament in Holland and there was literally no room in either of the dressing-rooms because there were so many players there. I counted them up, and there were 56 in all – 56 pros, I mean, because I'm not talking about apprentices or anything like that. There were probably another one or two I hadn't seen who'd got injuries. I was overwhelmed by numbers, if you like, and it put the wind up me. I'd never seen such a vast group of footballers before, and I thought, 'How the hell am I going to show in this situation? How am I going to project in this kind of crowd?' All your thoughts are selfish at times like that, and I just found it somewhat off-putting. When you're eighteen, just coming to terms with developing a man's body and half the time still thinking as a kid, you feel rather inadequate in a way when you see these guys with fully honed bodies getting changed in the dressing-room and going into the shower. It's very intimidating.

So there I was in this quandary. Do I take the plunge, take the chance? Such questions were still flying around in my head when Harry Haslam phoned me and, to my utter astonishment, said, 'I've left Tonbridge Football Club. I've joined Bobby Robson, who's just been appointed Fulham manager, and I'm to be his chief scout. Not only that, but Bobby wants you to come to Fulham too. So you've now got a choice.'

Immediately, heart started to rule head. Fulham was the club I'd always followed, and Bobby Robson was one of my heroes. He'd had two spells at Craven Cottage as a player, and one with West Bromwich Albion in between. And, of course, it was a place I knew well. I even knew the people on the terraces. So I went. I have to admit I felt a bit guilty about Bert Head and Palace because they'd done me no wrong at all. It was, for me, perhaps the first of those difficult decisions you have to take in life where somebody's always going to be disappointed at the end of it.

Having made my choice, I quickly discovered that I'd been better off financially playing for Tonbridge. The terms I accepted at Fulham, £20 a week, were identical to the ones I'd been offered by Palace, but it was a flat rate that came down to £15 after tax. Then I had to bear all the costs of travelling between London and Sussex, a round trip of about 70 miles a day for which I wasn't being reimbursed, as I had been at Tonbridge. So I'd been earning £17.50 a week in the Southern League and was now earning only £15 in the old Second Division of the Football League!

It wasn't a long time after the scrapping of the maximum wage in 1961, remember, and there was very much a class system in the game. Johnny Haynes, as had been announced with huge publicity at the time, had become England's first £100-a-week footballer. John drove a Jag, but there were still players arriving on the bus. Things had certainly improved financially for footballers across the board, but the trouble was you had to do an awful lot to get the extra money. 'Them and us' is the wrong way to describe the situation, but you really had to earn a reasonable wage. You certainly didn't start on one; clubs wanted to be sure you were of first-team quality before shelling out. Their attitude was, 'It's all very well having potential, but we ain't paying for potential, we're paying for the real thing.'

Despite George Eastham's success in challenging the retain and transfer system in 1963, contracts between club and player were still pretty restrictive too. I played under a certain type of contract throughout the whole of my career: whatever the number of years you signed on for, there was an equal number of years known as the 'option', and the option was entirely in the ownership of the clubs. Fulham signed me on a 'one and one', which meant I was contracted to play for a year and the club had an option on me for another year. Even at the end of the option, they still held my registration. You could go on indefinitely on that option, so the fact that it was called a one-year contract was a total nonsense. It was basically a never-ending contract that bound you to the club, full stop.

None of this could stop me signing for Fulham in the summer of 1968, of course. I was only too delighted to get the opportunity to play at that level. In fact, I was bursting for it. But there was a shock awaiting this part-timer joining a club of full-time professionals. The first thing you become aware of is the gulf between you and everybody else when it comes to fitness. It doesn't matter how hard you worked as a part-time pro, all of a sudden you are with senior professionals and their fitness has been honed over years. It's a type of fitness I still carry with me today, a muscle tone that's built year upon year, and I've not done a jot of training for maybe ten years now, certainly not since I last played squash. So trying to keep up with those guys at first was difficult. I was working hard, but the one thing I was very aware of, and was always being reminded of by coaches and other players, was that my stamina wasn't good enough. I was hopeless on distance runs, but when it was a question of tackling the shorter distances of 200 yards or less, I came into my own. As I worked at it day in, day out, I built my muscle tone purely and simply for sprinting.

I started my career with Fulham as a left-back in the reserves, but that season, 1968/69, an injury crisis hit the first team, particularly in attack. That September, Harry Haslam urged Bobby Robson to play me up front, telling him he'd done it at Tonbridge – which he had done on half a dozen occasions, and I always scored goals. One time, in fact, I scored a hat-trick. So I think that, always at the back of his mind, Harry knew eventually that would be the position I'd move into. 'Have no fear,' Harry told Bobby, 'stick him up front!' So that's how I started playing as a centre-forward in the old Second Division. But I was rough and raw, and my ball control left an awful lot to be desired. I was still playing like a Southern Leaguer, in fact. Nevertheless, once I got into the penalty area it was almost as if I became a different type of player, a different person even. I made things happen.

I came into a situation where the first team hadn't scored for four games. The next match was away to Oxford, and Bobby put me in the team. I managed to get the ball in the net twice, only to have both 'goals' disallowed for offside, so again Fulham didn't score and we lost 1–0. That was on the Saturday, and the following Friday night I made my senior home debut when we played Crystal Palace, of all teams. By then, the papers were having a field day because we'd gone 450 minutes without scoring, so all the reporters were at Craven Cottage, en masse, that night to report on Fulham passing the 500-minute mark scoreless. But I spoilt their story with the only goal of the night. It came from a ball knocked over the centre-halves, and I whizzed through, took it round John Jackson, the Palace keeper, and knocked it in the net. From then on, though, I missed an absolute hatful. Had I been the player I was at 26 playing in that game, I probably could have finished with eight or nine goals. But never mind, we won 1–0 and the hoodoo was broken.

I played in four more games for the first team and scored in all but one. There was Birmingham away, where we lost 5–4; then Blackburn at home was on *Match of the Day*. I remember rushing home and sitting down in front of the television, because I'd never seen myself play before. We drew 1–1, and, playing up front with that lovely guy Frank Large, I scored the equaliser.

Then, on the first day of November, just after this little six-game run during which I'd amassed five goals, Bobby Robson was sacked. I knew Bobby had been having problems with the senior players, but as I was still only a kid a lot of it went over my head. But I was certainly aware of the animosity being shown towards the manager by certain members of the team. What brought everything to a head and prompted Bobby's sacking, I believe, was the training session the day before he went. He staged what was virtually a practice match featuring the youngsters against the old guard, and everybody got the impression, from the way he was working with the youngsters, that it was Bobby's intention to play most of them on the Saturday. There was Ian Seymour in goal, Nicky Pentecost at right-back, Donny Kerrigan, Bobby Moss, Barry Salvage, and people like that in the team. Frank Large and I were also included, although Frank was one of the few old heads in our young team. The seniors almost treated this practice match as a joke, but I could sense Bobby was taking it a lot more seriously. That feeling grew a lot stronger at a meeting afterwards, when he told the youngsters who had taken part in the training session to keep ourselves right because we would be playing on the Saturday at Sheffield United.

The following day, as I said, Bobby was gone, and I'm sure it was because of pressure brought to bear on Tommy Trinder, the Fulham chairman, by the old guard of players. They knew full well what was in the offing, and more fool Trinder for bowing to their wishes. Fulham were at the bottom of the old Second Division, and it was the old guard, really, that had been responsible for putting them there. The club had been relegated from the First Division the previous season and gone straight to the bottom of the Second. There was no light at the end of the tunnel, so Bobby had decided to go with the kids. They were the future of the club, and quite rightly he reasoned that if Fulham were to go down again, it would be better to do so playing for the future rather than simply hanging on to the past.

Bobby has every right to feel bitter about what happened to him in that spell at Craven Cottage, because what I saw being done to him by the senior players was absolutely horrendous. He was guilty of trying to do nothing but good for the club, yet it seemed a lot of other people were hell-bent on committing professional suicide just to keep their jobs. He would have been 35 then, which was young for a manager. Haynesie was about the same age, of course, and that was basically the problem. In fact, if that episode taught me anything, it was never to try to manage players you've played with.

I joined Fulham after Bobby had been appointed, so I didn't see his initial spell in charge. It wouldn't surprise me, though, if he'd taken people by surprise with the way in which he wanted to dominate them to get the very best out of each player, to create a team and get the very best out of that. He was very specific about the way he wanted the game to be played, very specific indeed. We went through hour after hour after hour on the training ground with him. He would keep doing the same thing until we got it right. But what was happening was that people were purposely doing it wrong to thwart him. He'd just say, 'Let's start again. Go back to square one. Oh, come on, look at the time! We've got places to go.' That sort of thing. Having finally got it right, he'd move on to something else. But it would never be carried over into Saturday's match because everybody just reverted to type.

I suppose it was basically quite a simple thing he was seeking to do. He wanted us to get the ball to the full-back, who would then play it beyond the middle of the field to a diagonal-running centre-forward who would be supported by the midfield. The centre-forward would play it back into the middle, then the team could go and play, ensuring that when they did they always created width. But Haynesie didn't like the fact that the midfield was bypassed in the first instance. The ball didn't go into him, so he couldn't create the play. It was a battle between him and Bobby, and the other senior players – guys like Les Barrett, Jimmy Conway, Freddie Callaghan, Tony Macedo and Stan Brown – went with Haynesie in the main.

It was a crying shame actually to witness all that as a young pro. I knew what Bobby Robson was saying, then I was seeing people purposely doing something else. As far as I was concerned, if the manager said 'Jump!', I jumped. I followed his instructions implicitly, but others were just doing whatever they wanted. I know Bobby has said that it was his objection to interference in team affairs at boardroom level that cost him his job after only nine months as manager, but I believe the real reason was the hostility he encountered from senior players.

I was not at all surprised to see Bobby go on to be a very good manager. He had a very deep strength of will; one could sense it in him. In those days, of course, he would let his anger show. It's a lot more controlled now, although you can see it on occasion, and woe betide whoever's on the end of it. But it was hugely frustrating for him at Fulham because he knew that forces were ranged against him, players who simply ignored his instructions and didn't do what he wanted them to do. My abiding memory of the Fulham training field was not so much the good work of Bobby Robson, although it was there to be seen if you wanted to see it, but the blatant sabotage. The training session having gone wrong, half the people involved would start to laugh, and there was Bobby, going red in the face and wanting to break people's necks.

Bobby walked into a similar situation at Ipswich, of course, when he took over at Portman Road the following year after a short spell on the dole. Again there was opposition from the senior pros, but this time he tackled it head-on and sorted the situation out very quickly. He even had a fist-fight with some of the troublemakers on one occasion. What he did at Ipswich I think he realised he should have done at Fulham. He didn't allow the bad feeling to stay in there and fester to the point where it raged against him. Without a shadow of doubt, he was a man you would have marked out then as someone destined for future success. But, having suffered such an ignominious fate at Fulham, he had to win the battle at Ipswich. Had he not, that would have been the finish of him for all time, and I think he knew that. Had he lost, there would be no Sir Bobby Robson today.

Nowadays, of course, we see each other at every Newcastle home game and at functions on Tyneside, and we have a bit of a laugh about our time together at Fulham. He always has a dig at me, in fact. He'll say, 'I hear you praising every other manager you played under, but I was the first one to give you a chance and show you how it was done. You're always saying how great Stocky [Alec Stock] was, and Joe Harvey, but what about me? I started you off!' Bobby did help my development, without any doubt. He gave me the platform that allowed me to prove to myself that all things were possible. And he did it in the teeth of heavy criticism from within and without at Fulham, but mostly from within. Unfortunately, I never got to really appreciate him. In the short time we were together, there was everything else raging around him and his attention was as much on the civil war he was having to fight as it was on his job.

A couple of days after Bobby had been sacked, one of the coaches, Alan Humphreys, was taking us for the usual Friday morning sprints around the pitch at Craven Cottage, but he was telling people one by one to leave training and go up to the office, where sat Johnny Haynes, who'd been appointed caretaker-manager by Trinder. He was in that position for seventeen days, and one of his first acts was to tell me I wasn't playing the following day. 'But I'm your highest goalscorer! I'm the only goalscorer!' I protested. In response to that, Haynes said coldly, 'As far as I'm concerned, you can't play and you'll never make a career for yourself in the game. And while I'm at this club, you won't play here again.' So, along with a number of other players, I was thrown straight back into the reserves.

If I remember rightly, the reserves were runners-up to Arsenal in the Football Combination that season, and I think I finished as the highest scorer in the league with something like 25 goals. Meanwhile, the first team were relegated from the Second Division to the Third. Despite what Haynes had said, I was dragged into the seniors a couple of times as a substitute, and I even got on once as an outside-left against Middlesbrough at home. But it had become a pretty sick club. I think that's the only way to describe it. Fulham were terminally ill that season, and there was nothing anybody could do to save them.

Bill Dodgin Jr became the manager after Haynesie's short spell as caretaker. Dodgin, like Robson an ex-Fulham player, had his own particular way of doing the job, but Haynesie was always there in the middle of things. Dodgin wasn't the young radical Bobby Robson was; he had a tendency to go with the flow. But he was very similar to Bobby in as much as under him you got play started by getting the ball into your opponents' half first. In those days, there weren't the rigid crossfield lines

we have today, where the main formation is 4–4–2. The midfield worked
a lot more independently and played it as they saw it. But Bill's shout was
always, 'Get it to the full-back! Long ball, long ball!' The idea was to get
your opponents turning to face their own goal so that you could then
press in on them. So Dodgin's tactics were more rigidly long ball than
those Robson had been advocating. With Bobby, it was a question of
knocking it over the opposing full-back only when things were tight
in our half, but as far as Bill was concerned you played the long ball
whatever the circumstances, and it didn't matter whether it was done
with care or where it finished. I saw Haynesie and others doing this
happily, and I thought to myself, 'You load of two-faced bastards!' They
went along with Dodgin's route-one tactics because he kept playing
them, regardless of whether they played well or badly. As I said, the side
got demoted, miserably demoted, twice in successive seasons. What was
so awful about 1968/69 was that they seemed to go down happily just
because the status quo had been preserved among the senior players.
Dodgin went with the majority, and if Haynesie gave the nod to
something then the majority nodded also.

I didn't try to sort out my own differences with Haynes there and then
because he was always unapproachable. The only times we spoke were
when we had spats on the field, and he would come over to give me a
bollocking. In the game against Blackburn Rovers that was on *Match of the
Day*, for instance, at one point Haynesie was in the inside-right position
on the edge of their box and hit a cross-shot towards goal. Standing just
outside the six-yard area, I controlled the ball with my left foot and
smacked it into the net with my right. As I mentioned earlier, that was the
equaliser and a hugely important goal. Three or four team-mates came
over and said 'Well done!' but all Haynesie did was complain that I should
have let the ball go because it was going in! Don't forget, either, that I was
somewhat in awe of this guy, my boyhood hero. In fact, I really don't want
it to sound as though the only thing I'm trying to do is knock him. As
far as I was, and still am, concerned, Johnny was the supreme professional
beyond all others. He was so fit he could run all day; he could outrun the
youngsters, he could outrun anybody. And, by heavens, he couldn't half
play. He had wonderful skill on the ball, and his touch was so deft. His
passing ability with either foot, whether the distance was short or long,

was phenomenal; he could drop the ball on the proverbial sixpence. He'd even ask you which way you wanted the lace facing.

I'll give you an example of his brilliance, though it was at my expense. In that game I played against Middlesbrough at outside-left, while Haynesie was doing his usual trick of getting the ball in the middle of the park and turning, turning, I'd be looking to sprint beyond the full-back. But when the pass came, the clever so-and-so would measure it so that it just ran out of play before I could reach it. It seemed such an inviting pass that I had to go for it each time, but, quick as I was, I knew I wasn't going to get there. Haynesie, of course, would throw his arms up in the air in disgust. Then they would come down and he'd adopt that familiar hands-on-hips gesture of his. He'd look to the stand and his arms would go out from his hips, as if to say, 'Come on! I'm knocking in great balls here, and he's not good enough to get on the end of them.' Incensed as I was by that kind of treatment, I would be the first to admit that Johnny Haynes was an absolutely superb player. And, of course, at that age he was simply seeking to keep himself going as long as he could.

It was certainly a privilege to have a ringside seat watching a past master 'lending' the ball. That's where a player passes it to a team-mate in such a way that there's no pace on it; the ball gets to its destination, but it doesn't come at any pace, so all you can do is control it and knock it back where it came from. In that way, Haynesie made himself the pivot of everything that happened. He was just playing one-twos. He would run around all over the pitch and have every other touch. The game completely revolved around him, win, lose or draw.

Sadly, though, there was hardly a win to be had for Fulham at that time. When the season ended, I was bitterly unhappy and frustrated because I had matured a huge amount. That spell in the first team had done me a power of good in so many different ways. It had removed an awful lot of doubts I'd had about myself, and I had come to terms with a lot of things within myself. The best thing I had learnt was that you can promote a few strengths in such a fashion that you can hide all your weaknesses – provided, of course, your strengths are good enough. My strengths were lightning pace and physical power. For somebody who wasn't tall – I never stood above 5ft 10½in – I was good in the air, too. I also had a strength of will and a rocket shot in my left foot. Not only that, but I was an awful lot better with the other peg than most players. My right foot was by no means just for standing on. At that time, though, none of this seemed to cut any ice with the Fulham hierarchy. It hadn't helped cheer me up any, either, to see my mentor, Harry Haslam, depart for Luton Town, where he became their chief scout. I made regular phone calls to Harry as the season dragged on, just to keep him informed of what was going on back at Fulham. And he realised, as each month went by, that I was getting unhappier and unhappier with the whole thing.

In the summer of 1969, having been told I was being retained on my option, I requested an increase in salary, which I felt I deserved. After all, I had made seven full appearances for the first team, plus about three as a sub, and scored five goals. In fact, I'd finished as the first team's second highest scorer behind Brian Dear, who'd been bought from West Ham halfway through the season. He'd come in and scored six. But my request was met with a blunt refusal. So there I was, being told I had to continue living for at least another year on £20 a week (before tax).

I said, 'I can't do it. It's just not possible.'

They said, 'Well, we've been relegated.'

'That's not my fault,' I replied. 'I've done all that was ever asked of me. I cannot live another year on £20 a week. It's kid's money!'

I desperately needed a rise because I'd got married by then to my first wife, Julie, and we had a small flat in Wimbledon that was costing me £8 a week, with the services on top. That swallowed up most of my take-home pay, which was £15 a week.

That summer, I decided I had to go and get myself a second job. I found work in a factory that made supermarket shelves, the chrome wire type. They came off the production line in different lengths and widths, and it was my responsibility to take them off and store them in the warehouse. In the process, I also became a forklift truck driver of some expertise. It's amazing what you'll do when you are desperate for money. But as will perhaps be clear by now, I have never been afraid of hard work or of getting my hands dirty.

All the time I was stacking that supermarket shelving, I was wondering what the hell I could do about the unsatisfactory situation at Fulham. Apart from the fact that I wouldn't be able to live on the wage they were paying me, I had no desire at all to remain there, especially if it was going to be another year of the politics and infighting I'd had to put up with the previous season. I was now a young man of nineteen who needed somebody who appreciated me and allowed me to have my head so I could discover just how far I could go in the game.

So I phoned Harry Haslam again and said, 'H, we've reported back for pre-season training and nothing's changed. It's still the same divided dressing-room, it's still the same old story. Nothing's improved at all. I really don't know what to do. I'm at the end of my tether. It's been made clear to me I'm facing another season in the reserves and I'm not going to be playing in the first team.'

Harry had nothing to suggest at that point, but asked me to ring him back in a couple of days. When I did, he came up with a plan that sounded crazy, to say the least. Where on earth he got such an idea, I don't know. He said, 'Right! This is what you do, son. You get yourself an appointment to see the chairman, and this is what you say.' But when he told me exactly what it was I had to say, I couldn't believe my ears.

'I can't do that!' I protested.

'I'm telling you – do it!' was Harry's terse reply.

So, having plucked up the courage to go through with this outrageous plan, I got an appointment with the chairman, Tommy Trinder, and told him what Harry told me to tell him.

'I've spoken to the manager,' I announced, 'I've spoken to the secretary and now you're my final option. I cannot afford to live on the money you're paying me. I finished second top goalscorer last season, but that seems to have been totally ignored. So either give me a significant rise or let me go to another club.' Then, before Trinder could reply, and still following Harry's instructions to the letter, I added threateningly, 'The man who's caused me most misery here is your captain, Johnny Haynes. If you don't let me go, I'm going to stick him up against the wall and beat the living shit out of him.'

That, I swear, must have been the first time in the life of the great comedian when he was lost for words. The next thing I knew I was exiting Trinder's office and the meeting was over.

Worried, I phoned Harry and said, 'I think I've cooked my goose. I think I'm finished in the game, I really do. TT had me out of that office in a flash.'

But Harry said, 'Did you say what I told you to say?'

'Harry, I said it exactly as you suggested. I said it with all the venom I could muster, and that wasn't difficult to do. He was just dumbstruck. So what now?'

'You just sit tight, son, and keep turning up for training.'

Two days later, I signed for Luton. I'd seen Trinder on the Wednesday, and I signed for Luton on the Friday. Alec Stock, the Luton manager, did a deal with Fulham on the Thursday for £17,500, and I was told to report to Craven Cottage on the Friday morning. One of the girls in the office directed me to a little waiting room, and I sat there for an hour, then an hour and a half, and still nothing happened. At the time, I had no idea what had been going on and was worrying myself to death. 'I'm for the high jump,' I kept thinking. 'Are they going to suspend me or are they going to sack me?' Then, after two hours or more, a wheezing Alec Stock came up the steps of the Cottage and in through the door. I didn't know him from Adam then; all I remember is this man wheezing heavily. As I was to discover later, Alec suffered dreadfully with asthma. Anyway, coming up the steps behind him was Harry Haslam, who had his jacket off and whose shirt and arms were covered in grease. It turned out their car had broken down, and that had been the reason for the long delay.

Harry just gave me a little wink and, oh, the relief at seeing his cheery face was enormous. Suddenly, all the tumblers fell into place, and I was happy to sit there for as long as it took. The next thing, I was called in by Bill Dodgin.

'We've accepted an offer for you from Luton Town Football Club,' he said. 'Alec Stock, their manager, is in the next office. Do you want to go?'

To which I replied, with feeling, 'Let me get out of here!'

I sat down with Alec, and the terms he offered me were £35 a week, which was just music to my ears. Then he added, 'You'll also get a three-bedroom club house for as long as it takes you to sort out your own arrangements. There's no rush on that. If you need to be there a year or a year and a half, there's no problem. We'll charge you a nominal rent of £2.50 a week. And here's the bonus structure, here's the crowd bonus, here's this and here's that. Am I right in thinking you didn't put any transfer request in writing? Yes? In that case you'll be getting your signing-on fee, old son. It's half of £1,750 and payable in stages. But if you want to have a bit of a loan up front on the strength of that, we're always happy to oblige.'

I couldn't believe it. All of a sudden, here was a guy who was doing everything he could to help me. After my year of pain and anguish, of perpetually being in the doghouse for just being there, I'd sort of got the view that everybody in League football was a nasty bastard. Yet in the back of my mind I'd kept saying to myself, 'Surely it can't all be like this? There's got to be somewhere better!' And here it was, not much more than 30 miles up the M1.

A postscript to all this was provided in the 2001/02 season, when Newcastle played Fulham at Craven Cottage on the London club's return to the top flight. There was a whole host of ex-Fulham players there, all brought together by Mohammed Al Fayed, the present chairman and owner of the club, and I had been asked to go across to the new stand and do a talk. One of the questions I was asked was what caused me to leave Fulham, and I found myself telling the story while Haynesie was actually standing there listening. In fact, he was going to be next up. Of course, I was able to add the retrospective comment that what happened to me at Fulham probably made me a better and more determined player than ever I might have been. Often you need a setback in your early life, your early career, to make you a man, etc. Even so, what I'd said was not exactly flattering to Haynes, but he, as always, just stood silently and listened impassively. He made no comment, no reference, nothing whatsoever when he got up to speak, and it's not a subject he's ever been prepared to broach with me. Which makes me wonder. Leaving Fulham was a major event in my life, a major turning point in my career, but perhaps Haynesie struggles even to remember it.

We talked at the reunion, and he still looks remarkably fit. He was very pleasant to me, but, as always, totally reserved about everything. John is a very private man. He discusses nothing about his personal life at all and tells you nothing other than the fact that he lives in Edinburgh. That's about the only information you'll get out of him. But what a player he was!

# CHAPTER THREE
# LUTON: PARADISE REGAINED

I wasn't quite sure where to find Luton on the map. I'd been so keen to get away from Fulham that I hadn't given a thought to the exact location of my new club. Not only that but, like all real southerners, I hadn't much idea of what lay north of Watford. I was delighted, then, to discover that the town was only 30 miles from London when I travelled up the M1 for a medical. My delight increased when I arrived at Kenilworth Road. People talked about Fulham being the friendly club, but it had been just the opposite during the season I'd spent there. Little old Third Division Luton, on the other hand, beavered away to get you settled in, and to my mind were much more deserving of the title.

Having passed the medical, I reported for my first day. The club was already in the latter stages of pre-season training, close to starting friendly matches in fact, and during the first session the coach, Jimmy Andrews, set up a series of runs. He made a 250-yard circle by sticking white corner flags into the ground, and we ran around that. Wanting to impress, I went off like a rocket and amazed Jimmy with my pace. Unfortunately, I didn't realise that we had to do twelve of these runs and was on my knees by the last one. Jimmy remarked that it was a shame I couldn't maintain that kind of pace for anything over 60 yards, but others were less diplomatic. 'This feller will be great if you just play him for the first ten minutes,' someone said.

It was the old stamina problem again, combined with the fact that I was still coming to terms with having sprouted a man's body, which had sort of outgrown whatever strength I had. I had suddenly developed a barrel chest and broad shoulders. Jimmy sensed immediately what kind of work I required and sort of set out a plan for me. Having been a crafty little left-winger, Jimmy knew the potential of someone with lightning pace like mine, and I'd often sense that training sessions were actually being adapted to suit me. Whereas before I'd only ever been one of the crowd, now I was being given personalised treatment. And I responded to it eagerly.

When the pre-season friendlies started, Alec Stock wasn't quite sure where to play me. 'Is he a full-back, a forward, a winger? What exactly is he? How are we going to get the best out of him?' the Luton manager would say as he debated the issue with Harry Haslam and Jimmy Andrews behind closed doors. We played a couple of non-League sides to begin with, and I was used in one position, then another. It wasn't until we played the Italian under-23 side at Kenilworth Road in the first public match of the pre-season programme that Alec used me almost as an outside-left and became convinced my future was up front.

He then went the whole hog. It was the Friday morning prior to the first League game of the 1969/70 season and the team sheet was pinned up on the board. I don't think such things exist now, until a list of names is handed to the referee half an hour before the kick-off, but in those days there really was a team sheet pinned up on the dressing-room noticeboard. Everybody would scramble over to have a look at it, and there was my name next to number 10. Boy, oh boy, here I was in the old Third Division, picked to play purely on my own ability. I was chuffed to bits. I was going to give this everything, I really was.

But what happened in the next hour and a half reshaped my whole thinking about the game and my relationship with it. The events of that one Friday morning completely focused me for the rest of my career. So much so that I never needed another team talk for the rest of my life.

Once we'd all got changed after training and had a look at the team sheets, Jimmy Andrews said, 'Right, I want the twelve of you in the first-team squad to stay in the dressing-room. The rest of you can go.' Then he added, 'You see the numbers you'll be wearing? Well, I want you to sit in numerical order – goalkeeper, right-back, left-back and so on.' Having got us organised, Jimmy went off to make a phone call. It was the signal for Alec Stock to arrive. When he appeared about three minutes later, he was carrying a very large book.

'Well, here we are at the beginning of yet another August and another season,' he said. 'Isn't life grand? It gives us the opportunity to earn a living doing exactly what we love doing most, and it pays us well. It's not bad, is it? And that's all thanks to the good people of Luton Town, who come along to support us with their presence and the money they pay at the turnstiles. So it's our job to repay them. Now, who's up for a bit of promotion?'

When Alec asked this kind of question, the players had a tendency to look for guidance from the skipper, Mike Keen, who'd been a player under him for many seasons, not just at Luton but at Queens Park Rangers as well. So when Mike stuck his arm in the air and started chanting, 'Yeah, yeah, we go for promotion!' everybody else followed suit.

'Good,' said Alec when the hubbub had died down. 'Now I'm going to tell you how to do it. Here is a book that records every season I've ever spent in football, and from this book I can tell you precisely what you have to do over this coming season to get promotion. If you don't stick rigidly to what I tell you, you will not get promoted, so listen carefully.

'We're here in the Third Division, which means that we have 46 games to play. Of those 46, we cannot afford to lose more than nine. After that, the wins and the draws will take care of themselves. Now, how do we set about losing only nine? Well, we cannot, in those 46 games, afford to allow our opponents to score more than 35 goals against us. At the other end, we must score more than double that, and the minimum figure I'm setting you is 75. Now, how do we go about scoring 75 goals or more? Well, I'm going to tell you that as well.' With that, Alec turned to Tony Read, the goalkeeper, and said, 'Now, Tony, I don't expect you to score any goals.'

There was uproar at that because the previous season Readie had had to play out of goal for some reason and, if memory serves, had scored a hat-trick against Notts County. A used-car dealer in his spare time, big, lanky Tony always had a smile on his face and a ready quip on his lips. 'But, boss, you've forgotten the hat-trick I scored for you last season!' he protested. 'Does this mean I've got to stick to my goal-line?'

Pausing to let the banter subside, Alec replied, 'Yes. And I expect you to save at least three penalties!'

Moving on from Readie, the manager said, 'John Ryan, right-back. You're quick and you're strong, old son, and you love to overlap. You've got a fair old shot on you too, so I've got you down for five goals.' Having analysed John, Alec looked straight at Jack Bannister and said, 'Bannister, a left-back who shits himself every time he crosses the halfway line! Well, you're going to have to overcome that fear, because I've put you down for three.' As soon as the total was given, it was a dismissal and he moved on to the next one in line. There, with the number 4 shirt, was Mike Keen. 'Skipper. Loves a free-kick,' said Alec in the clipped, military manner he, the son of a Somerset miner, had acquired as a young army captain during the Second World War. 'I've got you down for eight.' From 4, he went on to 5, Terry Branston. He talked of the centre-half coming up for corners and free-kicks, adding, 'Who's going to be stupid enough to stand in this big man's way? I've got you down for . . .' And he gave a total to Terry, too.

I can't remember the figures Terry or John Moore at 6 were given, but Johnny Collins at 7 was expected to score eight goals, and Keith Allen, who wore the number 8 shirt, got a much higher total than that. Now Alec was up to number 9, my attacking partner, Laurie Sheffield. 'Laurie Sheffield,' he said, 'you've been about a bit, old son, haven't you? In fact, you've got more clubs than Jack Nicklaus! Although the legs are getting a bit old, they can still run a bit, still jump a bit. I've got you down for eighteen.'

I was next in line for the treatment, and I was thinking, 'Well, if he's got the experienced guy down for eighteen, he won't expect me to get more than that.' So imagine my shock when the manager of Luton Town stood in front of me and said, 'Macdonald. The new boy. Learning. Thirty goals.' He moved straight on without saying another word. There was nothing about my pace, and he didn't say I could do this or do that; all I was left with was this seemingly outrageous target of 30 goals. I almost slipped off the highly polished wooden bench we were sitting on.

From me, Alec went on to tell Graham French, our number 11, what he expected of him, but I don't remember a word of that. I just sat there in a daze, saying to myself, 'Thirty goals! He's expecting me to score 30 goals in 46 matches! I can't do that! It's a goal every one and a half games! That's a nonsense total!' But when I'd recovered from the shock, I began to think more positively. 'You've got to build yourself up for this, go for it,' I thought. 'You've got to make scoring opportunities for yourself, you've got to do this, got to do that.' I was running through the whole gamut of football striking in my head.

I don't remember anything else until I was on the field in our opening match, which was at home to Barrow. I started going here and going there, flying into the box, stretching for everything and trying to get on the end of something, but to no avail. Still, we came off the pitch 3–0 winners, a great start to the season. Two points (as it was then for a win) in the bag. Everybody came back into the dressing-room absolutely delighted. The manager was pleased, the coach was pleased, and the crowd had been thoroughly entertained and given great hope for the season.

But I sat down absolutely beside myself with fear and worry, panic almost. 'Well, that's it,' I was thinking. 'That's exactly one in every one and a half games now.' Meanwhile, all the players were coming up to me and saying, 'Well done, son, well played! You made this goal and you set that one up, too.' But all I could think of was goals, goals, goals – nothing but goals. Jimmy Andrews must have realised how I was feeling, because he came up to me quietly and said, 'How are you, son? The result's a perfect start. You just need to get the first one and the rest will all come.' But even those kind words were no solace to me at all.

The following Saturday, we went down to Bournemouth by train. It was a marvellous way to travel then. What Luton used to do was hire a train and have a first-class dining carriage put on the back for the players and officials of the club; the rest of the train they would sell to travelling supporters. We would leave Luton station early on the Saturday morning and be taken to the station nearest the club we were to play. It meant there was no need for expensive overnight accommodation in hotels.

That Bournemouth journey sticks in my mind because during the game, about fifteen minutes into the second half and with the score at 0–0, Mike Keen knocked the ball over the Bournemouth centre-halves and I was through. I took it round the keeper and, yes! I slotted it in. What a relief it was to see that ball trickling over the goal-line. To me, it was like it happened in slow motion. I just leapt for joy. Never had a goal been so important to a professional footballer as that one was to me. I remember lining up for the restart thinking, 'Yes, I'm away from that dreaded 30 figure. Now I'm into the twenties!' All of a sudden I felt lighter, fitter, stronger, faster. The burden had been removed, and I was flying. We won the game 1–0, and, oh, what bliss it was to soak up the congratulations of my team-mates in the dressing-room! I was responsible for the difference between a draw and a win. The trip back on the train just flew by. The supporters who came to ask for autographs just sat down and chatted about the game, and I couldn't get enough of it. It was marvellous, a wonderful feeling. Not only had a weight been lifted off my shoulders, but it was a new experience for me to be heartily congratulated by all ten players in the team. All I'd known before was one or two saying 'Well done'.

From then on, the games couldn't come quick enough for me. Luton began to extend a long unbeaten run at home that had begun the previous season, and which went from the twenties well into the thirties. All the way through the season we were neck and neck with Leyton Orient, both clubs swapping first and second places until we got to the last two games of the season. Both of ours were away from home, at Mansfield and Rochdale, and we needed just a point from them to go up. We got that at Mansfield, where we drew 0–0, and then went on to win at Rochdale.

We did get promotion, then, as runners-up, and we did lose only nine games, as ordered by Alec Stock. And if you go through the list of goals demanded by him from each player, everybody had got within one of his personal total. My haul that season was 29. I went to speak to Alec after the last game as the champagne was beginning to flow and everybody was letting their hair down.

'Boss,' I said, 'I want to apologise.'

'What have you got to apologise for?' he asked.

'I let you down. I only got 29 goals. I was one short of my target, and I'm sorry for that.'

Alec said, 'Don't worry, old son. You see, as long as everybody gets within one, up or down, it doesn't matter. You get there in the end; you get what you set out to achieve. Ours was promotion – that was the most important thing – and, by heavens, we got it. Everybody, more or less, got to his total, and that's good enough. Now we've got to look forward to next season in the Second Division, and don't forget, you owe me one!'

As usual, on the Friday before the first game of the new 1970/71 season, Jimmy Andrews got everybody organised in numerical order around the dressing-room and in came Alec with his book. There had been changes: we had a different goalkeeper, a different left-back and a different winger, but the manager's rigmarole was exactly the same as he set his stall out and let everybody know what he was demanding from them for the season.

I had switched from number 10 to number 9 by this time, and Alec just said to me, 'Nine. Macdonald, the not-so-new boy. Thirty.' But it wasn't a problem for me now. All this man demanded of me was that I go out every game of the season and do my utmost to score goals. He wasn't asking anything else of me at all. 'Score goals. That's your job, that's what I'm paying you for,' he would say. 'I'm not asking you for this, I'm not asking you for that. I'm not asking you to be able to turn centre-halves inside out.'

Alec was no coach. In fact, I never saw him out of his civvies. Jimmy Andrews did all that side of it, so for the most part you just picked up aspects of the game along the way. If you saw an opposing centre-half going up for a corner at your end, for example, you automatically went back with him and did your utmost to stop him scoring. But you wanted to play for Alec because he simplified the game for you, he brought it down to the very basics, all of it stemming from the statistics in that amazing book of his.

It was a pretty successful formula, too. Once the player-manager of Yeovil Town who established the Somerset non-League club's giant-killing reputation by taking them to the fifth round of the FA Cup in 1948/49, beating Sunderland along the way, Alec had managed Leyton Orient, Queens Park Rangers and, for a short time, Roma and Arsenal before taking over at Luton. Ironically, after four years at Kenilworth Road he moved on to Fulham, the club he had rescued me from, and took them to an FA Cup final against West Ham in 1975. He was deaf in one ear, and he turned that deafness to his advantage on more than one occasion. If a player came up to him to ask why he wasn't in the team and was looking for a ruck about it, Alec would just walk away. His excuse was that he hadn't heard him, and that he must have talked to him on his deaf side. The man was one of the greatest characters the game has ever seen, God rest his soul.

It was quite a partnership Luton had then with Alec as manager and Harry Haslam as chief scout. I mentioned that there had been changes in the team at the start of my second season there, and that was largely because of the amazing block signings Harry made. It was one of the most stupendous pieces of transfer business ever done. Just try to imagine it: four top-quality players moving from Manchester United to a Second Division club, all at the same time! One is good, two is great, but *four*? It was phenomenal. The four in question were winger Jimmy Ryan, striker Don Givens, left-back Peter Woods and centre-half Ken Goodman. We were never sure of the actual cost of the deal, but as far as we were aware it didn't cost us anything up front. The money wasn't there in the first place, so it was all very much a surprise to us. We knew the club didn't have the money, yet this incredible piece of business had been done. All we could do was wonder at how Harry had managed it. No doubt it had something to do with his marvellous contacts in Manchester and the fact that he and Matt Busby were old friends.

Jimmy Ryan, who is now back at Old Trafford as a coach, was needed because Frenchie – Graham French – was languishing in prison at the time. Graham was a bit of a lad. He'd got into bad company locally and was sent down for shooting someone. We missed him because he was a hugely important part of Luton's attacking strategy. As an outside-left, Frenchie was so deft and skilled that he could just ghost past full-backs, and the crosses he put over made life so easy for me, Laurie Sheffield and our other striker, Matt Tees. Graham's deputy, Mick Harrison, was a real flyer, but his career was blighted by short hamstring problems and his appearances were limited as a result.

You were always living on the edge with Frenchie. I remember one Saturday during the 1969/70 season when we were travelling by train to Bury and had to be at the station by 7.30 in the morning. There was no Frenchie, of course, but suddenly he turned up at the last minute looking terrible. We, the players, knew he'd been out all night because of the suit he was wearing. He had seven suits, each one a different colour – grey, white, yellow, pink, light blue, dark blue, and so on – for a particular day of the week. So you knew the day by the suit, and he came stepping on to the platform that Saturday morning in Friday's suit. If you can remember, think of the flamboyant TV character Jason King (played by Peter Wyngarde) without his moustache and you'll have a good idea of what Frenchie looked like. He had a roving eye, too, because he rented a house from the club and then let out rooms to air hostesses who flew out of Luton airport. So he brought the action in, so to speak, instead of going out to seek it. You should have seen the state of him that day. The players got round him, manoeuvred him into the carriage, sat him down and told him to go to sleep. He wanted to sing all the way, but eventually he dropped off and slept for the rest of the journey while we kept him hidden, as best we could, from prying managerial eyes. When we got to Bury, we woke him up and dragged him on to the team bus. The skipper, Mike Keen, spoke for us all when he said to him, 'You'd better have an absolute blinder today, Frenchie. You owe us.' Mike was as strait-laced as they came, but a great pro who had a wonderful ability to cope with Graham and get the best out of him.

It seemed to work that time, too, because after eighteen minutes we were 2–0 up with goals by me and Matt Tees, both of them from Frenchie's crosses. Then Graham said, 'Excuse me, lads,' went over to the touchline and honked up. 'Boss, boss, get me off!' he pleaded to Alec Stock.

'He's pissed!' Alec said dismissively. 'Get the sub on!'

Alec knew Frenchie always sailed close to the wind, and sometimes beyond, and seeing that the players were in control of the situation he didn't make a fuss. I think we went on to score another goal, but Frenchie's blinding twenty minutes had left Bury chasing the game.

The Luton players first heard about his arrest in the summer of 1970, at the start of my second season at Kenilworth Road. We were all on the bus outside the ground ready to go and play a pre-season friendly in Belgium, and there was a bit of a buzz among the players. I asked what was going on. 'Oh,' they said, 'it's Frenchie. It seems like he's in trouble. He's not here, that's for sure. There's something going on.' Jimmy Andrews came down the bus, told us there would be a bit of a delay, and asked us to be patient. Then Alec Stock climbed aboard and got into conversation with Jimmy. Finally, the club secretary joined them and whispered something in Alec's ear. At that, Alec stood up and said, 'Well, we're going to continue with the trip, but it's going to be minus Graham French. I might as well let you all know, because you're going to find out sooner or later, that Frenchie was arrested last night.' He explained that the incident had taken place at a pub called the Parrot, which was Frenchie's favourite haunt and also the haunt of a sort of hoodlum element in Luton, and he'd been arrested for shooting a man.

We all laughed at this unbelievable news and said, 'Are you serious?'

'I am,' replied Alec. 'He's in the cells now for shooting a man who is in hospital and is said to be comfortable, which says a lot for Frenchie's accuracy!'

I forget now what his sentence was. I think it could have been four years for wounding with intent, or maybe they talked it down to malicious wounding. The club was brilliant with him, though. When he got out, I'd already gone to Newcastle, but throughout his time in prison Luton kept him supplied with lager and cigarettes.

Jimmy Ryan played on the other side to Frenchie, of course, and I think the best way to describe him would be as a poor man's Ryan Giggs. I don't mean that disparagingly because Jim was a very good player, but he was not quite as good as Giggsy. Not many are, come to that. Don Givens was a bit special, too. Having come up through the ranks at Manchester United, he'd had a grandiose upbringing compared to me; he was steak and chips to my fish and chips. He was extremely long-legged and brilliant in the air. He hovered around quickly without ever seeming to move fast, and he could head it and shoot. In other words, this guy could play. His 56 caps for the Republic of Ireland are proof of that.

It was around the time that I was adjusting to a new attacking partnership with Don that a funny thing happened to me on the way to Luton's town centre. I'd gone shopping there after training one Monday afternoon when I was approached by a policeman in a very officious manner. Your knees wobble a bit, don't they, when a policeman gives you a hard stare and comes striding over with his full regalia on? Your knees wobble even though you know you're not guilty of anything! The policeman said to me, 'Are you Malcolm Macdonald, the Luton Town footballer?'

'Yes, I am,' I replied.

'Right,' he said. 'We've had a message. You must contact the football club as soon as possible.'

'Really?'

'Yes, it's an emergency.'

You start to imagine all sorts of terrible things when you hear something like that, but when I rang the club, they said, 'Get yourself ready. You've been called up for the England under-23 side.'

'For when?' I enquired.

'For today,' came the answer. 'You're the late call-up for the squad.'

'Oh, right. Where have I got to go to?'

'Come into the club first, then you're off to Glasgow.'

And so off to Scotland I went to join the under-23s at the Marine Hotel, Troon. That was my first meeting with Sir Alf Ramsey, who was in charge of the squad, and I found him to be one of the most polite men I have ever met in my life. He thanked me profusely for putting myself out and making the journey, and he hoped I hadn't been prevented from doing anything important. In fact, he made me feel like a million dollars! 'No, thank you for inviting me,' I said. 'It's come as a great surprise.' I was only twenty, and I was a substitute on the Wednesday night at Hampden Park. I didn't get on, but Alf made it quite clear to me that there was more to come. He asked me about Luton Town and what our plans were, and I just gave him an honest answer. 'We're hoping to get promotion again,' I said. 'We're just going for it.'

That first call-up was a wonderful experience. It was a great honour, and I was with players much older than I was. It was a great squad, and it broadened my horizons. It made me see the game in a greater perspective, and I feel sure that it enriched me. I'll certainly never forget returning to Luton and going into training on the Friday morning, because all the players were absolutely fascinated. 'Come on, tell us all about it,' they said. It seemed as if my status with them had gone up hugely, and they wanted to know everything. 'What's it like? What's Sir Alf like? What's the team like? What was the game like? What's Hampden Park like?' The questions never stopped coming.

It occurred to me later that I might not have got the call from England in time had I been playing for a bigger club. This was in the days long before mobile phones, and if I'd been with one of the top London clubs, for example, I wouldn't have known anything about it until the evening. By then it could have been too late and Alf would have put somebody else in. But that's how it worked in a small town like Luton. The club simply called the police and asked them to put out an all-points search for me.

I have many other reasons to remember the Bedfordshire club and town with affection. One of them was the recruitment of Eric Morecambe, one half of the celebrated and much-loved comedy duo, as a director of the club. In fact, Luton became nationally famous overnight because Eric, who lived just a few miles south in upmarket Harpenden, was persuaded to join the board. It goes without saying that we in the dressing room were tickled pink when we heard the news. It was, perhaps, the most famous signing a club of that size had ever made.

When Eric was introduced to us, he was in his element. I think he was far happier there with the lads, joining in the quick-fire banter, the rapid humour and the piss-taking, than he was up in the boardroom with the other directors. I suppose we got to know him pretty well, but the players were in for a big surprise when, in a complete reversal of a footballer's usual situation, they started to pester him for tickets for the recording of his shows. Eric kept putting them off and putting them off until finally, he said, 'Look, I'm going to have to talk to you lot, aren't I? Please try to understand when I say to you that I work very hard, and the last thing I want is you bunch of piss-takers in the audience when I'm trying to work.' In retaliation, we said in that case we didn't want him in the stand when we were playing. How dare he come and watch us work when we couldn't go and watch him! This brought on an immediate flurry of pipe-sucking from Eric, but he was adamant that none of us would be allowed to join his TV studio audience, and none of us ever was.

If that was Eric being the professional perfectionist, another incident showed us the sensitivity, insecurity even, that lay beneath the jocular front he presented to the world. It happened right at the end of a very long unbeaten run at home. We'd actually overtaken the previous record, so every time we won or drew it extended the new record by another game. The run finished up at 36 games in all. Anyway, Eric arrived at Kenilworth Road the day after Boxing Day in 1970 to watch us play Gillingham. Unexpectedly, we got beaten 2–1, and that ended this record, which had covered the whole of the previous season and gone way back into the one before. Players are somewhat philosophical when it comes to losing, because they know you can't win or draw all the time. Sportsmen have to get used to losing and use it as a springboard for improvement, but it doesn't take away the huge disappointment at the time. So we were all sitting there absolutely shattered physically, despondent and angry mentally, when Eric breezed into the dressing room. 'Never mind, guys, there's always another time,' he said, trying to cheer us up. Eleven pairs of muddy football boots flew instantly in the direction of his head. Eric was so shocked by this response that his face fell and he just turned and fled the dressing-room.

When he'd gone, we took a bath, got changed and went upstairs to the Hatters Club, which had been built out at the back of the club on pillars over a railway line. It held about 500 people and was where all the privileged supporters – shareholders, players' families and friends, and so on – used to gather. Usually, Eric would leave the boardroom and come and join us there, but there was no sign of him on this occasion. Not only had he scarpered from the dressing-room, we discovered, he had actually left the ground. In fact, nobody at the club saw him or heard from him for a week or two.

One of the players, Roger Hoy, had got to know Eric particularly well. Roger, a very forward guy, was very funny himself and good company, and he went to Eric's house on occasion. Roger decided to go and see him at home and find out what the problem was. When he saw us the following morning, he told us that Eric was absolutely heartbroken and full of apologies. He admitted to Roger he had done the one thing he would have so hated happening in his own dressing-room after he'd had a bad day on stage. He felt so guilty about breaking his own golden rule, as it were, that he couldn't face us. So Roger said to him, in effect, 'Wait a minute. You having a bad day on stage is a lot different to us losing because there's nobody seeking to stop you from being good. Football is a different way of life where you've got eleven guys and they're doing their utmost to beat us, and we accept there are times when the fates are conspiring in our opponents' favour rather than ours. Sooner or later, that unbeaten run had to come to an end. At that moment in time, when we were disappointed, we meant no animosity to you. Basically, it was just an obvious reaction to the first person who said a word.'

'So,' we asked Roger, 'is he coming back?'

'Yes, he'll be back,' came the reply.

Sure enough, the following Saturday, when we were playing at home again, a bespectacled face popped itself round the dressing-room door and said, 'Up yours too!' To which Eric, for it was he, got a loud response of, 'You can f★★k off again!' But the matter was closed and put behind us. What we came to realise, of course, was that beneath the mask, Eric was a very emotional, very caring guy who hated to do anything wrong at all and was absolutely unforgiving of himself.

What you saw of Eric on television is what you got in public. Every autograph hunter got the back of a hand under their chin with a 'Get out of that! You can't, can you?', while ladies who approached him would find their faces sort of cupped in his hand and given a gentle slap. A lot gentler than the ones he used to give Ernie Wise, that's for sure! All the time, though, you could see him watching situations develop. It was almost as if he was thinking, 'How can I do that? How can I incorporate it in the act?'

Which brings me to a rather amusing tale. One day, Alec Stock came into the dressing-room and said, 'Well, it's about time we had a shindig. But it'll be best bib and tucker, mind.' At this, us younger ones looked at one another as if to say, 'What's best bib and tucker?' Alec immediately picked up on that and explained. 'We're having a black tie evening, gentlemen, so you had better go and get your monkey suits. If you haven't got one, go and hire one.'

I didn't have a dinner suit. In fact, I'd only got two suits to my name at that stage in my life. After signing for Luton, I'd gone to the local Hepworths branch and had them made. So I asked Alan Starling, the goalkeeper, where I could hire a dinner suit, and he told me there was a Moss Bros in Dunstable, just down the road from Luton. I went there, got myself measured for a suit and bought a dress shirt and a dickie bow at the same time.

On the morning of the dinner dance that had been organised in the Hatters Club, I went back to Moss Bros to collect the suit. They gave it to me in a grey case and off I went home. That evening, having had a bath, I got my shirt and bow-tie on and opened up the case. I then took out a pair of trousers so big that I realised at once there had been an almighty cock-up – almighty being the operative word. Those trousers would have swamped a couple of Billy Bunters, never mind me! When I'd put them on and done everything up, you couldn't see my feet because the bottoms of the legs were all crinkly, and the beltline ballooned around my upper waist. The hire shop was shut by then, so emergency alterations had to be carried out quickly. The bottoms were folded under and the top pulled tight and sort of pinned together behind me. In the end, I thought I could just about get away with it if I put on two pairs of braces to make sure. Then I put the jacket on and discovered to my horror that where the lapels came down in a V you could see six inches of trousers across my chest. I didn't have another pair of black trousers, so I had to go as I was. I kept the jacket buttoned up, because when you are as young as I was at the time, you are so self-conscious about something like that. Particularly when you and your wife are seated on the same table as the famous Eric Morecambe and his wife.

Everything was fine for a while. We sat down and had our meal. But then a four-piece band struck up and Eric took his wife, Joan, up for a couple of dances. I just sat there, not wanting to move my bum off the seat, but Eric said, 'Come on, you miserable sod! Get up and dance!' With that, he invited my wife, Julie, to dance and sort of pulled me out of my seat to dance with his wife. Desperate now, I said, 'I don't really dance,' but Joan Morecambe, a lovely, lovely lady, insisted. 'Now come on,' she said, 'you can't sit there all night.'

The band were playing a fairly slow number, so I thought I might be able to get away with it. But no sooner had we got on the dance floor than the music changed to something quicker and Joan started jigging away in front of me saying, 'Come on, come on, come on!' Eric and my wife were doing the same thing, so I thought, 'Oh well, I'm going to have to join in.' But as soon as I started prancing about, the pin holding everything together at the back flew off and the trousers just went woof! and blew up like a balloon. There I was, jigging away, and the trousers were sort of bouncing up and down in front of me. Eric nearly pissed himself laughing at the sight of these incredible expanding strides. I cannot tell you how far gone he was; he was in utter hysterics. Joan was laughing too, and so was everybody else. So I just thought, 'Oh, to hell with it! Go with the flow!'

When we got back to the table, the trousers were so voluminous it was almost as if I'd got a hoop in them, just like those trousers the circus clowns wear. Then I noticed Eric had sat down and lit his pipe, his mind somewhere completely different. People would come up to ask for his autograph, but there would be no cheery greeting. He'd just hold the pen and sign, almost without looking. He was away, totally, in a world of his own, and you could practically see him working out how he could use what he'd just seen out there on the dance floor. In fact, when you think of all those Morecambe and Wise Christmas specials in the 1970s, just about every one had an ill-fitting item of clothing in it. Eric himself used to wear those ridiculous plus-fours that stuck out at the sides; and who could possibly forget Shirley Bassey and the outsize boot?

When not making a fool of myself in the Hatters Club and providing Eric Morecambe with inspiration for comic sketches, I was working hard to improve my ability as a striker. All the way through my career I had this great hunger for self-improvement, but never more so than when I was at Luton. As always, I didn't have to look much further than Harry Haslam for help. Harry gave me a huge amount of encouragement during my two seasons at Kenilworth Road. In fact, he gave a lot of people encouragement. A great talent-spotter, he was responsible for many youngsters coming through the lower grades and going on to do the business at the highest level. And in every case he established an everlasting personal friendship.

Harry had an office above Luton's souvenir shop on the corner of Oak Road, where I lived, and I would go and sit there the odd afternoon each week, have a cup of tea and just chat. He would make his wisecracks, and other people would come in and join the conversation. But those little chats were hugely advantageous because Harry, in a very different way to Alec Stock, was inspirational. It was not so much a father-and-son as a nephew-and-favourite-uncle relationship we had, but he had known me since I was sixteen, and he knew me almost better than I knew myself. If I had a problem of any kind, I would go and see Harry about it, not Alec Stock. He'd always come up with little thoughts. 'What you should do on Saturday...' he'd suggest, or, 'Have you thought about this and maybe that?' All the time, ideas were planted in my mind over those cups of tea with Harry.

He provided practical help, too. I don't know where Luton train now, but in those days we used to use the Vauxhall Motors sports ground. The facilities were fine in most respects, but there was no scope for the specialised training I was after. 'I'm not getting enough work in training for what I feel I need to do myself,' I told Harry. 'It's mostly teamwork and fitness training we do, but I need a whole host of stuff myself.' What I wanted was a place where I could concentrate intensively on honing my goalscoring technique.

I found it at first in a small room above that souvenir shop in Oak Road. It was meant to be a stock room, but it was never used by the people who ran the shop. I would practise in there using a plastic football with an autographed picture of Johnny Giles, then Leeds' gifted little midfield playmaker and occasional enforcer, on it. Giles kicked me a few times, but that was about the only time I ever managed to give him a good kicking back! When I had to find alternative premises because I was driving the people in the shop below mad, Harry found me an empty warehouse the Co-op no longer used. I'd get some training kit from the ground, go home after training for some lunch, collect the plastic ball from Harry and drive to the warehouse with the keys to unlock it.

It was about 40 yards from one side to the other, and the walls were constructed in such a way that you could imagine part of them to be the frame of a goal. Harry had said, 'What you need to work on is getting the ball, turning and shooting. Get it, turn, shoot; get it, turn, shoot. And you need to work on it so that you can do it quicker than you can say it.' So what I'd do was drive the ball against one wall and, no matter how it rebounded to me, control it with one touch, turn and shoot against the other wall. Get it, turn, shoot… get it, turn, shoot… get it, turn, shoot. I'd repeat the same exercise over and over again until I was so dizzy with exhaustion I nearly blacked out. I used to do it for two hours, sometimes four, on at least two afternoons a week. Those plastic balls fly all over the place, and I think it was a bit of psychology on Harry's part to make me use one. In other words, if I could learn to control that, I could control anything. Being naturally left-footed, I also used those private practice sessions to make myself as strong on my right side as I was on the left. Instead of controlling the ball with the right foot and turning and shooting with the left, I'd do it the other way round until I was satisfied I was completely two-footed. Just to make things a little bit more difficult for defenders, I worked on controlling the ball and shooting with the same foot too.

All the time, Harry kept saying to me, 'You have to shoot; the most important thing is to shoot. Twice on Saturday there was a shooting opportunity, but you laid the ball off to somebody else. You didn't take the opportunity at its optimum moment. You cannot afford to let those moments pass. OK, in the end you did something that might seem to be for the benefit of the team, but really it's not. You've missed your particular moment.' And if I protested that I hadn't seen it as a shooting opportunity, that it hadn't felt right, Harry would reply, 'Never mind if it doesn't feel right, just shoot. Shoot, shoot, shoot!' He came up with a little wheeze to ram home his advice. 'Look,' he said, 'I've done this before with people. Before you go out on Saturday, get two large wads of cotton wool and hold one in each fist. They are there to remind you that you are out on that pitch to shoot!' So, in my first season at Luton, I played with wads of cotton wool clenched tight in my hands. I only needed them for a couple of games; after that I would shoot from basically anywhere at what I felt was the optimum moment.

Something else I strove to perfect in that Luton warehouse was the art of mishitting a volley. Coaches will tell you that, to volley the ball properly, you must catch it in the centre with the meat of the foot. But when I was practising volleys one day and striking the ball perfectly, I found they were going over the bar. I began to wonder whether I might have more chance of scoring if I actually mishit the volley, and after a lot of practice I discovered that if you hit the top of the ball just right with your foot – that is, put topspin on it like a tennis player – and drove it downwards into the ground, you stood a good chance of surprising the goalkeeper with the bounce. I scored a lot of goals that way.

I would be the first to admit I was not technically gifted as a footballer, but nobody worked harder than I did to make myself better at what I was good at, which was scoring goals. I was quite content to let others do the fancy stuff; to my mind, I was the goalscorer and my whole attention had to be centred on that wooden frame at the end of the pitch, and on how I was going to get the ball into it. Fortunately, everybody at Luton was happy for me to do just that. I would take part in the general training, the coaching, the team plans, the formations and what have you, but I was excluded to a degree from most things because when somebody put a size nine leather to leather, my job was to tear off in pursuit of the ball, hunting it and knocking people all over the place in an effort to get control of it.

Nobody at that stage of my career sought to make the game confusing for me. Luton seemed to accept that the task of scoring goals was enough in itself, and for that I have remained eternally grateful to them. It was as if my personality changed when the ball crossed the halfway line; that's when I went into overdrive. Jimmy Andrews knew that, and so did Alec Stock and Harry Haslam. The players did too, and they were happy for me just to concentrate on scoring. They knew that once they got the ball up to or over the halfway line, it was mine. I scored a number of goals for Luton after receiving the ball around the middle of the pitch. It almost became a trademark for me, that run from the halfway line with the ball, out-sprinting centre-halves and full-backs alike, rounding the goalkeeper and slotting it home.

Every time I got the ball, my instant reaction was, 'How can I score?' I might be 50 yards from goal, but I would run at defenders and take them on. If I lost the ball, nobody said anything except, 'Hard luck! Keep going!' I would even get praised after losing the ball, and this just encouraged me more and more to seek every conceivable way of beating defenders, getting goalside and creating an angle. All the time at Luton it was encourage, encourage, encourage. I was chuffed with that. Nobody ever knocked me. Never was there a word of criticism. Later, at Newcastle and Arsenal, I found that other players would say, 'What the hell do you think you're doing, you greedy bastard?' But at Luton nobody ever called me that. The reason, I think, was the mentality Alec Stock created among his players: goalkeepers are there to make saves, defenders are there to stop balls and break down attacking play, midfielders are there to help defenders keep clean sheets, and forwards score goals. It didn't have to be clever or fancy or pretty; just make sure you keep peppering that goal. I could come off the pitch having missed chance after chance and the other players would just say, 'Well done, old son! You were murdering them!' We had a lot of intelligent players, and they knew that if I kept their defence worried stiff, the opposition would be less likely to present a problem as a whole. It can easily get to the point where you are more worried about what's happening behind you than in front of you. So it was all hugely encouraging, and I loved it. Every Saturday I just wanted to get in the dressing-room, get my kit on and shout, 'Come on, let's go out and get at the bastards!' I really couldn't wait for every match to come around.

My reputation for goalscoring was built at Luton. By the end of the 1970/71 season I still had an awful lot of developing to do, but the process had gone beyond the prototype stage. Scoring goals is not so much a physical thing as a state of mind. One hears the phrase 'he's not a natural goalscorer'. What the hell does that mean? What I think people are actually trying to say is that his be-all and end-all when on the field isn't to score goals. In my case, Harry Haslam had got me thinking totally about goals, about the need to shoot. People trivialise it with phrases like 'if you don't buy a ticket, you'll never win the raffle'. The process is deeper than that: it is a question of building up a fund of knowledge that develops into a goalscoring philosophy.

Alec Stock's statistics soon began to have a greater effect on me than just concentrating on reaching the target he had set. I began to log, in my mind, the number of times I struck the ball in our opponents' half, and what I actually did with it. I worked out that every six times I had the ball in the opposing half I had to have a goalscoring shot with at least one of them. The other five might hit the woodwork, or be saved by the keeper, or be blocked by a defender, or simply miss the target, but one of the six had to go in. That was the sort of mentality I was taking on to the field. I was thinking, 'OK, this half I need to get so many shots on goal. That means I've got to make myself space.' All the time I was working out how to create the space that enabled a team-mate to get the ball to me, be it to my feet or in behind the defence when I was ready to make a run.

In spite of everything, though, Luton's campaign for a second successive promotion didn't go well. The new players had strengthened the team and I was still scoring regularly, but we were losing matches we should have won. Easter is always the crucial time in the League, and we went into the holiday programme in fifth place in the Second Division, I think, but we took only one point from the two Easter games and dropped down to sixth.

Towards the end of the season, we'd just finished a training session at Kenilworth Road when Alec Stock came out and walked me from the perimeter track on to the pitch. As we walked, he kept looking over his shoulder, and then over my shoulder, as if he was looking for a tidemark on my neck. 'What on earth is going on?' I wondered.

'The club's got the bank on its back,' Alec began, 'and it looks like promotion's out of the window, so we're badly in need of something in the coffers. It's a terrible thing when a club finds itself in this kind of situation, because you have to sell your best. I have to tell you, then, that we are seriously considering letting you go to another club. But look at it from your point of view. It's a natural progression for you: you'll be going into the big league. It would have been nice if we could all have done it together, but that, I don't think, is to be. So you will not be playing here next season.' He went on to explain that three clubs had been showing an interest in me: Manchester United, Chelsea and Newcastle. Newcastle, Alec added, had easily been the most enthusiastic. 'They are very, very keen. From directors to manager to coach, they have been regular visitors to every game over the past few weeks, and we've even had official talks. Now that's just putting you in the picture, old son. The best thing you can do between now and the end of the season is just keep sticking them in the back of the net.'

'OK,' I said. 'Fair enough.'

My reaction was one of acceptance of the common sense he was giving me. I appreciated very much, too, the fact that he was keeping me informed of the situation. He was giving me plenty of warning, and yes, I was ready for the step up. I knew I had to go, and that this was the time to do it.

The last game of the season was a midweek match at Kenilworth Road against Cardiff City, who finished third that season. It turned out that we needed to beat them by two clear goals to qualify for the Watney Cup, a pre-season tournament open to the clubs that had scored the most goals in each of the four divisions of the old Football League. This competition didn't last long, but it was the lifeblood of smaller provincial clubs like Luton. So the talk before the game was, 'OK, we've missed out on promotion, but the least we can do for the good people of Luton is give them the opportunity of a further competition.'

I went on the field having already matched my 29 goals of the previous season, and I got the first against Cardiff. Then, in the second half, I got two more, and we won 3–0. I knew this was my last match for Luton Town, and I'm glad to be able to say I finished it in style, to use an Alec Stock phrase. When I came off the pitch, I went straight up to him and said, 'There you go, boss – not only my total for this season, but I got you the one back from last season, and there's one to spare as well!'

Smiling, because I was playing the game the way he liked it to be played, he said, 'Come and see me Friday morning. I'm going to have some news for you.'

I went on the Friday as requested and was told that Alec had been on the phone. He would be at the ground in about half an hour, and would I please wait. When he came breezing in, he said, 'Come on through, old son, come on through. I've got some interesting news for you.' I went into his office, and he continued, 'I've just been down at the Great Northern Hotel at King's Cross and had a very interesting chat with Joe Harvey, the Newcastle manager, and his board of directors. They're all down for tomorrow's FA Cup final and I have just agreed a fee of £185,000 for you to join them. Now, go and have a chat with them yourself and make yourself a bloody fortune. This is the big time, old son.'

Having driven down to the Great Northern, I asked at reception if

Mr Harvey of Newcastle United was available, and the lass behind the desk said, 'Oh, yes. He's in the lounge at the end of that corridor.' But as I was walking along the corridor, the large frame of Joe Harvey filled the doorway.

There was no mistaking Joe because I'd seen him play for Newcastle at Fulham when I was a kid. There's one game that sticks in my memory to this day. It was a fourth-round FA Cup tie in 1956 that brought all the Newcastle stars – Jimmy Scoular, Joe Harvey, Jackie Milburn and the rest – down to Craven Cottage. I was at primary school then, and I remember the headmistress calling an assembly and saying that if anybody wished to watch the game they could take the afternoon off (all matches had to be played in daylight at that time because there were no floodlights). Not only that, but the school was so close to Craven Cottage that there were going to be thousands of people milling around outside. If memory serves, they actually closed the school at lunchtime so the kids didn't have to go home through all the crowds. Needless to say, I went to the match, and it was one of the most fantastic games of football I have ever seen. Newcastle won 5–4, and one of the most influential players on the field was the no-nonsense midfield hardman Joe Harvey.

And there he was at the end of this corridor.

'Good morning, Mr Harvey,' I said. 'My name's Malcolm Macdonald. Alec Stock, the Luton manager, has asked me to come and meet with you.'

I was a little taken aback when his first words to me were, 'So, you're the little bastard who's just cost me another thirty-five grand. What the hell did you think you were doing scoring a hat-trick in your last game? Do you realise the deal was already done for £150,000 before your manager, with you scoring that bloody hat-trick, whacked the price up?' And then he laughed, and I laughed. After that, we sat down and got on like a house on fire. I loved Joe. He was very different to Alec Stock in a lot of ways, but at the same time very similar.

When I got back to Luton, I told Alec that everything had been agreed and that I'd signed for Newcastle, subject to a medical on the Monday.

'Oh, yes, Monday,' he said. 'Right. We've got a little bit of a surprise for you. You've done absolutely wonderfully for this football club. We shall never be able to thank you enough for all that you've done, and we wish you everything we can possibly wish you in terms of success for the rest of your career, and especially at Newcastle United. What we are putting in the bank from this deal [the fee of £185,000 was a record for both clubs at the time] is the saving of Luton Town for a long time to come. We are going to send you off in style, old son. What time are you leaving on Monday morning? Eight o'clock? Be here at that time then.'

When I turned up at Kenilworth Road at the appointed hour, there was a Rolls-Royce waiting for me. It had been organised by the club and one of the club's sponsors, and one of the directors was to act as my chauffeur and drive me all the way up to Newcastle. So I arrived at St James's Park for the medical in a Roller, and as we pulled into the big main gate there was a crowd of media people bigger than I had ever seen in my life. At Luton there had been just a couple of newspapermen, Roger Duckworth of the *Evening Post* and Eric Pugh of the *Luton News*. They were the only two pressmen I'd ever come across up to that point. But here was a heaving media mob. There were television cameras, flash cameras, microphones and about 50 notebooks and pencils at the ready.

The Rolls-Royce stopped by the steps and the driver got out, came round the back and opened the door for me. As I got out, someone remarked, 'F★★k me! This is the first time I've ever seen a football player actually arrive in his signing-on fee!' It turned out to be that great joker Bob Cass, lately of the *Mail on Sunday* but then the *Sun's* man in the north-east, and his crack broke the ice.

# CHAPTER FOUR
# NEWCASTLE: TALK OF THE TOON

Having made my grand entrance at St James's Park, I went inside for the medical, which was a formality because I'd never had an injury and clubs send the injury file on. I'd had a bit of ankle trouble at Luton, but that didn't cause me to miss any games because the one I would have missed had been postponed owing to bad weather. So I'd played in every single game, and when a 100 per cent playing record over two seasons appears, the medical just flies through. There was a quick check of the joints, and I passed A1.

Then it was on to the press conference, where the football reporters told me there was some surprise at my willingness to join Newcastle because normally it was players in the north who travelled south, and this was a reversal of that trend. When they asked what my reasons were, I talked about my desire to play for a club that had a great tradition, particularly where goalscorers were concerned. The tradition at Newcastle, I said, was a nationally known thing going back to Jackie Milburn and Hughie Gallacher.

So far, so good. But then I was asked whether I was setting any targets for myself. Automatically, I said, 'Yes. I look to score 30 goals every season.' I didn't know any different, because that was the figure Alec Stock had set for me. I had just missed it the first season but reached it the second time around, so as far as I was concerned it wasn't impossible. But the intake of breath when I said it was audible, and the muttering started: 'The flash git! Who does he think he is, a London loudmouth coming up here full of bullshit?' The press put me down as a cocky bastard from the start, but I'd been asked a question and had just given an honest answer. I was setting out at Newcastle to do exactly what I'd done at Luton – score 30 goals a season. It just seemed a natural thing for me to do. The general consensus, however, seemed to be that I was off my head. Bob Cass came up to me after the press conference and said, 'Are you quite serious about it?' I said I was, and told him the story behind what I'd said. Even Joe Harvey pulled me aside.

'Don't you think you've put yourself under a bit of pressure?' he said.

'Joe,' I replied, 'nobody could put me under the pressure Alec Stock did, just by giving me that total in the first place. I missed it by one in the first season, then went two over it the next. That's what I'm here for.'

Impressed, Joe enthused, 'I f★★★ing love it! It'll do for me!'

The following day, the reaction to what I'd said was very mixed. In a number of papers I was called a loudmouth, but others were saying that this guy means business. Overall, though, there were reservations about me because I hadn't played at the highest level of the game, and most people were questioning the arrogance, the brashness of somebody like that thinking he would automatically succeed and figure somewhere around the top of the goalscoring charts. From then on the press attention on me was more acute, and I was often asked why I had put myself under such pressure. My answer was the same one I'd given Joe Harvey: 'I'm here to score goals. I only talk about goals and the targets I'm aiming at. Why is that naive? That's not putting yourself under pressure. You are under pressure just by being a footballer in the first place. I'm setting out to prove myself as a goalscorer.'

Unqualified support came from a mild-mannered, quietly spoken chap who wandered up to me at the end of the press conference and started talking in a very knowledgeable fashion about football in general and Newcastle United in particular. Suddenly, it dawned on me who I was talking to: he was the player I'd seen terrorising Fulham with his pace when I was a lad. I was talking to the great Jackie Milburn himself. You can imagine how grateful and privileged I felt, then, when Jackie, who was working as a journalist for the *News of the World* at the time, said he would give me the low-down on playing for Newcastle. He said some lovely, flattering things and clearly knew what kind of a player I was. 'The crowd here will adore you,' he reassured me. 'You're quick and you're strong, and they will love the way you play. What you have to do is exactly what you've been doing at Luton. Don't change your ways and try to play the game. You just think goals – that's all they want of you. There's more I can tell you, but first and foremost you need to get settled in. You don't want all that hassle of staying in hotels. When do you intend to start house-hunting?' When I told him I was going back to Luton to sort various things out and planned to return later in the week, he told me to give him a ring when I was coming up. 'I'll meet you at the ground,' he said. 'You leave your car here and we'll go off and I'll show you Tyneside.'

Sure enough, there was Jackie, good as gold, waiting for me when I returned. He popped me into his car and drove me down the coast road. We went to Tynemouth and Whitley Bay, up the coast, then we came across through Morpeth, Cramlington and Stannington to Gosforth and Jesmond. They were the areas of Tyneside in which I should be looking to live, he told me. I was very impressed, but it was the conversation as we were driving around that really fascinated me. Jackie talked of the Geordie public who revered their number 9s. It was a magical, spellbinding number to them, he stressed, and they looked to the man in that shirt to create the week's conversation for them. 'You have to understand the people and what their lives are like,' he told me. As we were driving, he pointed out the shipyards at Wallsend, and when we were up around the Ashington area he took me to the coal mines. He showed me where the industrial estates and factories were built on the edge of residential areas. Jackie took me along the famous Scotswood Road too. 'Now you know the song "Blaydon Races"?' he said. 'Well, this is Scotswood Road, and these are the kind of people who used to go along it on their way to the Blaydon Races.' And there really was a pub on every corner then, although none of them is there now. He gave me an almost street-by-street, pub-by-pub tour. You go along Scotswood

Road and you come to Vickers Armstrong. He talked of the armaments that came out of there – tanks and God knows what else – and the thousands of people who worked there and what their lives were like.

'These people,' he explained, 'their lives are humdrum, the jobs make them humdrum. They don't have much money in their pockets, but they like a pint and they want to talk football. So it's your job, on a Saturday afternoon, to give these hard-working people enough conversation for the whole week. You've got 90 minutes every week to do it. It's your job to get on that field and have as many shots at goal as possible, to create as much excitement in the opposing penalty area as you possibly can. Every time you get the ball, you've got to give them something to remember, something for their weekly conversation in the pubs. Above all, don't let coaches talk you into anything other than what you've been bought for. That is to score goals. Every time you get the ball, you must think, "How can I score a goal?" You've got to do your damnedest to stick it in the net. Remember, the opposing half is your stage. There are ten others in the team to look after everything in the other half, and eleven being there is not going to make that much difference.

'There is one thing you must ensure. It is that, during a game, you maintain enough fitness, strength and stamina to be a threat right to the end. In the last minute, when the ball is just booted out of defence, you've got to fight tooth and nail to get it, control it and then be able to run with it from the halfway line. You are going to have people kicking at you, pulling you and doing everything in their power to stop you, but you've got to have the strength to see them off. Then, when you've got to the opposing penalty area, you've still got to have the stamina to compose yourself and beat the goalkeeper. All this because you are the match-winner. Let nobody talk you into being anything else.'

What he said was music to my ears, of course. Jackie was echoing exactly what Alec Stock had always told me.

'But that's how I am on the football field, anyway,' I said. 'Alec Stock told me to be like that.'

'Well, he's a shrewd old feller, that Alec Stock,' said Jackie. 'And don't think I'm telling you any tales out of school either, because Joe Harvey and I are great friends. Joe has told me exactly why he's bought you and what he wants from you. He knows, like I do, what the crowd want to see. So don't let the coaches or the defenders tell you any different.'

'All right,' I said, 'they won't.'

Before even having kicked a ball, then, or even tried on the Newcastle kit, my mind was being prepared as to what exactly I needed to do. And as I've said, it was no different from what I'd done at Luton. But when you actually hear it being spelt out by somebody who's been there at the top and has already done the business, it has a big impact on you. And, you know, Jackie never once told me a single anecdote from his playing days in a Newcastle shirt. He didn't say, 'When I was playing...', he only said, 'When you go out there on Saturday ...' It was just naturally assumed between the two of us that he was talking from a wealth of experience and didn't need to recount a particular moment. He talked of the big picture, but he still had me at the centre of it; he never put himself there.

Nor did Jackie's invaluable assistance end at that point. After spending a week in Bedfordshire, I made contact with him again. 'Come on,' he said. 'I've made a few phone calls and I've now got something definite to show you.' He showed me houses in all the various regions, but left Morpeth till last. When we got there, he commented, 'I think you might get a nice deal here. If ever there was a good place to buy at this particular time, it's Morpeth.'

Thanks to Jackie, I found a pleasant new house on the edge of an estate that has since been hugely developed. Morpeth is a lovely area only twenty minutes from Newcastle, and the deal was done after Jackie had taken me in and introduced me to the managing director of the building company. In my second season at Luton, Julie and I had moved out of the club house in Oak Road and bought a three-bedroom link detached house in Flitwick, a village about twelve miles north of the town. I got that for £6,250 and sold it a matter of months later for £7,250. A grand was a lot of money in those days, and it helped us purchase the four-bedroom detached house in Morpeth for £7,500.

During those early trips of mine down south, I went to see my agent, Reg Hayter, in London. Before the end of my time at Luton, Alec Stock had said he wanted to introduce me to a very good friend of his. That friend was Reg, and Alec spelt out to me that what he was capable of doing for me went beyond what anybody in a football club could do. Reg's main occupation was as a journalist. He ran London's famous

Hayters Sports Agency, which has schooled celebrities such as the Sky Sports and BBC Television presenters Richard Keys and Steve Rider as well as many of the national newspapers' leading sports writers. At the time he took me on, Reg was representing Bob Wilson, then the Arsenal and Scotland goalkeeper, and Basil D'Oliveira, the Worcestershire and England cricketer. Later, Ian Botham became his fourth and last client, so I like to think I was in select company.

Anyway, when I went down to London to see Reg, he said I was causing a stir not just on Tyneside but all over the country before I'd even kicked a ball for Newcastle. He asked if I was all right.

'Yeah, don't worry about me,' I said. 'I'm all right.'

'OK,' said Reg, 'then let's go and have something to eat. We're having lunch with Frank Nicklin, the sports editor of the *Sun*.'

'That's interesting,' I replied, 'because I've been getting some very positive feedback from their two guys up there, Bob Cass and the photographer Keith Perry. They seemed to be certain something was on involving me.'

'Oh, it's on all right,' said Reg. 'The *Sun* loved the way you handled yourself at the press conference.'

So I went and had lunch with perhaps two of the most fascinating men I've ever met in my life. There I was, only 21 years old, having lunch in the old Fleet Street Press Club, which is long gone now. As we ate, we talked about what the *Sun* wanted, the kind of things they were after, what the *Sun* newspaper was all about in terms of sport. Frank Nicklin said that 70 per cent of all newspaper readers look first at the back page and then read towards the front. 'That's what we aim to exploit,' he added. By the end of the meal we had got round to talking about deals. The upshot was that the *Sun* offered me £250 a week to do a column for them, which put me in the strange position of earning more from a newspaper than I was from my football club, my primary employer. At that time, I was on just £100 a week at Newcastle, so when Frank mentioned the figure he was prepared to pay you can imagine how far my jaw dropped. It wasn't long, remember, since I'd been earning a paltry £20 a week, and here I was being asked by a national newspaper to write one column a week for a sum more than ten times that.

It took me a while to get my head round the idea of being so well paid, but I was only too happy to do the deal, of course. In fact, I thought to myself, 'Isn't negotiation easy!' You could hardly blame me, because the offers were just tumbling in: first Newcastle, then the *Sun* newspaper. It was then that Reg proved his worth by giving me some very good advice. 'You cannot ignore all the other newspapers,' he said, 'but keep the two totally separate. Make sure that what you give to the *Sun* is good and juicy and keep the banalities for the others. But don't ignore them, whatever you do, because you'll only annoy them that way and they'll gang up on you.' That was fine by me; I was happy with that. Frank Nicklin was dead chuffed too, because he now had on the payroll a well-known player in every geographical region. I, of course, was his man in the north-east.

The champagne came out, and we began what was the first bout of drinking with the flute I'd experienced. It was one of the funniest times of my life too. We laughed and laughed as Frank and Reg started telling stories, and I could have gone on listening to them all day, every day. Then we moved from the restaurant to the bar, and it was a case of 'Oh, meet the editor of so-and-so!' as and when people came in. It was my first time ever in the Press Club, and I soon realised that it was a real corridor of power – perhaps even greater than what we generally accept as a corridor of power.

Eventually I tore myself away from this glamorous setting and set off in a taxi to get the train up to Luton. En route, I had time to reflect on the fact that in the space of a few days I'd signed two phenomenal deals. Financially, my life had been transformed completely at a time when I suppose the average wage nationally was about £25 a week. It was all a far cry, certainly, from an embarrassing situation I'd found myself in when I first had to get from Fulham to Luton. Then, I was so short of money to buy petrol for the car that I'd had to risk bouncing a cheque for a couple of quid at the local off-licence to get my hands on some cash. And I'd had to plead with the shopkeeper to do that. Having secured the deal with Luton, I was then able to phone the bank, explain the situation and ask them to honour the £2 cheque because there would be plenty more coming in.

Although I was more than happy with the deals that had been struck, and delighted with the money they were bringing in, I still had a little doubt nagging away at the back of my mind. 'You don't think I've made a mistake signing for Newcastle, do you?' I asked Reg. 'I was told by Alec Stock that Chelsea and Man United had been in for me as well.'

'Yeah,' he replied, 'but in life you have to go where the need is greatest, and Newcastle displayed their need of you more than the others. They didn't mess about. They just came straight in, put their money where their mouth was and sorted out the deal. When people do that, you know you can deal with them. If you'd said no to Newcastle, you could have finished up in a sort of will-they-won't-they no-man's land.'

Before I knew it, pre-season was upon us. I absolutely loathed this time of the year. I hated the training because it was the stamina-building part of the football calendar and entailed long, hard slogs. As I've said before, I wasn't built for that; I was made for the short stuff. So I found it difficult to summon up much enthusiasm when, on the first day of training with Newcastle in July 1971, we were told we would be going out for a run on the Town Moor. The plan afterwards was to get changed, go and have some lunch, and then return to the ground for the annual photo-call for all the newspapers and agencies.

For the benefit of those not familiar with Newcastle, Town Moor is a huge swathe of green pasture land that begins just behind St James's Park and extends over the whole of the north of the city. It is so big that it has a nine-hole golf course on it, and there's cows grazing on it too. It's deeply historical as well. I think it was signed over to the good people of Newcastle by the Tudors' all-powerful Star Chamber as a reward for their bravery in fighting off one of the Scottish kings, and for being a barrier to the marauding Scots over many years. It was to be run for the benefit of the citizens by the freemen of the city, who were granted the right to graze their cattle on it free of charge. A Star Chamber ruling cannot be overruled, it seems – there is no power in the land high enough – so the Town Moor remains for ever. That's why Newcastle had so much trouble trying to expand St James's Park, because it is in fact part of the moor.

There was a laid-out route for us, but pretty soon I was lagging miles behind. I got further and further detached from the others until, in the end, the main group disappeared out of sight over one of the hills. I just kept running in what I thought was the right direction until I came to the brow of a hill and couldn't see anybody. I thought they must be heading back to the ground, so, seeing the floodlights in the distance, I ran in that direction. I finished up near a hospital, the moor having come to an end, so I stopped a passer-by and said, 'Excuse me, but could you tell me where St James's Park is, please?' The woman took one look at me and exclaimed, 'Ooh, you're 'im out the papers!' Then she came to her senses enough to tell me where the ground was and how to get there. By the time I arrived, though, the rest of the lads had already changed and showered and were going off for lunch.

Mine was a pretty rushed affair after that, but at least I made it to the photo-call – only to run across another problem. All shorts were tight and skimpy in the 1970s. That was the new fashion, a reaction to the baggier numbers of old that, ironically, have become fashionable again now. Anyway, I absolutely hated the size of them, and the shiny synthetic material they were made of. When you have thighs as heavily muscled as mine, the things restricted your movement, and were at full stretch and beyond when you sat down. 'You're not expecting me to play in these, are you?' I said. 'Having a photograph taken is one thing, but playing in them will be impossible for me.' When I was told they were part of the standard playing kit for the season, I insisted the club get me another pair. I told them I not only wanted a bigger size, but that I much preferred cotton to the man-made nylon stuff the regulation issue were made of. Reluctantly, Newcastle asked the manufacturers to provide me with an alternative pair of shorts, but that started off a story that I was getting preferential treatment. Who said what, I don't know, and the whispers never really found their way into a definite story, but the rumour went around that I was demanding to be treated differently from the other players. I wasn't, of course. It all came down to the fact that I just couldn't get those bloody little shiny shorts on!

As the pre-season training progressed, periodically we were bussed off to just beyond Seahouses on the coast. We'd go running on the sand, and it was during those punishing long runs that I first came to appreciate the beauty of the north-east coastline. It is absolutely spectacular. I remember one run in particular that took us up the coast to Bamburgh Castle, which is one of the most breathtaking sights in Europe, never mind the north-east of England. This incredible redstone building sits on a headland and looks as though it is protruding out into the sea. I was just in awe of the place. I tend to get that way at the amazing accomplishments of man. I marvel that they were able to dream up and construct these phenomenal structures back in the days when they did not have mechanical aids. The amount of toil and effort that must have gone into it, not to mention all the planning, is staggering to contemplate. So it seemed a complete misuse of such a grand edifice when the Newcastle coach, Keith Burkinshaw, ordered us to go running 'doggies' (sprints) along the sand and up the rock incline to the castle; you had to touch the castle wall, then get back to the starting-point. I was always struck by the irony of that. Bamburgh Castle, an Anglo-Saxon stronghold dating from the twelfth century, was not built for Newcastle United footballers to touch on the uphill leg of a 'doggie'. However, such thoughts, I have to say, did get my mind off the physical pain I always endured at that time of year.

Eventually we got ourselves fit and settled into a team structure. Then, one day after training, Joe Harvey came into the dressing-room and drew himself up to his full height in front of us. He stood with his feet apart, his hands sort of turned in so that his wrists were resting on his hips, and he rocked slightly on his heels. Standing right in front of me, he said, 'Well, big Mal, I have just signed the man who is going to make the bullets for you to fire!'

Everybody in the dressing-room was agog and could hardly wait for him to reveal the player's name. 'Come on, boss,' we all said, 'tell us who it is!'

To which Joe replied, 'I've just bought, for £30,000, Terry Hibbitt from Leeds.'

We were impressed. We knew what a good player Terry was. He couldn't get into the Leeds side on a regular basis because the great Johnny Giles played in his position, and Giles' recognised deputy was Mick Bates. But Terry had made frequent appearances as a substitute. The previous season, I'd seen him on *Match of the Day* coming on for Leeds just about every Saturday, and it was obvious he had a great left peg and a wonderful ability to ping the ball about.

Joe, having imparted his big news, turned on his heel and went to the door. But just as he opened it he halted, looked over his shoulder and said, 'Mind, he'd cause trouble in an empty house!' And, by heavens, he wasn't kidding.

Later that season, John Tudor, my partner up front at Newcastle, and I were in the players' bar after a match at Elland Road chatting to Norman Hunter, the Leeds and England defender. 'Hey, Norman,' said John, 'how on earth did Joe Harvey nick, for the paltry sum of £30,000, Terry Hibbitt off you?'

Norman is like a wise old owl, and he looked at us with those droopy, sad eyes of his and said, 'Oh, he had to go! He definitely had to go!'

'What do you mean, he had to go?'

'You don't know the story?' Norman asked.

'No,' we chorused. 'What happened?'

Norman looked over his shoulder to make sure he couldn't be overheard, then said, 'Well, it was round about the end of last season. We'd done a training session, and at the end of it we were having a bit of a five-a-side, with the goalkeepers playing out. All five-a-sides here are pretty competitive, and Gary Sprake and Paul Reaney have tackled each other, neither liking the way the other has gone in. So they are on their feet now with fists clenched, squaring up to each other. At that point, little Hibby's come running straight over to them and gone, "Yak, yak, yak, yak." So Paul's turned to him and said, "Terry, this hasn't got anything to do with you. Piss off!" The warning falls on deaf ears, because Hibby's gone "Yak, yak, yak" again and given Paul a mouthful. Then Gary has a go. "Terry," he says, "you've been told once. It's nothing to do with you. Keep your nose out of it!" And Terry's turned to Gary and said, "Talking of noses, what about your wife's!" As I said, he had to go.'

John Tudor and I were very different types of strikers. John was very much a textbook and coaching-manual sort of player. He was somebody who would study the opposition carefully and work out all the ways of getting past them and defeating them. And there he was, saddled with someone like yours truly who said, 'Just give me the ball and let me get at 'em!' He must have thought, 'What on earth have they got here? I want to coach this lad and teach him all the finer intricacies of playing up front.' But all I was interested in was getting the ball and running the bastards into the ground. It soon dawned on John that he wasn't going to change me and that he was going to have to adapt to how I played. As far as I was concerned, the coaching manual was out the window. If I didn't see a scoring chance, I wouldn't go; if I did, I went. That was the way I played the game.

We went to Crystal Palace for the opening game of the season, and they beat us 2–0. We stayed over in London to play Tottenham on the Wednesday night at White Hart Lane, and picked up our first point there with a no-score draw. It was a rather ignominious start to the season, not just for the team but for me particularly, the man who had said he was going to get 30 goals a season. It goes without saying, then, that an awful lot of questions were already being asked in Newcastle and elsewhere about my ability as a goalscorer at that level.

What changed everything was our next game, my home debut, against Liverpool on 21 August – no easy fixture. Under the shrewd, inspiring management of Bill Shankly, Liverpool had established themselves as one of the best sides in the country, if not in Europe. In the 1960s, they had won the old First Division championship twice and the FA Cup, and had reached the final of the European Cup-Winners Cup. Understandably, then, everybody in the city was talking about what was going to happen that afternoon. Everything seemed new when I got to the ground. The whole thing was strange, totally different from anything I'd experienced before. In those days, there were so few season-ticket holders that the fans would start arriving at about one o'clock to be sure of getting in, and that day the place was absolutely jam-packed when I got there. I had to fight my way through the gates and through the crowds. It was a twenty-minute job just to park the car. Once out of the car, I was surrounded by hundreds of kids and adults wanting my autograph. There must have been about 500 of them swarming around. I'd never known anything like it in my life. At Luton, I think I'd had a queue of three autograph hunters at the very most; here you disappeared under a sea of bodies. It was just impossible to sign so many autographs. There's no way I could have done them all and got to the dressing-room in time for the game. In those days security wasn't an issue, so there weren't the stewards or police about that there are today.

I firmly believe it is a player's duty to sign autographs when asked, but you can't do it before a game when the requests come like an avalanche. Trying to explain my refusals to everybody was a nightmare. Because of the tremendous clamour, it was difficult to make myself heard as I said, as politely as I could, 'After the game, after the game. I'll sign all the autographs after the game. Now I've got to get into the dressing-room to get ready.' This was to become a ritual for me at St James's Park, but, being a realist, I did wonder at the time whether they would still be crowding round my car after that afternoon's game.

At last I made it to the steps, where the ground was policed and stewarded, and wormed my way through a little cordon and on to the dressing-room. But it was as if the atmosphere around the ground was sucking not only the energy from the players, but their thought processes as well. One could sense in the crowd's expectancy their huge desire for victory. You can't help but arrive in the dressing-room a different person to the one who drove the car to the ground. It was an experience in itself for someone like me, who'd been used to strolling up to Kenilworth Road, where just a few supporters might say, 'Hello, Mal. You all right? Good luck this afternoon!'

When I reached the Newcastle dressing-room, I said, 'Thanks for warning me about what to expect at the ground! I really appreciate that!' But of course the players had never thought to tell me because to them it was the norm. It was what they experienced every other week. Although this was my third Football League game in Newcastle colours, and we were supposed to be enjoying the familiarity of playing at home, it was all completely alien to me. At least they'd sorted out my shorts. In fact, the physio made quite a piss-taking thing out of it by staging a special presentation of my simple black cotton pair in front of the other players.

At five to three, the skipper, Bobby Moncur, ball under his arm, said, 'Right, lads, when you're ready!' And out we went.

In the dressing-room, you get yourself oiled up – before going out I used to smear my eyebrows with Vaseline to prevent the sweat from going in my eyes – and partially warmed up, but when we got out on the field a horde of photographers enveloped me and everybody wanted a photograph. All I wanted to do was get fully warmed up. I was thinking, 'Why do they always come before the start of the game, when you're not done up for photographs?' You're smeared in Vaseline, you're about to play an important game of football, and they want you to smile? I'm going into battle. There's nowt to smile about.

The photo session over, we lined up for kick-off. While we were waiting for the referee's whistle, what I noticed most of all was the density of the huge crowd. If memory serves, there were not many short of 50,000 people filling the stadium that Saturday afternoon. There was not a seat to be had, not a space on the terraces to be seen, and it all made the pitch appear much smaller than it really was. The crowd were very close to the touchline at St James's Park in those days, and everybody on the pitch seemed to be in much closer proximity than perhaps was really the case. It was almost like an optical illusion.

Then, all of a sudden, we're off, playing against Liverpool, in 1971 one of the four outstanding sides in English football alongside Arsenal, Leeds and Everton. Early on there were a couple of skirmishes between me and Liverpool's legendary hardman defender Tommy Smith, who was marking me. Big Tom always had something to say. 'You'll find it a lot f★★★ing harder up here, son!' he quipped, and he'd say such things almost at the same time as he was kicking you. He'd just keep on chipping in with comments like that, all in an effort to diminish you, of course. But I just kept thinking to myself, 'If I can survive Don Murray at Cardiff, I can survive anybody.' Murray had kicked lumps out of me when I played against him for Luton at Ninian Park.

Liverpool quickly moved into a slick passing mode. They were absolutely great at creating their little triangles, and their growing pressure brought them a penalty which Emlyn Hughes scored to put us 1–0 down. That simply prompted the crowd to shout even more loudly in support of Newcastle. The noise was quite incredible. It was almost as if they were trying to blow you from your own goal down to the other one.

That day we had a guy called David Young in the side. For the life of me I can't remember what position he was playing, because usually he was Bob Moncur's understudy at number 6 in the middle of the defence, but Bob was playing in this game so all I can think is that David had come into the centre of midfield. Anyway, he made a run into the Liverpool penalty area and the ball was slotted into him, but Youngie had been tracked back by someone who I think at the time was the youngest player in the Liverpool side, a lad by the name of Kevin Keegan. As the ball came down the outside of David's run, Kevin, who was on the inside, went across Youngie, didn't make contact with the ball and sent him over. The penalty decision of a few minutes earlier was reversed, and it was down to me to take it. In the dressing-room before the game, Joe had said, 'Should we get one, who's going to take a penalty?', and my hand had just gone straight up.

As I went across to pick the ball up, the Liverpool players were creating all sorts of unsettling arguments, which was so typical of them in situations like that. There were unhelpful comments from Smith, full-back Chris Lawler and goalkeeper Ray Clemence, but eventually the referee got the nonsense over and done with. I put the ball on the spot and walked back for my run-up. I decided I was going to go for my left-hand side, Clemence's right, but just as I got to the ball my standing foot shifted a bit. It meant I skied the shot slightly, but that was a good thing: Clemence dived the right way but the ball was above his outstretched upper arm and crept in just under the bar. It was a vital goal at a vital stage in a vital match, and the Newcastle players were ecstatic. As for the noise that came from the crowd, that was absolutely deafening.

From then on the game became very much a midfield battle. It meant I was having to come off the front line an awful lot to help out. Liverpool had a tendency to crowd that area of the pitch until they'd gained control of the situation; then they'd go off and play their football in threes and fours. But the battle wasn't so easily won this time. Newcastle kept the scrap going and Liverpool were never able to settle on the ball and get their passing movements going.

I think it was Tommy Gibb who finally broke the deadlock by getting the ball in the inside-left position in the middle of the park. What he was doing across there heaven knows, because he was the right-sided midfielder, but he knocked a straight ball into my feet. Instead of taking it square-on, I dummied so that as I received the ball I was more or less facing goal. Having come off the centre-half, I controlled the ball, knocked it outside Tommy Smith, accelerated past him and smacked a left-footed shot towards the far post. For a split-second there was a stunned silence; 'Where's that going to end up?' everyone seemed to be thinking. And then it hit the roof of the net. This time, the noise was quite the most incredible thing I had heard in my life. It was beyond description. I put my arms in the air and the other players enveloped me.

I knew I had just scored a goal that was a bit special, but I wasn't prepared for what happened next. As we returned to our places for the restart, it suddenly came rolling down the terraces. The hit musical in London at the time was *Jesus Christ Superstar*, and to the tune of the title song the Geordies started singing, 'Supermac, superstar, how many goals have you scored so far?' They did it over and over again, and that's how the tag Supermac was born.

We went in at half-time 2–1 up, to the most phenomenal applause. It was literally a standing ovation from 50,000 people. The goals apart, they had been treated to a fantastic spectacle with no quarter given. The tackles had been flying in to such an extent that had those 45 minutes of football been played today there would probably have been about four players left on the pitch, two of them goalkeepers and two of them wingers. But that was the way football was in those days. The current generation of football-watchers probably aren't aware of just how rough and tough it was then. It was a physical contact sport; people kicked, barged and elbowed one another. It was only the extremes of that kind of behaviour that were ever punished.

When we reached the dressing-room, Joe Harvey was like a peacock with a full fantail. That's what he reminded me of. 'That's the way to do it!' he said. 'You can't do better than that! You're bossing them, you're pushing them about!' Joe related to that rough side of the game. As far as he was concerned, you had to win more physical challenges than you lost if you were to win the game. Joe just loved that kind of thing. 'You've got another 45,' he said, 'and you've got to win every tackle you go for. You can't allow them to start pushing you about or bossing you. You have to boss them.'

And when we went out for the second half, it was Newcastle who started to play the football. It was almost as if the physical battles of the first half had set Liverpool back on their heels. We started to find space in possession and began to play. We were knocking it about, and knocking it about well. The crowd were in full voice, and it wasn't 'Supermac, superstar' they were singing but their old favourite, 'Blaydon Races'.

Midway through the second half, the ball found its way to Terry Hibbitt, who was in space on the left wing inside our own half. He started to motor up the wing, and as Lawler came towards him he knocked a deft little ball diagonally inside to John Tudor, who just touched it on again. By this time I had come in on the diagonal, and across my marker, from the centre to inside-left on the edge of the box. Touching the ball with my left foot to make half a yard of space, I smacked it across Clemence again because I was going away from goal and the goalkeeper was coming across to cover his near post. This time the shot went past his left hand and into the bottom corner.

We were 3–1 up, and 'Supermac, superstar' filled the city of Newcastle, never mind the stadium. Two goals to the good against one of the best sides in Europe and flying. I'd got a hat-trick in my home debut, and all I wanted now was to get another, and another. You could see Liverpool had been rocked to the core because they were arguing among themselves and calling one another some very unpleasant names. We knew we were on top and were determined not to give anything away or to do anything silly. 'Let's keep playing it forward,' we said, and we did.

With about eighteen minutes to go, Liverpool were awarded a goal-kick, and Clemence took it. Now I've always thought Ray was one of the most elegant goalkeepers I've seen – elegant in the way he would come to catch a cross, elegant in the way he would set himself up for a dive, and elegant, certainly, in the way he kicked a ball. This time, though, he duffed the goal-kick, really duffed it. I don't think I ever saw him do that before or after in the whole of his career. Sometimes, in view of what happened subsequently, I even wonder whether he did it deliberately.

I was standing in the centre circle in the Liverpool half, and Larry Lloyd, their other centre-back, was five or six yards closer to the Liverpool goal when Clemence's goal-kick came trundling towards me. The ball took a huge bobble as it reached me and then bounced too high for me to get my foot to it. In fact, it hit my shin and looped back towards the Liverpool goal. So I set off after it, Lloyd set off after me, and Clemence set off out of his goal. The ball had gone way up in the air, so I was willing it to come down as I gave chase. I was already goalside of Lloyd, so all I needed was that damned ball. When it finally started to come down, I realised I couldn't afford to delay my shot for a second; I had to take it at the earliest possible moment. So I leapt in the air and with my left foot lobbed the ball over the advancing Clemence. As I met terra firma again I continued to run, all the time watching the flight of the ball. Would it come down this side of the crossbar or the other? To my disappointment, it landed on the roof of the net. At that exact moment, out of the corner of my eye I saw Clemence leap off the ground. I was still going full pelt towards the Liverpool goal in case the ball hit the bar and bounced back out, and Ray was in top gear too. You can imagine the sort of impact there was when six studs, with the full weight of the Liverpool goalkeeper behind them, hit me smack in the side of the face. I was just pole-axed. The first thing that hit the floor was the back of my head.

Suddenly, consciousness was a very distant thing. I was just about aware of an inability to move my limbs. I remember thinking, 'Come on, get up!' but nothing was responding to the signals my brain was sending out. The next thing I knew there was a huddle of people around me attempting to put me on a stretcher. But I said, 'No, no. I'm not being carried off. I haven't been carried off yet and I never will be!' Instead, my arms were put round the shoulders of the physio, Alex Mutch, and the coach, Keith Burkinshaw, and I attempted to walk off. All I could hear was this enormous roar, a feeling of drowning, a wave of blackness that sounded like rushing water. And that was it – I was gone. Alex and Keith had to carry me off.

When I came to, I was on the couch in the physio's room. I saw Frank Clark, our left-back, standing at the foot of the couch and I said, 'Hey, Clarkie, I've had this weird dream. I dreamt that we went out and beat Liverpool!' As I was on the physio's couch and didn't know how I'd got there, I assumed the game had not yet taken place.

Frank said, 'Oh yes, we beat Liverpool all right, old son, and you scored a hat-trick!'

'What?' I said. 'What was the score?'

'3–2,' he replied. 'They got one back late on, but we hung on.'

I had absolutely no recollection of it, but fortunately the game was televised by Tyne-Tees TV in the north-east and was shown the next day. I had to watch the game on the Sunday afternoon for it all to become crystal clear to me, and to discover why my face was such a mess. My lip was gashed and swollen, my cheekbone was the size of a cricket ball and my left eye was blackened. In other words, one side of my face was smashed to smithereens. Oh, and I'd lost my four front teeth. I thought, 'Oh dear, I've got hours to face in a dentist's chair.' And once they've gone, they've gone for life. You know the sentence that's bestowed upon you when your teeth have gone. Later, people told me that the loss of my teeth gave me a more fearsome appearance on the pitch. I suppose it did, but I could have done without it. I had to have a denture made, and there was no way it was possible to play wearing a denture for fear of getting a whack in the mouth and having it go down your throat. There was no alternative but to take it out before every game.

The worst discovery of all was that Ray Clemence had got off scot-free for what he'd done to me. The referee and his linesmen had taken no action at all; they'd not even given us a free-kick! Watching it on television, I noticed that the game had restarted with a goal-kick. Nothing was said to Clemence. The ball was a long way behind him when he hit me about eight yards outside his area, but his run never faltered. He jumped in the air, and it was studs first. He didn't look to see where the ball had gone either; he kept his eyes firmly fixed on me. No doubt he would argue it was a complete accident, but I couldn't help thinking it might have been his way of exacting revenge for having a hat-trick put past him.

The ironic thing is that all this happened just after a refereeing clampdown had been introduced. In our previous game at Spurs, five players had been booked. That may be the norm today, but back then it was unheard of. Deliberate hand-ball was one of the offences they had decided to crack down on, and Joe Kinnear, the Spurs full-back, had been shown the yellow card simply for grabbing the ball for a throw-in when he thought it had gone out of play. Mike England, Tottenham's big, rugged Welsh international centre-half, was cautioned too. His mistake was to go through me from behind, a tackle the authorities were no longer prepared to tolerate, it seemed.

But the fact was that we had won the game against Liverpool, and that was the most important thing. Not only that, but the whole team had been brilliant and we'd actually out-footballed one of the best teams in the country. It had been fantastic entertainment for everybody who was there, and on top of that I'd got a hat-trick. It was the least I could do, I suppose, after two goalless matches, and it sort of corrected the situation. That third goal did not just put me in the history books, it put me into the hearts of all Newcastle fans. For everybody at St James's that day, certainly, it's one of those moments to treasure for ever.

Not so long ago, I was out walking the dog near my home in Co.

Durham and a chap came along with his two kids, the younger of whom was a boy. The father recognised me, turned to his son and said, 'Son, in the first game my father took me to when I was your age, I saw this man score a hat-trick on his home debut.' That's how it's remembered in the north-east, as a magical moment, and I have to say it's very gratifying to be the subject of that. There is an affinity now between the people of Tyneside and me that nothing whatsoever can break. The bond is unbreakable because we were there together, back in August 1971 when we beat Liverpool. It was a really historic moment for Tyneside.

I have to admit I did take the opportunity to get a bit of my own back on Clemence later in the season. Ray had a habit, when poor crosses came over and forwards weren't able to make a challenge, of taking the ball between his hands and immediately bouncing it at his feet. At one point during the return game at Anfield in March 1972, Clemence was on his goal-line and a bad cross was heading for him head-high. It was too late for me to get to the ball, but I started sprinting anyway because I expected him to bounce it as usual and thought I would try to reach it before he got it back in his hands. Sure enough, Ray collected the ball and bounced it, so I steamed in and hit it and him, the two of us ending up in the net with the ball. I got back on my feet with my hand in the air claiming a goal because I'd played the ball first, but as I came running out of the net Tommy Smith smacked me from the side with a right-hander that stung my neck. I didn't go down, but he stopped me dead in my tracks. I was thinking, 'Bloody hell! What was that?' It was the dreaded Tommy, nose to nose with me, wanting to tear me limb from limb. He was not a pretty sight, I have to say. Smithy was fearsome at the best of times, but in this occasion he was snarling and spitting out his words, most of them consisting of just four letters. Then the referee blew his whistle, came striding over and sort of put his arm across Tommy, doing his best to push him back. And booked me.

'What have you booked me for?' I asked. 'I haven't right-handed anybody.'

'For kicking the goalkeeper,' he replied.

'But I kicked the ball first,' I protested. 'If I got the goalkeeper afterwards, tough luck! The ball was in play, and if he wants to bounce it—'

'No, no,' insisted the ref, 'you kicked the goalkeeper.'

So I got punched and booked for being quick off the mark. But it was worth it.

Although I enjoyed most of my five years at Newcastle enormously, I have to say the club and the ground were far from perfect then. St James's Park was certainly big because it had once been a cricket ground, but the surface was a bit up and down and it was in an elevated position, which left it open to the elements. In truth, it really was a bit archaic. You had the one stand on the west side of the ground which was nothing more than a huge corrugated hut. At the back of it, there was a spiral staircase that went up to the very top of the roof, where the press box was. It certainly made for a grand view, although I felt it removed you too much from the game itself. I don't think it would have passed a modern safety inspection, but then nor would much else in all probability. The only modernisation that had taken place anywhere was at the main entrance, which had had a sort of new façade put on it.

And that's pretty much what Newcastle United was at the time – a façade to hide the decay. That decay came not from the state of the ground, rather from the attitude that emanated from the boardroom. Everything that was done out of the spotlight was done on the cheap. They'd go and break their transfer record, as they did in my case, then they would ask the players to get changed every day for training in a freezing-cold cricket pavilion that had no heating whatsoever. August, September and October weren't so bad, but then we'd get to November and December and the winds would start to bite. They talk about southern softies up here, and I have to say I did find a bit of a difference in the winters at first. The bitterly cold wind would whip along the training ground, which was also in an elevated position, and it was so strong at times that we literally ended up running on the spot. You'd run as hard as you could and hardly move a pace forward.

The place where we got changed was that standard sort of 1920s cricket pavilion. There was a bay window to the left and the right, and behind them were the dressing-rooms; in the middle was the bar. The first-team squad of fourteen or fifteen would change on one side and the rest would change on the other. But the bay windows had panes of glass missing, so when January came around the wind came whistling through. It wasn't so bad before training, but afterwards, when you'd just had a hot bath and were standing there dripping wet, it was freezing. I thought to myself, 'I can't believe this! The club can go out and spend a fortune on some guy, then ask him and others to risk colds and even pneumonia because of a few missing panes of glass.' We kept on at Joe Harvey to get something done about it, but it wasn't until about the third season I was there that they finally did do something. But they didn't do the obvious and patch up the windows; what they did was put on the floor a free-standing two-bar electric fire! Think about it. After training, there were about fifteen bodies dripping with water, and there was this two-bar electric fire in the middle of the floor. Everybody avoided it like the plague.

Our infuriation with that strange attitude to expenditure built up over the years. If we were playing away from home and had to go south down the A1, for instance, we'd travel for just an hour to Boroughbridge, then stop and have this grandiose tea with the whole works. But we, the players, had eaten lunch only an hour and half earlier, so why were we stopping? If we went west to go down the M6, we would stop at a tea shop at Brampton, near Carlisle, a lovely old thatched cottage, where another huge spread would be laid out. Eventually, we realised this was all for the benefit of the directors. They'd get stuck into those teas as though there was no tomorrow. Then, when we got to our hotel for the overnight stop on Friday, the directors would scrutinise the menu. When we, the players, came down from our rooms to go to the restaurant for dinner at the appointed time, we'd be given a list of what we couldn't order because it was too expensive. Steak, would you believe, was often off the menu. The feeding ritual would continue on the Saturday evening after an away game. On the way back to Newcastle, we'd stop off again so the directors could have another slap-up meal. What really annoyed the players was not just the gluttony itself, but the time it consumed. We always had to leave an hour earlier than necessary on the Friday, and on the Saturday night we would always arrive back late in Newcastle because we'd had to stop and have yet another banquet.

Here, then, was a football club that was superbly supported but did little to deserve that support. The conditions for the fans were awful too. Not a thing had been done to the ground since it was built at the turn of the century, and if the supporters stood in three feet of pee, so what?

The Newcastle board knew the fans just wanted to see the lads play. Their support was total and undemanding. All they wanted was to be entertained. So for a very long time the club did nothing to improve their lot.

The Newcastle supporters *are* something very special. I think they get better as the years go by because, if you think about it, it's an awfully long time since they won anything. You have to go back as far as 1969, when they won the Fairs Cup. They've won nothing since, yet the supporters are still there, more eager than ever, saying, 'This is going to be the year.' They've been to three FA Cup finals and lost them all, but it still doesn't deter them in any shape or form. I was once asked an intriguing question: 'What separates Southampton, Leicester, Luton and a lot of smaller clubs from Newcastle?' The answer is that they have all won a trophy since Newcastle last won one. It's just incredible that they get that level of support without winning anything. People are there just for the love of the club and they are happy if the team can give them reasons to hold their heads up high. They are happy just to see exciting football. As Jackie Milburn told me, if you give them plenty to talk about through the week, they will keep turning up on a Saturday.

What they love above all, of course, is the FA Cup. I think it's the sudden-death element about it that appeals to them; nothing is more likely to produce exciting football. But it also has something to do with tradition. It's football's oldest cup competition, and those great Newcastle teams Jackie and Joe played in won it three times in five years back in the 1950s. The club might not have won it since, but the legend lives on. So you can imagine what the atmosphere was like on Tyneside when in 1974 we got to Wembley for the first time since Milburn, Jimmy Scoular and company beat Manchester City 3–1 there in 1955.

If I'm to be brutally honest, though, our cup run that year was football bordering on farce. It started when we were drawn to play non-League Hendon at home in the third round. Straight away, all the local papers and the north-east editions of the nationals immediately delved into their archives to find out when Newcastle had last been beaten by a non-League side. They didn't have to look very far, because we had gone down two years earlier to Hereford – Ronnie Radford, Ricky George, John Motson and all that – and our embarrassment had been captured by BBC

Television for posterity and the nation's delight.

People tend to forget what a saga that third-round tie against Hereford in 1972 was. For a start, the weather that January was so bad, the original game at St James's had to be postponed for nine days and played as a midweek match. Even then, the surface was difficult, but all credit to our opponents, who were then in the Southern League: they ran their socks off and finished up with a 2–2 draw. John Tudor and I scored for Newcastle, but what I remember most about that game was the 30-yard screamer Colin Addison, Hereford's player-manager, scored for them out of absolutely nothing when we were leading. It was one of the best goals I've ever seen. It came like a bolt out of the blue and gave Hereford the impetus to go on and force a replay.

The next ten days or so became more and more farcical. We went down to Hereford the following day ready to play the game again, but it was postponed because of the state of the pitch. So we went back home, played a game on the Saturday, then travelled down the following week to try again, only to find that the replay had been postponed a second time. And that's how it was day after day. Monday, Tuesday, Wednesday and Thursday came and went without a ball being kicked in anger.

We were living in a hotel in Worcester, but as we hadn't anticipated such a long stay we soon began to run out of clothes. We all had to go round to the local Cecil Gee shop and buy shirts, underpants, socks – all sorts of stuff. They couldn't believe their luck! Every day a big group of guys came in wanting to buy clothes. We also found this wonderful pub in Worcester called the Dirty Duck, or something like that. They had live music, country and western or the blues, provided by local singers, and we'd wander down there and have a couple of pints after eating our evening meal in the hotel.

But, to tell the truth, we were desperately bored and frustrated. It was difficult finding somewhere to train each day for a start, and two or three hours of training still left many hours to be filled. We were totally isolated, and organising things back home was a nightmare without the aid of mobile phones, which make rearranging your life so much easier these days. All we wanted to do was play the game, get it over with, and go back to Newcastle. But every time we prepared for the following day, we'd be told it was off again.

*Me at ten months. Note the firm set of the mouth and the prominent left leg.*

*Posing in the garden of 33 Finlay Street, Fulham, with my dad and younger brother, David.*

*This school picture was taken in my first year at Sloane Grammar School, Chelsea. I may have looked the model pupil, but looks can deceive.*

*My first team picture. This was the Queen's Manor Primary School, Fulham, side, and I'm on the far right of the front row.*

*An early sign, at Sloane Grammar, of the ability that won me a BBC TV long throw competition in the 1970s, beating Tottenham's Martin Chivers in the final.*

*My first Match of the Day goal and the one that annoyed Johnny Haynes (in the background) so much. I control his cross-shot and score for Fulham against Blackburn.*

*On the rampage for Luton Town.*

*Giving my all for Newcastle at St James' Park in a game against Carlisle.*

*Sitting on the Rolls-Royce transport so kindly provided by Luton, I pose with a Newcastle shirt after my arrival at St James' Park.*

*Interviewing the legendary Jackie Milburn for BBC Radio Newcastle. The look on my face tells you how much I was in awe of the great man.*

*I prepare to take on Manchester City defender Mick Doyle in the 1976 League Cup final at Wembley.*

*Concussed and missing four front teeth, I am helped off following a collision with Liverpool goalkeeper Ray Clemence during my three-goal home debut for Newcastle.*

*Alan Kennedy, Keith Burkinshaw and I inspect the Wembley pitch before the 1974 FA Cup final against Liverpool. Newcastle's tracksuit fiasco and a heavy defeat followed.*

*There goes another one! I score against Wolves at St James' Park with that trusty left foot.*

*The scoreboard at Highfield Road tells its own story. That's the way to leave the opposition — in need of the emergency services!*

*Manchester City defenders look thunderstruck as I celebrate scoring with a header direct from a corner swung under their bar by Terry Hibbitt.*

*Leicester's Jon Sammels is too late to stop me letting fly with my left foot from inside the centre circle.*

*Leicester's goalkeeper, the airborne Mark Wallington, is well beaten as my 40-yard shot flashes past him into the net.*

*Irving Nattrass helps me celebrate one of the most spectacular goals of my career.*

*Joe Harvey's Newcastle line up for what was the first team photo following my arrival from Luton in 1971.*

*Different team, same old left foot. Here, I spray the ball around for Arsenal.*

*Alan Ball congratulates me for scoring the goal against Newcastle we had planned in advance.*

*Chatting to three Arsenal apprentices just after my transfer from Newcastle. Ironically, the one nearest to me, Derek Wright, is now the physio at St James' Park.*

*Now where's that goal? Playing for Arsenal, I prepare to make a beeline for it while Leicester's Steve Sims (get those fancy epaulettes!) tries to intervene.*

It got to the point, on the Thursday of that week, where it looked as though the winners of the tie would have to play another FA Cup tie on the Saturday, on which day the fourth-round ties were scheduled to be played. When Thursday was a no-go as well, it was decided our third-round replay would have to take place on the same day as the fourth-round games. Absolutely desperate now to get the match on, the whole of Hereford was galvanised into making the pitch playable for the Saturday. Local farmers laid straw on it to keep it warm, then cleared the straw off on the morning of the match.

Even so, when we arrived at the ground the surface was a total quagmire. It took some getting used to, but we were the quicker side and were knocking it about quite well up to half-time, when it was 0–0. Terry Hibbitt had hit the bar, if I remember correctly. Then, quite late in the second half, Viv Busby, who was on loan to Newcastle from Luton at the time, sent over a cross from the right that I nodded in at the far post. We were confident we could go on to win and get this bloody game out of the way, but then Hereford took a big, deep breath and really came at us.

We were coping until the ball was knocked past me to Ronnie Radford. I was two yards behind him, looking over his shoulder and trying to get to him for the tackle. Just before I could get there, though, the ball sat up nicely off a divot, and I had a perfect view of his famous shot as he hit it. Now, with the best will in the world, Ronnie was just about the most inelegant player on the field and the least likely to hit a ball as cleanly and sweetly as he did from long range. But as the shot set off I could see that our goalkeeper, Willie McFaul, didn't have a hope of saving it. Sure enough, the ball crashed into the top corner. Then, of course, Hereford sent on Ricky George as a substitute, and he scored the winner with a shot across Willie that went in at the far post. That was the cue for a mass invasion of the pitch by hundreds of kids, and it took ages to get them off. But we knew we were out, and all credit to Hereford. They scored tremendous goals against us and dumped us out. People can talk about the conditions suiting them more, but I'll have none of that. The truth is simply that they really played out of their skins. Our opportunity came at St James's Park, but we didn't put them to the sword. The only thing that grates is having to watch that Ronnie Radford goal all over again every time the BBC show their historic films when they're covering the FA Cup. Even now I kick myself mentally for not having got to him.

Ricky George has almost made a living out of his winner, and there was an amusing postscript to the story involving him. Our paths crossed again prior to the 1974 FA Cup final, by which time he was working for Adidas. His job on that occasion was to paint the trademark three stripes on our boots with luminous paint. Having collected them all up on the Friday afternoon, he needed somewhere to do his painting, so I told him to go ahead and do it in my hotel room. The Newcastle squad went off to the cinema to see a film on the Friday night, and when we returned we found Ricky fast asleep in my room. The fumes from the paint were so strong they had knocked him out! We thought he was dead for a minute. He was completely gone, and it took us ages to wake him up. We had to open all the windows.

When it comes to the FA Cup, the one thing Newcastle players dread is getting drawn at home against a non-League side, or a side from the bottom of the Football League. Arsenal or Man United away is no problem, but facing so-called minnows at St James's Park sets in motion this press vehicle that brings up every conceivable bad result there's ever been in the history of the club, and it remains headline news until the day of the game. The papers make out that they are pleading for it not to happen again, but it's almost as if they are preparing everyone for inevitable failure.

So in January 1974 we trotted out at our place with everyone waiting to see if we were going to fall flat on our faces again. Typically, Hendon were absolutely brilliant. They ran their socks off. It wasn't as if we went out with an arrogant attitude against them either. Only a late equaliser got us back into the game, and it finished 1–1. That meant we had to go down south that week for the replay, but about 10,000 Geordies wanted to make the trip and Hendon decided their little ground couldn't cope with Newcastle's huge following. The game was switched to Watford's Vicarage Road, where, I remember, I scored with a rare right-footer from the edge of the box and we went on to score four. Fine, got them off our backs.

The draw for the fourth round, which had already been made, paired us with Scunthorpe at St James's Park. Scunthorpe might have been only

Fourth Division opposition, but they soon went one up against us. They were useless, and we were even worse! They were still ahead with just a few minutes left on the clock, then, just as panic was kicking in, Terry McDermott suddenly hit a screamer into the top corner from 30 yards. Yet again we drew 1–1 with a team we should have beaten easily, though thankfully we saw them off in style at the Old Show Ground in the replay.

It got tougher in the fifth round, drawn away from home against another First Division side, West Bromwich Albion. To make matters worse, Terry Hibbitt got injured in the first few minutes and had to go off. He was replaced by Jimmy Smith, a player I had hardly played with in my three years at Newcastle because of all the injuries he'd suffered; no sooner had he played for an hour than he was back in the treatment room for another three, four, five, six or seven months. Everybody kept telling me what a wonderful footballer 'Jinky' was, and what little I'd seen of him suggested they were right. He confirmed it that day by orchestrating one of the finest team performances I ever played in. With the ball at his feet, Smithy slowed the game down. He just passed it and got it back, passed it and got it back; then he would play it or ping it. He knocked one cross over and I headed it in. Thank you very much, that's 1–0. With Jinky linking in midfield with Tommy Cassidy, Terry McDermott and Stewart Barrowclough, and them supplying John Tudor and me up front, it all just clicked beautifully. John got the second goal and Stewart the third in a 3–0 win. John Wile, their centre-half and captain, was pulling his hair out trying to cope. He didn't know what to do next. We slaughtered them.

In the quarter-finals in March, we got another home draw, this time against Second Division Nottingham Forest. But now that we were back at St James's, we suffered another attack of the collywobbles. We went 1–0 down, 2–0 down, 3–0 down before pulling one back, then Paddy Howard, one of our central defenders, got sent off. Down to ten men and losing 3–1 at home! In the second half, out of pure frustration, the crowd at the Leazes End invaded the pitch. It was frightening, I tell you. It was frightening for us Newcastle players, so what it must have been like for the Forest players I can only imagine. It must have been like facing Genghis Khan and his hordes coming over the hill. Hundreds and hundreds of supporters had come running on, and I saw the Forest players going down on their knees. I never saw anything serious happen, but it became a question of every man for himself and all the players were shouting, 'Head for the tunnel, head for the tunnel!' We all sprinted in that direction as hard as we could.

Back in the safety of the dressing-room, we wondered what was going to happen next. Joe Harvey went to see the referee, Gordon Kew. He returned after about fifteen minutes and said, 'Right, I have persuaded the referee not to abandon the game. We are going to go out and complete it. The police have cleared the pitch. You've got to go out and salvage what you can from this disaster.' And, amazingly, we did. We were suddenly full of a motivation we'd lacked prior to the invasion, but the Forest players, who had been full of confidence, were now haggard and gaunt. Fired up, we started playing for the first time. We knocked in one, and suddenly it became a steamroller job. We got a third, then, in the dying seconds, we made it 4–3. The stadium erupted; I have to say I have never known anything like it. It was an unbelievable turnaround, and the poor Forest players were gone; their hearts and minds had just utterly vanished. But there was a nasty surprise for us around the corner.

Over the weekend, the Football Association decided that an unfair advantage had been gained by the pitch invasion. They penalised Newcastle, decreed that the result would not stand, and said that the game must be played again, but on a neutral ground. Forest argued that the game should be played on their ground, and we in Newcastle had a certain sympathy with their argument, but Goodison Park was chosen by the FA as the venue.

It was goalless there after 90 minutes, and as this was supposed to be the original tie there was no extra time. That meant a replay, and we all assumed it would be held at the City Ground, but the FA had another meeting and, for reasons that are still beyond me, decided we should all go back to Goodison Park. I remember writing in my column in the *Sun*, 'As a Newcastle player, I have to say we are staggered that Nottingham Forest are not being given the opportunity to play at home.' Understandably, Forest were livid, and to this day nobody knows why the FA came to this decision. It was another tight contest at Goodison, but I managed to nick the only goal of the game and continued my record of having scored in every round.

So, in probably the most controversial and bizarre manner in the history of the FA Cup, or any other top competition for that matter, we were through to the semi-finals. The whole thing was quite unbelievable. We couldn't beat Hendon at home, we couldn't beat Scunthorpe at home, but here we were in the semi-finals. 'Bloody hell,' we thought, 'has somebody written our name on the cup? It's almost as if the fates are conspiring in our favour.'

Burnley, then in the old First Division, were our semi-final opponents at Hillsborough, and they didn't half have a good side under Jimmy Adamson. But, good as they were, we always felt we had the upper hand. Because we also had to meet Burnley in the two-legged final of the Texaco Cup, a competition for clubs from the four home countries and the Republic of Ireland that had not qualified for Europe, and twice in the League, we played them five times that April, if memory serves. And of those, I think we won three, drew one and lost one.

We certainly looked like losing the FA Cup semi-final. In the first half, Burnley absolutely wiped the floor with us. We couldn't get the ball off them. They were brilliant. Their football just flowed down the right and the left, and our keeper, Willie McFaul, was on overtime. In fact, Burnley did everything except put the ball in the net. The second half started in exactly the same vein too, with them camped around our penalty area, but then a cross from the left was cleared to the edge of the area, where John Tudor sort of flicked it on. It was met by Terry Hibbitt as he, too, emerged from the penalty area, and he half-volleyed the ball with the inside of his left foot from about five yards outside our box. Terry had less flesh on him than my little finger, but this ball flew upfield as straight as if Jack Nicklaus had taken his driver to it.

At that moment, I felt Colin Waldron, the Burnley centre-half, come tight because he expected the ball to drop in front of me. Suddenly, however, he realised it was going to fly way over his head. I turned, and Waldron got hold of my shirt; then he grabbed me round the neck. I was still running, but he was holding on. All I could see was the goal and the goalkeeper. There was no one else to beat, other than the fourteen-stone centre-half hanging on to my neck. I was thinking, 'Don't go down, whatever you do! Don't go down! Stay on your feet! Try and shake him off!' Gradually, his grip loosened and he started to sort of slide down me, still going for hand-holds in the way someone falling down a crumbling cliff would do. In the end, he went down in a heap, and then I began to catch up with the ball, which had bounced, gone on and bounced again. But having had Waldron's weight on my back while still trying to run at pace, I struggled to regain my balance, almost falling over to my right. Alan Stevenson, the Burnley keeper, was coming at me, so I volleyed the ball with my left foot, almost falling over at the same time. Stevenson parried the shot with his hands, but the rebound came back to me slightly to my right, which was the way I was falling. Managing to get myself upright again, I took the ball with my right foot and went square of Stevenson, putting him out of the game. The Burnley left-back had tracked back by now and was trying to get to the goal-line, but from about fifteen or sixteen yards I rolled the ball in at a fair pace, and there was nothing he could do.

What I found amazing about the saga of having Colin Waldron on my back was that the referee, Gordon Hill, didn't blow for a foul. After the game, I asked him why he had decided not to punish such an obvious offence, and he gave me a brilliant answer. 'I get to know the players I referee,' he said, 'and, of all of them, if there's one who's going to stand on his feet and make a goalscoring chance, it's you. Despite the mauling you were getting, I backed you to stay on your feet and score. So I allowed you the advantage.'

'Thank you very much,' I said. 'I'm pleased that you did.'

Now that's the kind of knowledgeable person football needs to referee it, somebody who knows and understands the players exactly for what they are. Eternally, I shall be grateful to Gordon Hill for that. It was a brilliant delaying of a certain decision in my favour that, in the end, never had to be made and allowed me to score.

It was the first of two goals I scored that day. The second wasn't dissimilar, in that Burnley were again laying siege to our goal when Terry McDermott broke free from the area and knocked the ball straight down the middle. Away I went, and Waldron didn't get hold of me this time. Again Stevenson came straight out at me, but this time I drove the ball between his legs. So we took an absolute battering from Burnley and came off 2–0 winners. Anything up to 16,000 Geordies had swathed the old Kop End at Hillsborough in black and white, and after the final whistle we went down there and celebrated with them for a long time before going back to the dressing-room and the flowing champagne.

You never know what it's going to be like getting to an FA Cup final, and this was my first experience of it. Tyneside worked itself up to fever pitch. The hype and the expectations leading up to the semi-final had been massive, but now that we were in the final against Liverpool, the whole place was in ferment. Everything was still getting done in the city of Newcastle, but nobody was thinking about what they were actually doing. No other sport existed; there was no talk of anything else. The Geordie nation was going to Wembley, and the only problem was getting enough tickets.

Before the switch to Cardiff, what Newcastle fans liked about the FA Cup, apart from the sudden-death element and the tradition, was the opportunity it gave them to go down to London for the final. Newcastle is the furthest English club from the capital and they relished the thought of being able to fly the black and white Magpie banner down there and remind everyone of their existence. To watch Newcastle play in the final at Wembley was something the fans would plead for; they lived their lives to be part of the occasion. You can win the League championship, but you don't usually do it on one particular day. I think this is what Jackie Milburn had been talking about. The FA Cup final is something that can take people out of their humdrum existences and afford them one moment of history in their lives.

There was another factor in all this cup final fever on Tyneside in 1974, of course. The previous year, Newcastle had been upstaged by their bitterest north-east rivals when Sunderland beat Leeds 1–0 at Wembley. What had galled Tyneside was that Sunderland, then in the Second Division, had not only won the FA Cup, but overcome one of the best sides in the country to do it. So it was of paramount importance for Geordie prestige that Newcastle showed they could follow suit.

Unfortunately, we got things wrong from the start. Looking back now, it was a serious mistake to go down to the Selsdon Park Hotel in Surrey and spend a full week there preparing for the final. Like dogs, footballers love routine, and this arrangement took us out of our routine. It's all very well to go away, but do it when all the major work has been done. I speak with the benefit of hindsight here, of course, and I have to admit that at the time I felt it was probably the right thing to do. I'd been away with England before big matches, and because that's the way it's done in so many other countries, you almost accept it without question. But what we discovered was that we had simply made ourselves the focus for the world's media, who knew exactly where to find us. We were all together under the one roof, and we were bombarded with requests for interviews from the word go. We had the media living in our pockets every day of the week. In addition, our training routine was upset and we were sleeping in strange beds, living in unfamiliar surroundings and eating far richer food than we would have had at home.

Liverpool, on the other hand, travelled down on the Friday, stayed only the one night and went straight to Wembley the next day. They treated it just like any other League game in the capital, whereas we made this big thing about it. The city of Newcastle was at fever pitch, of course, and the week at the Selsdon Park Hotel was designed, I suppose, to take us away from all that. But, as I've said, it didn't have the desired effect. Training became almost a series of photographic stunts rather than the proper preparation it should have been. Keith Burkinshaw used to get angry with the media, but Joe was soft with them, and I felt there was a falling-out between the coach and the manager over it.

Then, on the Thursday morning, another wrong decision was taken, in my opinion. Thursday was always our main tactical day in readiness for the Saturday, and John Tudor and I couldn't believe it when it became apparent that Stewart Barrowclough would not play in the final. All that season, and the season before, we had used a formation that was 4–4–2 when we were defending and 4–3–3 when we were attacking. Stewart was the midfielder who would join me and John up front as a right-winger when we went on the attack. He was super quick – almost as quick as me – and he would whip in his crosses like a shot, which was great for strikers like John and me. Anyway, at that Thursday morning training session, Keith Burkinshaw started rearranging the team to play four straight midfield players, Stewart not among them. Barra himself was gobsmacked, absolutely shocked, at being left out, and John and I were very dubious about it. We wondered at first whether it might just be something to try out in training in case somebody got injured, but we gradually realised that this was the team that was going to play in the final.

We questioned the strategy, pointing out to Burky that Liverpool had, in Alec Lindsay, one of the slowest left-backs in the First Division. Lindsay hated playing against Barra, whose pace frightened him to death, and Stewart frightening Lindsay could cause panic among the rest of the Liverpool side. But it made no difference. Stewart was out, and Tommy Cassidy, who had played in the semi-final and the sixth-round second replay, was in. On paper, a midfield of Terry McDermott, Cassidy, Terry Hibbitt and Jimmy Smith looked exceedingly good. The plan was for McDermott to get wide and go like Barra, but it just didn't happen. That's hardly surprising since we'd only had that one Thursday morning to readjust to the new system and get it right. John Tudor and I were also worried about the tactical frailty of it. If you want to play negatively against Liverpool, you fill your midfield; if you want to attack them, you play with width. So it seemed to us we were taking the negative option. But, as footballers you say, 'OK, perhaps they know best', and you go out with a will to try to make it work.

The final disadvantage of staying at Selsdon Park became apparent when we set off for Wembley on the Saturday morning. The hotel is just south of Crystal Palace, and anyone who has tried to get to Selhurst Park from north London will know just how difficult it is to drive across the capital from that southern suburb to Wembley. It's one hell of a trek around the South and North Circular. There was an ominous atmosphere on that long road journey, too. I sensed a nervous tension I had never experienced before on a Newcastle team bus. Nerves I understood, but not nervous tension.

When we finally arrived at Wembley, we took a stroll up the tunnel and had a look at the hallowed turf. It was a bright, warm day, with some clouds dotted about. It got cloudier as the day wore on, but even when it was fairly cloudy, Wembley used to get quite stuffy. In fact, when people ask what I remember most about the famous old place, my answer is always the same: the smell of frying onions from the hotdog stands. The stadium reeked, absolutely reeked, of fried onions when you were on the pitch.

Then came another shock. When we went to the dressing-room, we found we were expected to wear tracksuits on what was a warm day. Not only that, but they were in a hideous combination of lilac and yellow. What those horrible colours had to do with Newcastle United, nobody could work out. And there was worse to follow. When we started to put the tracksuits on, we discovered they were way too big. Little Terry Hibbitt said, 'It's taken me two minutes to put my kit on and an hour and a half to pull my tracksuit bottoms up!' When he stood up, the waistband of his bottoms, which would have fitted Billy Bunter, was actually underneath his armpits. So the shout went out for safety pins so that we could look half decent when we went out. Later, we discovered how the tracksuits had come to be foisted on us. Stan Seymour Jr, one of the Newcastle directors, owned a sports shop, and it turned out that he'd got a whole load of outsize tracksuits he couldn't get rid of, so he did a deal with the club to sell them off as a job lot. All this, too, at a time when kit companies were falling over themselves to supply clubs with sportswear for the big occasions. But that farce over the FA Cup final tracksuits, I'm afraid, was typical of the board's thinking back then. Liverpool, in contrast, went out for the pre-match preliminaries wearing just tracksuit tops to go with their all-red strip. Psychologically, we were a goal down before the kick-off.

The game itself, when it started, seemed to fly by. It felt like just the blink of an eye before we were coming off at half-time with the score at 0–0, but not because the first half had been a thriller. I remember walking towards the tunnel and saying to Frank Clark, 'That's the worst we've ever played. There's no way we can play as badly as that in the second half. We've got a shout here, and we've been absolute rubbish.' Frank agreed that we'd been terrible. We couldn't string a pass together, we weren't getting forward and, incredibly, Liverpool were just as bad.

It all changed in the second half, though. The writing was on the wall for us when Alec Lindsay began to stride into the acre of space in front him that was going to become our downfall. Our four midfield players were tightly grouped in the middle of the park, and without Stewart Barrowclough there to put any pressure on him, Lindsay was just dribbling the ball forward and playing almost like an outside-left, not a left-back. Steve Heighway, in front of Lindsay, was making his runs from the left wing across the field in an effort to drag the right full-back across, but on one occasion he came forward into the safer space and smacked one from outside the box. It flew into the top corner, but the linesman on the far side stood there with his flag up. Offside! As I say, though, the writing was on the wall. We were all shouting and screaming that we had to fill that hole on our right, but it never happened. Liverpool just steamrollered forward as if we didn't exist and ran out 3–0 winners. It was all too easy.

I don't think I had a single shot at goal. Yes, I had one, which missed by a mile. It was a shot from distance because I'd seen Ray Clemence come off his line. It was the worst game I had ever had personally and the worst team performance I'd ever been part of. The irony of it was that Liverpool had been there for the taking. They had never before won an FA Cup final with such a poor performance as the one they put in that day.

The result meant I was there to be shot at, of course, mainly because the *Daily Mirror* had carried a back-page story on the morning of the final claiming I had said Newcastle were going to slaughter Liverpool and I was going to score a hatful. But I had never even spoken to them; as far as I could make out, they had just made it up. It was all part of the circulation war between the *Mirror* and the *Sun*. I had done a column for the *Sun* that day, of course, and I imagined the *Mirror* had simply concocted something to trump it. On reflection, however, I have to admit that Joe Harvey instigated some of this stuff in the papers as much as anybody. He had a real canny relationship with the press and would suggest little bits and pieces to them. I often wondered whether Joe was responsible for things like that, because when they appeared he never came over to me and said anything. I used to say, 'What's this shit?' and he'd say, 'Don't worry about it, son. It's all good publicity.' I wasn't worried about it, but it would have been nice had it been reported accurately.

I think one or two of the Newcastle players were shocked by our defeat in that final. Some, I felt, had been beginning to think the fickle finger of fate was pointing at us, what with the way our run to Wembley had gone. There was a feeling that our name was on the cup, that we only had to turn up to win it. I have to admit I was guilty of that myself. The discovery that we were all sadly mistaken cast a bit of a pall over what had been intended as a celebration dinner for the club and their guests at the Grosvenor House Hotel in Park Lane on the Saturday night.

What we were dreading even more was the return to Tyneside the following day. We travelled back by train, and it had been arranged for us to board an open-topped bus at the station to go around the town centre and up to St James's Park. There was a lot of anger in the players, not just because we'd got beaten, but because of the manner in which we'd been beaten. We'd lost 3–0 without even offering a whimper in return. Bob Moncur was so ashamed that as we were coming over the high level bridge above the Tyne he went to the window and threw his runners-up medal into the river. 'Why do I need a medal to be reminded I'm a loser?' he said bitterly.

That defeat hurt, and hurt badly. I think we'd have preferred to get back to Newcastle and be ignored by everybody. We would have deserved that. But it didn't happen. Instead, we were confronted by a city packed with people. I saw footage of Liverpool's return to their city with the cup, and we must have had four times the number of people turn out. They were all cheering so much you'd have thought we'd won the final. At that moment, I saw Geordie support for what it was. They were still there, saying, 'Thanks for a memorable occasion, even though we lost.' When we arrived at St James's Park, the ground was full, absolutely packed. We went in the directors' box and they wanted each player to say something to the crowd. But there's nothing original to say if you're eighth or ninth in line, so the mike was handed to me to speak on behalf of everybody. 'We'll do our damnedest to get back there next season and win,' I said. That was reported the following day in the *Mirror* as 'We'll win the cup next year!' They just don't stop, these people.

Most of us were just thankful it was the end of the season and we could slink away. Not so in my case, however. A few days later, I had to join up with an England squad full of Liverpool players for the summer tour of East Germany, Bulgaria and Yugoslavia, undertaken as a result of England failing to book a place in the 1974 World Cup finals. Not that Ray Clemence, Kevin Keegan, Emlyn Hughes and Alec Lindsay said a word about the FA Cup final, of course.

# CHAPTER FIVE
# NEWCASTLE: OUT OF TOON

The season that followed our FA Cup final defeat, 1974/75, was very much a case of after the Lord Mayor's show. Something had gone out of the club and the Joe Harvey magic wasn't there any more. We certainly felt that a gulf had been created between the board and Joe, and that they had lost the confidence they had had in him for thirteen years. Our tame surrender to Liverpool at Wembley was probably the last in a sequence of events leading to his removal as manager. You could trace it back a couple of years to the time we beat Fiorentina in Florence to win the Anglo-Italian Cup.

I didn't play in that final because I was away with England at the time, but I got all the stories from the lads when I returned to Newcastle before going on holiday. And there were plenty to tell, because it seemed there had been ructions over in Florence about a new contract Keith Burkinshaw had been promised. Joe Harvey was not particularly well paid, not by any stretch of the imagination, and Keith was pretty much on a pittance, but he was hoping that would be rectified by his new contract. So when he was told the contract offer had been rescinded,

Burky was absolutely furious and refused to prepare the team until such time as the situation was sorted out to his satisfaction. His show of militancy surprised the players, who thought he might have put the argument to one side until the Anglo-Italian final, the last game of the season, had been played. But, as I've pointed out already, Burky could be a very stubborn man when he thought he was in the right. He used to do all the tactical work with the players, of course, and his absence on this occasion meant that Joe had to give his first team talk for yonks.

Joe decided to leave it until the squad had arrived at the ground and were all in the dressing-room. He told them what the team was going to be, then proceeded to say the following: 'I have been at this club as a player, as a coach and as a manager, and at all three levels I have got to cup finals. I've never, ever lost a cup final as player, coach or manager either, so I'm not going to have you lot ruining my record. If you don't get out there and beat this lot of Eye-ties, you've got me to deal with when you come off the field.' And with that, he walked out. That was his team talk. Left with just the physios in the dressing-room, the Newcastle players got on with the game plan themselves. They went through the set pieces – free-kicks and corner kicks, for and against – and got themselves organised tactically. Then they went out and beat Fiorentina 2–1.

At first, Joe's unusual team talk was hailed as a wonderful battle cry, a sort of Geordie version of 'Cry, "God for Harry! England and St George!"' But the more the story was told, the more denigratory to him it became. People were saying it just showed that he had no tactical knowledge, that he was not able to coach players, that he wasn't able to do this, wasn't able to do that. It was perhaps the perfect team talk for that particular moment, but it was beginning to be used against him. For a while, the players told the tale in a jokey fashion; then, when they realised it was harming Joe, they stopped in an effort to protect him.

The previous season, of course, Newcastle had suffered the embarrassment of that famous FA Cup defeat at the hands of non-League Hereford; then came the Anglo-Italian team talk that should have glorified Joe but ended up vilifying him; and now there was the FA Cup final débâcle against Liverpool at Wembley painfully fresh in the memory. The pressure started to mount on our manager, and I became aware of this throughout the 1974/75 season.

As secretive and removed as the board were, bits of information started to filter out – as they always do – and there were rumblings afoot. There was a change in Joe, too. The big man who used to swan up to the training ground and watch things going on wasn't doing it with the boyish confidence he once did, and as the season progressed he developed something of a stoop. Nothing changed much on the field, and that hardly helped Joe. We had our highs and lows, as we did every season. We would slaughter some sides, then get slaughtered by others. We were brilliant, then awful. Peaks and troughs, peaks and troughs; we never seemed able to achieve any consistency and finished mid-table as usual.

Towards the end of the season, Frank Clark was nearing the end of his contract. That didn't seem to matter much because he was the vice-captain and the regular left-back, so it was taken for granted the club would automatically take up the option on his contract, as they did with each player who had done well. Not only that, but Frank had been promised a new contract by Joe. 'Not a problem, Frank, I'll look after you,' he'd said. But when the retained list came out, Frank's name wasn't on it. He was given a free transfer. Frank was devastated, absolutely devastated. Newcastle United had been his life, and he was in his late twenties now. As it happens, things turned out brilliantly for him and he was snapped up by Brian Clough at Nottingham Forest, who went on to win both the First Division title and the European Cup, but no one was to know that when Newcastle cast him aside.

Then, in the summer of 1975, the final blow: Joe was sacked. Perhaps sacked is not quite the right word. According to the board he was not being sacked, just moved to another position. But when questioned closely about whether he was still with the club, the board were not prepared to give a straight answer; all they were prepared to say was that he was not the manager of Newcastle United any longer. What it amounted to was that they had sort of sacked him but had shied away from cutting ties altogether, which left Joe in complete limbo. It was a shabby way to treat a man who had served the club so well and so loyally as player, coach and manager for some 30 years. He had played in the first two of those three legendary FA Cup triumphs of the 1950s, and as manager had won the Fairs Cup, forerunner of the UEFA Cup, in 1969. That remains the only success Newcastle have had in European football, and the only major trophy they have lifted in any competition since 1955. Under Joe, Newcastle also won the Anglo-Italian Cup, the Texaco Cup twice and got to the final of the FA Cup. It was quite a record for someone who supposedly couldn't coach.

Rather like Kevin Keegan when he got the job many years later, Joe had a very simple philosophy as manager of Newcastle United. Basically, he was looking to the team to score goals all the while without worrying too much about the defence. If things started to go wrong and the rumblings started, he'd just get into the transfer market and go and buy a bloody good player for a hundred grand. That's how he came to sign Tony Green, for instance. There was no grand master plan or anything like that. He also bought Paddy Howard from Barnsley to play at centre-half, and relied heavily on his skipper, Bob Moncur, who played alongside Paddy. Paddy was one hell of a customer to deal with, and pretty mobile. Monc, for his part, was a great reader of the game and a powerful leader for both Newcastle and Scotland, but he suffered from a serious lack of pace. In fact, the pairing reminded me a bit of the one West Ham had at the time between Bobby Moore and Tommy Taylor. This may sound like sacrilege, but I loved playing against Mooro because, great reader of the game and tremendous passer of the ball that he was, he had no pace at all. A young, quick whippersnapper like myself could cause him nightmares. Taylor was just as slow; I used to run riot against him when he was playing for Leyton Orient and I was with Luton. I have to say I was at my happiest playing against West Ham.

It made me uneasy, though, to think that our central defence was so similar. At the top level of the game, I believe, at least one of your centre-halves has to be quick. That was as true then as it is today. Looking back to those days, there was Martin Buchan at Manchester United, Kevin Beattie at Ipswich and Colin Todd at Derby, and each one played off a big centre-half: Jim Holton at United, Alan Hunter at Ipswich and Roy McFarland at Derby. Todd and McFarland were the finest central defenders I ever played against. When people ask me who was the best I faced, I always say those two.

To make matters worse, I thought Joe Harvey had our central defensive partnership the wrong way round. Instead of asking Paddy Howard, the more mobile of the two, to pick up the opposition's quickest striker, Joe had him doing the big centre-half's job, challenging in the air dangerous headers of the ball like Wyn Davies and Derek Dougan. The problem when a defence lacks pace is that they drop off and defend deep. Ours, certainly, would finish up defending on the toes of the goalkeeper. That meant I was having to deal with an awful lot of long balls because, to find me on the halfway line, defenders had to ping it 50 or 60 yards. If we were on top, the defence would push up, but we had to be well on top for it to happen, so we tended to lose games we could have contested more seriously. It was sad, really, because we had two quick full-backs in David Craig and Frank Clark, and if Craigie was injured there was a young lad called Irving Nattrass who was as quick as the wind and could run all day. Irving was a great athlete. I used to think we'd be laughing if we could have put four of him along the back.

Under these circumstances, Monday mornings following Saturday games would become very argumentative. Keith Burkinshaw would sit us down and we'd have a sort of team meeting at which nobody could agree. The attacking players felt things weren't right at the back, and the defensive players felt they could be better supported when the opposition had the ball. The attackers contended that the best way to defend was as far from the goal as possible, but the defenders disagreed. So there was this huge difference of opinion that never really got sorted.

I have to admit I finished up having major arguments with Burky. He'd been a centre-half with Liverpool but had never really established himself in the first team and had had to retire from the game early, but he still possessed a tremendous footballing mind as he proved a few years later by becoming a surprisingly imaginative manager at Tottenham. He would argue that I hadn't done this or hadn't done that to help the team out defensively, and I, echoing Jackie Milburn, would say, 'Why are you telling me this, Keith? There's nine others and a goalkeeper to do that. OK, once an attack of ours breaks down and the ball's with the opposing goalkeeper, where do you want me to go? I can stop it going to the centre-halves or the full-backs, but what more do you want me to do after that?' The arguments would be relentless, with no conclusion ever reached. It seemed to me the defenders wanted superhumans up front. Having done everything in your power to finish with a goalscoring opportunity, done your damnedest to get the ball in the net despite all the kicks and the hacks, the shoves, the elbows and the head-butts, there was no time to recover. It seemed to be forgotten, too, that up front there were two of us playing against four, but four against two at the back. This was always one of my premises for an argument.

I thought the world of Frank Clark, and still do, but I couldn't agree with him when he said, 'When we defend, we defend as eleven. That's how it's got to be.' OK then, think about this. If I'm on the halfway line and I've got two guys who remain goalside of me, and there's a third who sits back just in front of me, I'm occupying three plus the goalkeeper. That's four out of eleven, and you've then only seven to deal with. But if I come back, all I do is drag with me the one in front of me and possibly one of the others. So how am I supposed then to mark two men near our goal? Keith's argument was that it didn't matter if I did bring them back with me because the more bodies there were, the less likely it was a goal would be scored against us. His theory was that even opposing players could act as a shield in our box. But I wasn't buying that. It was a dispute that continued for a very long time, and one that formulated a great deal of my thinking when I became a manager myself. Hardly ever did I put a defensive responsibility on either of my two strikers.

Keith and I got on all right most of the time, though; it was just over tactics that we agreed to differ. Burky was fearsome when riled, and we nearly came to blows over it at times. I often used to go and have a chat with Jackie Milburn about it and tell him Keith always wanted me to come back and help out. 'Of course he will,' said Jackie. 'He's a centre-half. He's thinking like a centre-half, not a coach. All defenders think everybody else has got to defend, but you've got your job and you can occupy 90 minutes very well working out how you are going to score goals. You just stick to it!' It was, I suppose, all a bit unfair on John Tudor, because I wasn't doing all the attacking on my own and he, willing as ever, would get back and play a centre-half's role if required. John sought a kind of middle ground between Keith and me and would say, 'Look, Burky, I'm getting back and I'm doing this and I'm doing that, but when the ball does get cleared, Mal is always the "out" ball for us. He takes the weight off us that way. If he comes back, then we haven't got any "out" ball.' But Burky was totally stubborn over it. So was I.

Joe Harvey would just let these arguments run their course without taking part. Sometimes he'd be there, sometimes he'd leave halfway through, sometimes he wasn't there at all. He liked to hear other people voicing their opinions, but he rarely offered his own. Then he'd sidle up to me as we were going out to training afterwards and say, 'You're doing all right, son. You just keep going forward,' thus undermining Burky completely after the two hours of argument that had just taken place.

I find it difficult to criticise Joe because he always treated me superbly. Apart from all the verbal encouragement he gave, he was very generous when it came to pay rises. For four seasons, I never had to knock on his door with a query about money or contracts. Every year, before negotiating time came, Joe nipped in and increased my pay. He always showed his appreciation before I had to ask. If I ever did knock on his door, it would be because he had asked me to come to his office so he could tell me I was in the England squad. He would then call Russell Cushing, the secretary of the club, to sort out travel arrangements for me.

Joe was also kind enough to allow me to go on what proved to be the trip of a lifetime in the summer of 1975. Because there was no England tour, and because I didn't like long breaks away from football, I persuaded Joe to let me be transferred temporarily to a club in South Africa called Lusitano, which was run by leading members of the Portuguese community in Johannesburg. They played at the Rand Stadium, the major venue in South Africa at that time, and I was contracted to play a few games for them along with two guys from Portsmouth, Eoin Hand and Norman Piper. We were booked to fly TAP, the Portuguese airline, from Heathrow to Lisbon, then on from there to Johannesburg. Unfortunately, the connecting flight was postponed until the following morning, so we were put up overnight in a Lisbon hotel. When I woke up the next day, I discovered I'd developed a rather large pimple in a very awkward place on my backside. It seemed to get bigger when we took off, and I was shifting about, trying to get comfortable, in my airline seat at 37,000 feet. But, oh, what a relief, a refuelling stop was scheduled for Luanda, the capital of Angola, so we landed... and looked out of the windows to see tanks ringing the airport. Soldiers with a million pips on the shoulders of their uniforms came on board and told the crew a state of emergency had been declared. We had to disembark and go to the transit lounge, where we would be looked after.

When we got there, we discovered that the air conditioning had broken down, and the heat as we'd come off the aircraft was absolutely phenomenal. It just stole all the oxygen out of the air, making it almost impossible to breathe. It felt like 50°C out there, and the sweat was just pouring out of us. Our clothes were drenched within a minute, and then we were told there was going to be a delay of an hour and a half. Eoin, Norman and I headed for the bar to get a cold beer. I perched my bum precariously on a waist-high stool at the bar because the pimple was really starting to annoy me now. To get a bit of relief, I hitched my right buttock up and pulled my cheeks apart in the process. But as the three of us were chatting away and getting to know each other, the stool beneath me suddenly gave way. The seat came away, my weight was on it, and I went straight down and hit the stem of the seat with the most tender part of my posterior. Whoo! I didn't need that, I can tell you. I could feel this thing starting to throb, and I realised I had a problem.

By the time we were shepherded back on to the plane by armed government troops, there were still another three hours to go before we reached Jo'burg. During the flight, this growth on my bum went on the rampage. By the time we landed at our final destination, it had swollen to the size of an egg. We were met in the airport by a couple of Portuguese officials from the Lusitano club, and the manager. I immediately pulled him aside and explained my not-so-little problem to him.

'Don't worry,' he said, 'we'll get a doctor to look at you straight away. Have you ever had anything like it before?'

I replied, 'No, this is the first time. I've been taking antibiotics for something else, and maybe they've inflamed it.'

The doctor told me I needed an operation, so not long after landing in Johannesburg I was booked into hospital. It turned out that my 'pimple' was actually an abscess caused by hairs that had started to grow out, then turned back in and got infected. They cleaned the thing out that night, but in such cases the incision has to be kept open so that it heals from the inside out. The problem was that Lusitano were scheduled to play their first game three or four days after my op, so the manager came in to see me and said, 'I don't know what to do. There was big press coverage before you arrived saying you were coming, but what do we do now?'

Ever the optimist, I replied, 'Don't worry, it'll be all right.'

'But the medical people are saying you've got to stay in hospital for seven to ten days.'

'OK, then I'll check myself out.'

I had to sign forms to say I'd take full responsibility for anything that might go wrong and that the club had arranged for me to see a doctor every day. They also put a drain in the wound, but when I checked in at the hotel I found that my trousers were being soiled by what was coming through it. I went straight off to a chemist and bought some sanitary towels, because they seemed the obvious answer to the problem. Now I could wear underpants with a sanitary towel stuck inside them and wouldn't mess them up.

Everything was fine for a while after that. I went along to Lusitano to meet everybody and watch a training session. When the day of the first game arrived, I got to the ground and went through to the dressing-room to get changed. I took my trousers and underpants off, and by now it was second nature to me to remove this sanitary towel covering the open wound on my backside. But suddenly I became aware that the other players were looking at me, watching closely as I peeled off this sanitary towel, rolled it into a little ball and put it in the waste bin. The players gave one another a little nod and disappeared to have a team meeting out in the corridor.

'What on earth is this guy doing wearing sanitary towels?' they asked the manager. 'What is he? We want to know what's going on! You've brought over this feller from England who's supposed to be some sort of sensational goalscoring type, and he comes here wearing sanitary towels!'

To placate them, the manager had to tell them the story. 'But,' he added, 'we don't want the press making mountains out of abscesses, so just keep it quiet, lads, and let's get on with it.'

They were happy with that, and we went out and won 5–0.

Apartheid was at its height at the time, of course, and I have to say that a lot of what I saw shocked me. I couldn't believe the attention to detail when it came to segregating blacks and whites. Wherever you went, there were arrows saying 'this way' if you were white or 'that way' if you were black; every door had a sign on it telling you whether you could go through it or not. At first, if you were white, it gave you a feeling of superiority because you were going through the best doors, but once I started to realise the absolute severity of what it meant for the vast majority of people, I came to despise it. Perhaps I was wrong to have gone there in the first place, but then I wasn't as aware of the implications as I might have been. I knew South Africa were barred from playing cricket anywhere in the world because of apartheid, but that was it. Now, though, I was seeing the situation at first hand. At the Rand Stadium, both ends of the ground and the main stand were for whites only; the far side, where the spectators were packed in like sardines, was full of black faces. It had a very distinctive smell, too. When I asked what it was, I was told it was the ganja (marijuana) they smoked. They certainly loved their football.

The hotel we stayed in was also rather amazing; it was generally referred to by its nickname, 'the Sportsmen's'. Its claim to fame was that it was the only hotel in South Africa that allowed black and white occupancy. There were black floors and white floors, a black restaurant and a white restaurant, a black bar and a white bar. Everything was segregated, including the lifts. It was bizarre, to say the least, to find you couldn't go one way and had to go another.

It was at the Sportsmen's that I met a well-to-do black guy I liked a lot. He spoke with an American accent and had a lot of fun, a lot of devilment, about him. He had the confidence of a successful man and didn't shuffle about like most of the blacks I saw. Neither did he kowtow to anybody; he stood erect and proud. We kept meeting up, but it wasn't as though we could go to the bar together and have a drink. Even so, we managed to spend some social time together. I told him I couldn't help but notice that he seemed altogether different from other blacks, and asked him the reason why. He told me that he had got out of Soweto as a lad and had gone to the United States where he'd become a petrol attendant on a garage forecourt working all hours and saving his money. Then the breaks had come his way, he'd got a petrol franchise and opened his own garage. He now owned a major chain of gas stations and had become a very wealthy man.

He was back in Johannesburg, he added, because one route out of

Soweto for the black kids was football, and he was there on a scouting mission. He was looking for youngsters between the ages of fifteen and seventeen to place in teams back in the States. 'There's big money to be had over there,' he said, 'and what I do is get these kids to sign a contract with me personally. I own them, if you like. It is a kind of black on black form of slavery, but it's all to a good end. I give them enough money over there to live reasonably, and the rest of it is put away for their futures. I control all the finances so that they don't go and blow it. They come out of Soweto uneducated and unworldly, and they don't know what to do with a lot of money other than to blow it. I set up trust funds, pensions and all sorts of things to make sure they and their families are going to be well looked after for the rest of their lives.' In effect, he was one of the first football agents. He still had his chain of gas stations, but, as he said, 'This is my way of helping the kids who come from the same place I came from, but who don't get the breaks I've had in my life.'

I found this guy so fascinating that I invited him to come and see one of our games at the Rand Stadium as my guest. That presented certain problems, so I went to see the Portuguese president of Lusitano and explained the situation. I'd spent time at the home of the president and sensed he was anti-apartheid. Sure enough, after a lot of deliberation, the president gave the idea the green light. On the day, my black friend turned up in this great big white Cadillac which he parked in the white car park before going through the white entrance and making his way up to the directors' box in the main stand. There, he was fêted. No doubt the wealthy Portuguese guys in charge of the club realised this fellow was something out of the ordinary. They could, perhaps, sniff business to be had at some time in the future. Anyway, my friend had the front to carry it all off in great style.

Imagine my shock, then, when, sitting at home a couple of years later watching the Soweto riots on television, I saw him. The camera view was from behind the police lines, so it showed the backs of the policemen, three, four and five deep with their riot shields. Some 60 yards beyond them there was this huge, milling mob of black people which was just starting to come forward when suddenly, from the side, there appeared a black figure in a white suit. Instantly, I recognised the guy I'd met in Johannesburg. He was holding his arms up to the crowd as if to say, 'Don't go any further, don't do this! Whatever you do, don't do this!' Then a youth came out of the crowd and went up to the guy in the suit, who then promptly crumpled to the ground. Hardly able to believe what I was seeing, I heard the commentator's voice saying, 'The leader of the blacks was knifed and killed by his own people.' It was a shocking act that encapsulated the whole situation in South Africa for me. There was only one word to describe it, and that was 'insanity'. And do you know what? I can't even remember that magnificent man's name. It makes me feel so sad and guilty.

But not all my memories of those six weeks in South Africa have unhappy postscripts. On a trip down to Cape Town we met a bookie called King Louis who liked a drink and a game of poker. His great love, though, was horseracing, and he was an avid punter. When he heard that we intended to go to the races before returning to Jo'burg, he gave us a tip, a horse called Farci. 'Put your brains on it,' he urged. 'It'll win. Don't let anything anybody says deter you from backing Farci. You'll hear a lot of negativity about it, but this is my present to you.' King Louis was white, of Italian descent, and everything about him suggested links with the Mafia. 'I just ask you to promise one thing,' he added. 'Don't bet at my stall.' There were no betting shops in South Africa; the only place you could bet was at the racecourse itself.

We were advised not to take anything less than 3/1 on Farci, but the opening price was 5/2. It went from there to 11/4, then, suddenly, to 3/1. Norman Piper hit one bookie, I hit another and Eoin Hand a third. It was the biggest bet I'd ever had in my life. I don't know what the others put on, but my stake was 2,000 rand, and it was something like two rand to the pound in those days. It was a sprint, and the horse didn't show until about two furlongs out, but then it went like greased lightning and won by about four lengths. But when I went back to the bookie with my ticket I found he couldn't pay me. He apologised and asked where I was staying. When I told him, he said he'd be there first thing in the morning with my winnings. I didn't believe him, of course, and demanded my stake money back, at the very least. 'I haven't even got that,' he said. 'I've been cleaned out on that race.' So I went to see King Louis and told him what had happened with the bookie. 'Don't worry,' he said, 'he'll be there. If he says he'll be there, he will be.' And, blow me down, he turned up! He gave me the whole 8,000 rand, which made me wonder what the hell I was going to do with so much money. I couldn't just carry it around with me, so I went to the bank and opened an account.

The next day I got a call from an old friend in England, the *Newcastle Evening Chronicle*'s John Gibson, then one of their football reporters and now the paper's executive sports editor. After asking me how I was enjoying life and my football in the sun, and after being told about my big win on the horses, Gibbo said he'd got a bit of news for me.

'Oh, yes?' said I. 'What is it?'

'If you're feeling that lucky,' he replied, 'see how you do on this one. I'll give you three guesses as to who is the new Newcastle manager.'

'Brian Clough?' I said.

'No, he wasn't even mentioned in the raffle.'

'Bobby Robson?'

'No, they weren't interested in him either. This is your last guess.'

'Please don't tell me they've appointed Jackie Charlton!'

'No, not him either.'

'Well, go on then, John, tell me who it is.'

'Gordon Lee,' Gibbo replied.

'Gordon who?' I said instinctively, because I'd honestly never heard of the feller, even though he had been manager of Blackburn.

It was an unfortunate thing to have said, because the next day, and unbeknown to me, the back-page headline in the *Evening Chronicle* was GORDON WHO? SAYS SUPERMAC FROM SOUTH AFRICA. So, without even knowing it, I was completely at odds with the new manager before he'd even set foot in Newcastle, before we'd even so much as exchanged a word. And he really took it badly. When I returned from Johannesburg for pre-season training at the end of what had been an absolutely fantastic trip, I was immediately shown that edition of the *Evening Chronicle* and asked by the other press guys if I had actually said what I had been quoted as saying. Yes, I had, I told them, but it was just an instinctive reaction and I never imagined it would be used as a headline for the piece.

I thought it might be a good idea to go to St James's Park, introduce myself to Gordon Lee and explain what had happened. I studied the *Chronicle* hard because I had no idea what Lee looked like, and there was a photograph of him in the paper. There was also a head-and-shoulders mugshot of his coach, Richard Dinnis, whom I had not heard of either. 'What's he done?' I thought, but I couldn't find anything in the reference books about him as a coach or a player. As I was making my way towards the glass doors at the main entrance of St James's Park, they swung open, and out came the face I had last been looking at in the paper. Realising who it was, I stuck out my right arm to offer a handshake and uttered the immortal words, 'Hello, Dennis. I'm Malcolm Macdonald.' I'd only forgotten the poor bloke's name, thinking it was Dennis Richards! Not surprisingly, he blanked me. What a good start!

It got worse. When I introduced myself to Gordon Lee, he didn't say anything by way of a greeting; all he said was, 'Come into my office,' and then told me to sit down. He sat down as well, looked at me and opened the conversation with this: 'Tell me about Terry Hibbitt. I hear he's a troublemaker.'

I couldn't believe it! I'd just rushed all the way back from Johannesburg only to be sat down in the manager's office and quizzed about Terry Hibbitt being a troublemaker! 'Let me tell you this,' I said, anger already rising in me, 'Hibby's a great player, and that's all you need to know. Beyond that, this conversation is terminated. I'm off. I'll see you next in training.' And away I went.

It seemed to me that Lee had allowed himself to be affected by publicity about Terry without getting to know the facts, and I was next in the firing line. In an article by the new manager, he was quoted as saying 'I will not tolerate superstars!' and he went on to say that one man didn't make a team, etc., etc. As I read through the article, I realised he had named me and only me. It couldn't have been construed as anything other than an attack on yours truly. All the other players had seen the article, of course, and it provided them with all the ammunition they needed to wind up the new manager. Whenever I went in for pre-season training, the rest of the lads would refer to me as 'Superstar' whenever Lee was within earshot. 'Did you hear what Superstar said? Did you see what Superstar did?' they would say. At the same time, I might add, they were referring to him as 'Gordon Question Mark' (as in Gordon who?), or just plain 'Question Mark'.

Footballers are the world's worst for seizing on something like that and stirring it up for a laugh. Me? I found it funny. But as the next three or four weeks went by, we sensed an antagonism building twixt manager and dressing-room. Lee brought in some players and talked of them as 'my players', whereas the others were just 'the players'. And he was segregating the dressing-room at a time when I could not have felt more rebellious.

He came into the dressing-room one day and, pointing at me, said, 'I've just signed a player who is going to score more goals than you!'

I just looked at him with contempt and said, 'In your dreams! I don't think that bloke's been born yet,' or words to that effect. But the other players were curious and wanted to know who it was he'd signed. I knew he wanted me to bite first, though, so I said, 'I tell you what, Gordon. If you're so convinced this guy is going to score more goals than me, I'll have a little wager with you. I bet you a week's wages of your money against a week's wages of mine that I finish up with more goals come the end of the season. And I know how much you're earning, remember, so I know I'm giving you odds of better than two to one.' That brought the other players up short because I'd just announced to them that I was earning more than twice as much as the manager!

Lee went outside and brought in Alan Gowling. Now, Alan was a nice enough guy and quite an intelligent lad, and he didn't need to be in the middle of something like that. I think what Lee had intended as a clever wind-up on his part left him with egg all over his face in the end. As soon as John Tudor saw Gowling, he turned to me and said, 'Well, that's me on my bike!'

The unrest in the dressing-room escalated very quickly from that point, and what had been a very integrated and solid unit suddenly had this bloody great dividing line down it. When team spirit is undermined at any club it's usually the players who do it, but in this case we had a manager and his coach who were responsible.

There was another occasion when Lee walked into the dressing-room and dramatically announced a signing. This time, though, he came out with the most audacious prophecy about a young player I've ever heard in my life: he told us all that he'd just signed the new Bobby Moore. We all sat back, waiting, then in through the door came this tall, well-built lad Lee introduced as Graham Oates from Blackburn. Lee officially welcomed him to the club, but unfortunately, as the poor lad attempted to reply, we all realised that he had an awful stutter. 'Mmm,' we thought, 'could be a problem there with communication on the field.'

The following Saturday we were playing Leeds United. They won the toss, decided which way they were going to kick and left us with the kick-off. Graham Oates was in the side in central defence, and I was up front with Alan Gowling. I said to Alan, 'Knock me the ball, and I'll give the new boy his first touch in the game.' The whistle was blown, Alan touched the ball to me, and I drove it straight at Oates's feet. He went to control the ball but failed to do so; it hit his foot, came up towards his knee, hit his chest, bounced on his shoulder and went over behind him. He quickly turned round to rescue the situation only to thrust out a foot and lob the goalkeeper. The ball having been retrieved from the back of our net, I carried it to the halfway line, put it on the centre spot and remarked to Alan, 'I have to say, I never saw Bobby Moore do that.' There we were, restarting the game with Leeds 1–0 up without even having touched the ball!

'What now?' Alan asked.

'Give it me again.'

I did exactly the same thing again, pinging the ball straight at Graham and thinking, 'I'll give you a second chance, old son.' But once again Oates couldn't control it, and he treated us to a near action replay of the first, bizarre incident. This time, though, the keeper saw the lob coming and back-pedalled like crazy to tip the ball over the bar. Strangely enough, despite that comical, self-destructive start, we went on to win the game.

I couldn't resist having a go at Gordon Lee at half-time, though. He wanted everybody to call him 'Boss', but I couldn't bring myself to do that. I called Joe Harvey, Alec Stock and Harry Haslam 'Boss', but it was a term of endearment in their case. People had to earn my respect before I called them that. I repeated what I'd said on the pitch to Alan Gowling. 'Well, Gordon,' I said, deadpan, in front of the whole team, 'I don't remember Bobby Moore doing anything like Graham has just done!' He was flummoxed, and angry, and from there the rift between us became a chasm. He started to play me deep, though I don't know whether or not that was to prevent me scoring and winning the bet.

Before the end of that 1975/76 season, other things happened to make me think it was perhaps time to move on from Newcastle. The previous summer, none of us had been able to believe it when Frank Clark was given a free transfer. He was still a very good player, as Brian Clough had confirmed by signing him for Forest. Because Frank was an old friend, I went and played in Paul Hart's testimonial at the City Ground. It was a team of international footballers that Forest played against, and after the game Cloughie came into our dressing-room. 'I want you, you and you in my office as soon as you're ready,' he said, pointing to Roy McFarland, Colin Todd and me.

You don't turn down a summons like that, so we went and sat in Cloughie's office. Frank was already well and truly ensconced in there – Cloughie thought the world of him – and so was Archie Gemmill; there was also a Forest director in the group, though I think they called them committee members in those days. Anyway, Cloughie sat behind his desk and for a long time didn't say a word; he just listened to all the chat that was going on. But every now and then, suddenly, he'd come out with a remark that just cut through the conversation, a remark so pointed it was, literally, remarkable. I'd never before sat through a session like that, where somebody could be so pointed, not in a scathing way but rather in a way that hit home on a truth.

I was sitting there with a light ale in my hand, but then I became aware that Cloughie was looking at me intently. His gaze wasn't shifting, so I turned and looked him directly in the eye. 'Time for a move, young man, time for a move!' he said, pointing at me. 'There's no more you can do up there. It's time for a move.' That said, his gaze moved elsewhere, and the next time he spoke to me it was to say, 'Cheerio, thank you for coming.' I went off into the night with the Cloughism 'It's time for a move!' ringing in my ears.

It hit a chord in me. The idea had been floating vaguely round in my head, and I realised Clough had forced me to confront it. I was now well and truly established as a First Division footballer, and at 25 going on 26 I was at the peak of my career. I'd finished top League goalscorer once, and when I wasn't top I was either second or joint second. Every season I'd scored between 27 and 32 goals, which meant I'd created a reputation as a consistent marksman – one of the danger men of the game, as it were. So it shouldn't really have mattered to me who became manager of Newcastle United, because no self-respecting manager turns his back on goals. Unfortunately, instead of going with the flow and making the most of my scoring record, Gordon Lee decided to battle against it. He had to do it his way, hence the signing of Alan Gowling. That was fine by me. I was still going to notch up my 30 goals, and if somebody could improve on the fifteen or sixteen John Tudor always got, then all well and good. In fact, I have to say that, working by Alec Stock's statistics, the 46 to 50 goals John and I scored between us each season were the reason Newcastle did not get relegated. Whatever came from the rest of the team would be what took us up the division and through the cup rounds, but it was John and I who saw to it that we stayed healthily in the top flight.

I was still enjoying my football at St James's Park under Gordon Lee, mainly because I found putting up with him a challenging lark. I'd sometimes have him pulling his hair out at comments I made, and other players would make remarks he fell for every time. There was one particularly memorable occasion when he came into the dressing-room and asked if Aiden McCaffery, our eighteen-year-old reserve centre-half, was Irish.

'No,' we chorused, 'he's Geordie born and bred.'

'Well,' said Lee, 'I still want to nominate him for the Irish international team.'

To which I replied facetiously, 'Well, he owns his own boots. That always gets you into the Irish team!'

'His parents must be Irish!' snapped Lee in return.

'No, they're not,' we said, looking round at one another. 'They're Geordies born and bred as well.'

'How dare he have a name like Aiden McCaffery and not be Irish,' Lee continued to complain.

'Oh, that's stupid, Gordon,' I said. 'My name's Malcolm Ian Macdonald. You can't get more Scottish than that, and I play for England.'

'You... you should not play for England with a name like yours!' he spluttered.

At which point somebody – I think it was Tommy Cassidy – came out with one of the greatest one-liners I have ever heard. 'Excuse me, boss,' he said, all innocence, 'how many times have you played for China?'

There wasn't a lot to say after that.

So little respect for Gordon Lee did some of us have that our dealings with him increasingly became a mickey-taking exercise. I remember Paddy Howard and I were having a jog round the training pitch one day before the 1976 League Cup final against Manchester City when Gordon came over and started jogging alongside us.

'What's it like to play at Wembley?' he asked.

Perhaps he meant it as a serious question, I don't know, but it came over as sheer stupidity. We certainly regarded it as such, and replied, 'Oh, it's different to anywhere else. It's got two big white towers!' Then we carried on jogging.

Although Newcastle did qualify for the UEFA Cup the season after I left, reaching that League Cup final was the club's only really significant achievement during Gordon Lee's two years in charge – and I don't know whether we got there because of him or in spite of him. I rather fancy it was the latter. One of the things that sticks in my mind about that cup run was the save Pat Jennings, then still Tottenham Hotspur's goalkeeper, made from Tommy Craig in the first leg of the semi-final. The score stood at 0–0 when Tommy struck the ball very well from about 25 yards. I had pulled away to the left, so I was looking at the shot side on. From there, I watched Jennings go up and backwards, then stretch out an arm in a way that reminded me of Twizzle, the kids' television character that had extendable limbs. He just got his fingertips to the ball and tipped it over the bar. It was a glorious sight, one of the greatest saves I have ever seen.

We lost 1–0 at White Hart Lane but absolutely murdered Spurs in the second leg at St James's Park. That gave us Manchester City in the final at the end of February, and we proved to be two very evenly matched sides. The deciding factor was not just the second goal City scored, but the manner in which it was scored. We'd gone a goal down, then got one back, and we really thought we could go on and win it from there. But not long after half-time Dennis Tueart scored with a wonderful bicycle kick. It was a great piece of athleticism on his part, and well done to him. It knocked the stuffing out of us, and it was a real uphill battle from then until the final whistle.

So my Wembley record with Newcastle was two finals, two defeats. But the one thing that has to be said about the second one was that it wasn't a poor performance against Manchester City. Unlike the FA Cup final against Liverpool two years earlier, it was a damned good game of football, and one brilliant goal was the difference between the sides. Of course it was disappointing to lose at Wembley again, but the second defeat did not feel as bad as the first.

Meanwhile, Gordon Lee was being as petty as ever. Once, when bad weather forced us to train indoors in the gym, the first-team squad was divided into four small teams to run relay races as part of a game designed to make training more interesting. The first runner in each team was given a piece of chalk, and he had to run from one end of the gym to the other and draw a circle on the wall. Then the rest of us, in turn, had to use the circle to create a clock face with a time and a maker's name on it. The teams had been picked at random, but it just so happened that ours contained the four quickest players in the club: Irving Nattrass, Alan Kennedy, Stewart Barrowclough and me. We were miles ahead of the others, and when it came to putting the finishing touch – the maker's name – on our clock face, it was my turn to go. Now I knew there was a small and little-known Swiss firm of decorative watchmakers called Bueche Girod – they make dress watches in gold – so I wrote this across the clock face. Irving, though, sensed that Lee was going to do everything in his power to stop us winning. 'We're absolutely pissing this,' he said, 'but he's going to try and find some way to scrub us out cos you're in the team.' Sure enough, Gordon Lee being Gordon Lee, he couldn't just accept things at face value, if you'll excuse the pun; he had to go and inspect the clocks to make sure everything had been done properly.

He came marching back after checking ours and said, 'What the hell is written on that?'

'Bueche Girod,' I replied.

'What's that when it's at home?' he said.

'It's a watchmaker,' I said.

'Well, I've never heard of it,' he retorted, 'so I'm dropping you back down to fourth out of the four teams.'

He just had to make a fuss about it in order to have a go at me.

'You couldn't simply have put Smith on there, could you?' he snapped.

'Why should I?' I snapped back. 'It's my prerogative. You said you wanted a maker's name. I think we should get an extra mark for artistic merit.'

That is how it was all the time. He was constantly seeking to pick a fight with me, and in such a childish fashion. We would be on the coach for away trips, and there'd be four of us sitting there playing cards. We used to enjoy playing hearts, aces and kings, or what have you, something to get the brain working. There would be Paddy Howard, Mick Mahoney, me and perhaps Tommy Cassidy, and Lee would walk down the coach and start berating us for being the 'mindless set' because we were playing cards.

'Have you seen what these lot are doing?' he said once, pointing to another group of players. 'There are five of them poring over the *Guardian* crossword. *That's* how to put your minds to work!'

So I said, 'Are you familiar with the *Daily Telegraph's* cryptic crossword?'

'What's that got to do with it?'

'Well,' I added, reaching into my bag and producing the *Telegraph*, 'I did it at lunchtime. That's why I'm playing cards now.' I showed him the evidence, which took the wind right out of his sails again.

Gordon Lee also had a ruthless side to his nature, which showed itself after a midweek game at Derby. I think it was Micky Burns who got sent off after about only five minutes, but the point is we were down to ten men away from home against a good side. They went 1–0 up, we equalised, and then they went one up for a second time, only for us to fight our way back on to level terms again. It was 2–2 going into the last few minutes, then Derby nicked it at the death. Now, Terry Hibbitt was outstanding for us, a true hero on the night. He'd run himself into the ground and hardly had enough energy to walk off the pitch at the end. It had been a fantastic game that had called for superhuman efforts from all of us, but nobody had responded to that challenge better than Hibby.

We all walked off the pitch together and got into the big players' bath at the Baseball Ground. Soon it was just the two of us left there talking. I can still hear Terry saying over and over again, 'I'm f★★★ing knackered! I am so f★★★ing knackered!' I finally interrupted his chuntering by saying, 'Come on, we've got a long trip back. Let's go and get a beer before we leave.' So we got out of the bath and went into the dressing-room, which was now empty apart from Richard Dinnis, the physios and the two wicker skips in which they packed the kit and the boots. One skip was on top of the other, and on top of that was a brown paper parcel. It was obvious the parcel contained a pair of football boots, so Terry, who never missed a trick, said jokingly, 'Who's not travelling back to Newcastle, then?' Dinnis and the physios went scarlet at that, for at that very moment Gordon Lee had come through the door. He picked up the brown parcel, shoved it into Terry's chest and said, 'You're not.'

Terry was so shocked by this that all he could say was 'What?'

'Freddie Goodwin, the manager of Birmingham, is outside in the corridor waiting to talk to you,' Lee added. 'I've agreed a deal with him, so go out and talk to him.' And with that, he turned round and marched out.

Never in my life had I witnessed anything so callous and cruel. Here was Terry, after one of his best ever games, just sitting there completely stunned by what his manager had just told him. I went over and sat down next to him, both of us still with towels round our waists, dripping wet and absolutely knackered after our efforts that night.

'I don't f***ing believe that!' growled Terry. 'Have you ever seen anything like that?'

Trying to lighten the mood, I said, 'Well, it's the first time I've ever seen you almost speechless, that's for sure! Look, you've got to think about this logically. I've never heard anything so drastic and dramatic in my life explained to anyone in that way, but you've got to remember you've got a wife, you've got a home, you've got kids, you've got their schooling. You've got an awful lot to think about apart from yourself. So don't go rushing into anything because it's only them you'll hurt. Why don't you go and have a chat with Freddie Goodwin? But tell him you're going home to talk to your wife before making any decisions.'

Terry agreed to do that, and we got changed. Then I went off to the players' lounge, leaving Terry and Goodwin talking in our empty dressing-room. But before I'd had time to get myself a beer, Gordon Lee came marching into the lounge and ordered all the Newcastle players to board the team bus immediately. He followed us on to it and said, 'Right. Everybody here? Driver, let's go!'

But I said, 'No, no. Hang on, Gordon, the wee feller's still inside talking to Freddie Goodwin.'

'Yes, fine, we can leave him,' he replied. 'He'll be in Birmingham tomorrow.'

'You what?' I said. 'No, I'm telling you he isn't going to make any decisions tonight. He's got a wife and kids to think about and he'll be wanting to go home and talk with them before he decides anything. He's coming home with us tonight.'

'No he isn't,' Lee insisted. 'He'll be Birmingham's problem from now on. Driver, drive on!'

The driver, a lovely feller called Bob Green, was put in an awful position by all this. He just sat there knowing that the right thing was to wait for Terry Hibbitt, not to leave him stranded hundreds of miles from home at eleven o'clock at night, yet worried at the same time about what might happen to his job if he disobeyed the manager of Newcastle United.

'Come on, get this bus moving!' Lee began to shout. 'We've a long journey to make.'

At the same time, there are all sorts of catcalls coming from the back of the coach. Most of the players were unaware of what actually was going on; they only knew that Terry was missing. Then, as Bob Green clunked the gears and moved the coach very slowly up the road, Hibby came out of the main doors and started looking left and right for the bus. He spotted it and started running, that brown paper parcel under his arm, and we yelled, 'Bob, stop the bus! The wee feller's on his way!'

Still Lee was having none of it. 'Driver,' he said grimly, 'if you value your job, drive off now. We're leaving the little bastard here.'

I was so angry by this stage that I wanted to get hold of him and throttle him. Fortunately, I have great control over what temper I have, and it takes an awful lot for me to snap. But though I managed not to hit him, I did go and give him a piece of my mind. 'You do not leave anybody stranded miles from home,' I said. 'Get this bus stopped now, pick him up, and let's get back home!' But he refused absolutely to allow the bus to be turned round, so we left poor Hibby there standing in the middle of the road outside the Baseball Ground. All he could do was go back into the club and order a taxi to the railway station. There, he had to wait for a train from Derby to Chesterfield, and after another wait at Chesterfield he got a connection to York. He finished up catching the milk train to Newcastle at about six o'clock in the morning, and got home at about nine.

On the bus back, I sat there thinking, 'That is it. I've put up with playing for this plonker long enough. He can go whistle now. I'm not interested in him or the club.' And when we got back to Newcastle, I made sure the directors found out exactly what had gone on. They knew that if they tolerated a manager who behaved in such a shoddy, callous way, there would be an uprising from within the dressing-room, because it wasn't just me who was unhappy about it. Even some of Gordon Lee's men in the dressing-room, so to speak, were appalled by what he had done. I, for my part, resolved that I wouldn't play another season at Newcastle if Gordon Lee was staying.

As for Terry, he went home and talked to his family and, yes, he went and signed for Birmingham. And, yes, he could be a bit of a scallywag, and, yes, he could let his mouth run away with him – on one occasion he got my goat so much by doing a 'Johnny Haynes' on me that I picked him up by his shirt front and hung him on a peg in the dressing-room – but, by heavens, there was no excuse for Gordon Lee treating another human being in that fashion. From that moment on, I made up my mind to go out and play for myself. I decided the best thing to do in circumstances like that was just to keep scoring goals. In fact, I resolved to finish top of the 1975/76 First Division scoring chart. Alan Gowling had got quite a few, so I thought, 'Right, I'm going to come out on top!' and spent the rest of the season trying to score as many goals as I could.

With Terry gone, Lee wanted me to start playing deep and wide, but it didn't matter where he played me; I just kept popping up and scoring. In fact, I went on a hell of a scoring run. I think it helped me to play deeper and wider because Alan and I were not an ideal partnership. I much preferred a situation where one striker went one way and I went the other, but I was like a magnet for Alan, who used to follow me everywhere. As for my bet with Gordon Lee, it all depended on how you looked at the goalscoring charts at the end of the season. Alan scored more than me overall – 30 goals to my 24 – but I got more than him in the League – 19 to his 16 – and I felt that was where it really counted. We agreed to differ.

What really annoyed me about the Terry Hibbitt incident, aside from Lee's behaviour, was the reluctance of most of the other Newcastle players to take the issue a stage further. We discussed the incident in the dressing-room, of course, but although the majority of the players felt the manager had been in the wrong, they did not appear to do very much about it. I was so angry that I said to them, 'If you can meekly sit back and let that happen to one of your team-mates, when is it going to happen to you? Is that how you want your career at this club to end? Do you want to live under that threat for the rest of your playing days, to be treated with disdain and a complete lack of respect?' But there were only three of us incensed enough actually to be prepared to speak up about the matter: Paddy Howard, Mick Mahoney the goalkeeper, and me. We came to be regarded as the rebels in the camp.

Events were pushing me firmly towards the exit door at St James's Park. I had kept in regular contact with Harry Haslam, who was now manager of Luton Town, and I had told him how bad the situation was getting. 'It's time to get away, Harry,' I said. 'I'm doing everything right: I'm going out there and giving it everything, sticking the ball in the net as many times as I can. But it's time to go.'

My itchy feet weren't entirely Gordon Lee's fault, I should say. Back in the 1973/74 season, when Joe Harvey was still manager, I had been made aware that Anderlecht, Belgium's most famous club, were interested in signing me. Bizarrely, the news was broken to me by George Bayley, who was head of sports broadcasting with Radio Newcastle at the time. He later joined BBC Radio and became known as 'Whispering George' for the restrained way in which he covered golf. I owe George a lot because not only did he hire me to do a half-hour pre-recorded programme for Radio Newcastle that went out on a Saturday lunchtime, he also taught me all he knew about radio technique, which was just about everything. It was a programme about football, but I was able to invite guests from outside the game like Mike and Bernie Winters to take part, and I also went down to London to interview Eric Morecambe. George and I would put the show together every Thursday afternoon, but we would meet up first in an Italian restaurant for some soup and pasta.

We were having lunch one day when George said, 'I've been

contacted by a Belgian lawyer who wants to know if you are interested in playing football abroad – in Belgium, in fact.' At that time, it was still pretty unusual for a British footballer to play abroad. There had been John Charles, Gerry Hitchins, Denis Law and Jimmy Greaves in Italy, but it was still a rather rare thing. Not only that, but Anderlecht, the club seeking my services, were then a major force in Europe; in the 1970s they appeared in no fewer than four European finals. We spent the rest of our lunch discussing the pros and cons of such a move, but what really made me sit up and take notice was George's remark that Belgium were streets ahead of the rest of Europe in terms of footballers' contracts. Even then, long before the Bosman case blew the whole transfer system wide open, it seems that Belgian footballers virtually had freedom of contract. I made it clear to George that I was definitely interested in the proposition, but that I wanted to know an awful lot more about it.

By the following Thursday, he had spoken to his Belgian lawyer friend again and was in a position to give me more information. 'You've got a lovely surprise coming,' he said. 'Let me explain to you how the deal works in Belgium. As Anderlecht would be the signing club, the rules of the transfer would be regulated by the Belgian FA – theirs and nobody else's. That means, whatever fee is agreed, you would take a third of it.'

'Are you serious?' I said.

'Absolutely. The rules of the Belgian FA are that any player who is transferred and has not asked for a transfer will receive one third of the transfer fee.'

'Bloody hell!' said I. 'So what kind of money are the Belgians talking about?'

'Well,' George replied, 'from what I can gather, they are talking about a fee of £300,000. Not only that, but your weekly earnings would be far, far superior over there. You've got to consider what your taxable situation is. You're being caned for tax over here.'

That was true enough. Throughout my career in the old First Division, the elite of English football, I paid 82.5 per cent tax, which meant that for every £100 I earned only £17.50 of it went into my bank account. There were restrictions, too, on what I could put into my pension. You will not be surprised, then, to learn that I said to George,

'Go for it! Tell them I want to go for it!'

Everything went quiet after that, but when George and I met up some weeks later, he said, 'The situation is that they've actually put in an offer of £300,000 for you, and it's been accepted. Just wait and see!'

So I waited and waited, and nobody said a word. This, remember, was the season we went to the FA Cup final, so I wasn't getting unsettled or anything. I was too pragmatic to hold out too many hopes anyway. You wait and see what happens; you don't take anything for granted. All the same, a third of £300,000 was an awful lot of money in those days.

George and I just couldn't understand the long silence, so he decided to investigate.

'There's a problem,' he reported back. 'Newcastle don't want to do the transfer under Belgian FA rules. Lord Westwood told Anderlecht that while he was alive and chairman of Newcastle United he would not see a player take one third of his transfer fee.' We are talking lords and servants here. My aristocratic chairman was apoplectic at the thought that I, a mere footballer, might pick up such a large sum of money. He insisted that the whole of the £300,000 be paid to Newcastle, but Anderlecht responded by saying that under Belgian rules the fee would have to be raised to something like £433,000 if I were to get my third and United were to clear about £300,000, and they were not prepared to do that.

So, nothing ever came of Anderlecht's attempt to sign me, but it was an interesting experience to have gone through. Nobody ever said a word to me at Newcastle – not the chairman, not a director, not the manager. In fact, I don't even know whether Joe Harvey ever knew anything about it. As far as I could tell, the only person who had spoken to the Belgians on the matter was Lord Westwood. The upshot of it all was that my mind was now alerted to the fact that there were other, more attractive ways of being a professional footballer abroad.

Later, opportunities opened up at home, too. During one of my regular telephone conversations with Harry Haslam, he asked me if I had any thoughts about what I wanted to do with my career. 'Of course I have, Harry,' I said. 'I tell you who I fancy in this country: I think Arsenal are going to have one of the best sides in the First Division. They've got some tremendously experienced players in Alan Ball, Peter Storey, George

Armstrong and Bob McNab, and they've got some great youngsters coming through. Look at the kids they've got – Liam Brady, David O'Leary and a host of others.'

'And if not Arsenal?' asked Harry.

'To be quite honest,' I replied, 'I think I'd look at moving abroad, and I'm not sure whether that's my first or second option.'

'Oh, I see,' said Harry. 'Right, leave it with me. I'll have words.'

When Harry said that, you knew you could rely on his contacts base, which was second to none. Sure enough, as we were moving towards the end of the 1975/76 season and had a game in London, Harry suggested I stay down for the weekend and invited me to dinner at his house just outside Luton. I was not entirely surprised when I arrived at Harry's place to discover that Bertie Mee, the Arsenal manager, and one of his staff were also among the dinner guests. During the meal, we talked without going into specifics. Basically, Bertie just wanted to know what my situation was at Newcastle, and I told him it precisely. 'The manager and I are completely at odds,' I said, 'and that's been the case from the moment he first set foot in the place. He doesn't want me there, and things have happened that tell me I'm on my bike. So, rather than just sit there and let things happen to me, I'm looking to maintain control of my own destiny.'

Imagine my shock, then, when I heard in the summer of 1976 that Bertie Mee had been sacked as manager of Arsenal. There was I, sitting on the papers from the solicitors, confident the London club were going to come in for me, and now the manager who wanted to buy me had been relieved of his position. I'd been so sure I was going to be on the move that I'd even sold my house. I was thinking, 'What the hell do I do now? Do we go into rented accommodation for a while?' There were quite a few days of agonising before I thought, 'Sod it! I'm probably one of the most wanted assets in English football right now. The one thing that will always talk with regard to Newcastle is money. That's the strongest language they understand.' So I signed the papers and agreed on a moving date.

In the meantime, Terry Neill was appointed the new manager of Arsenal. It was quite a surprise at the time because he was moving from Tottenham Hotspur, the Gunners' great north London rivals. I'd known him on a casual basis; we'd played against each other a number of times and he seemed an all right bloke. He'd also done a stint at the PFA (Professional Footballers' Association), and you'd get to converse on a whole host of issues whenever there was a union meeting. But I didn't know whether the Arsenal board were aware of the interest Bertie Mee had shown in me, or whether it had been passed on to Neill. Nothing was appearing in the papers to suggest that my move was imminent, and everything was being played very close to everybody's chests.

Then, out of the blue, I received a phone call from one of the lasses at Newcastle United. She asked me if I would go and meet Gordon Lee at Newcastle airport.

'Why would I want to go and meet the Newcastle manager at the airport?' I asked. 'Why not at St James's Park?'

'I'm just passing on the message,' she said.

Putting two and two together, I packed a bag, put it into the boot of my car and drove to the airport. I met up with Gordon Lee, and hadn't been there two minutes when, lo and behold, there was Terry Neill as well. I have to say I wasn't surprised one little bit. Almost immediately, Gordon and Terry excused themselves and went off in a little huddle. When they came back, it was Terry who took the lead. He was clearly a man who knew how to deal with a situation like this – unlike Lee, who was completely out of his depth.

'Look,' said Terry, 'I've come up in a private jet and I want to take you back to Arsenal. My chairman has agreed a fee with the chairman of Newcastle and I want to get you down to London. We can talk on the way down.'

I went straight off to get my bag from the car and took great pleasure in saying to Gordon Lee, 'I hope this is the last time we'll meet as employees of the same club,' before going off with Terry Neill.

We boarded this private plane and took off for Luton airport, of all places. In fact, I couldn't help but say to Terry, 'I've got to tell you this: Alec Stock thought he was sending me from Luton to Newcastle in ultimate style when he provided me with a Rolls-Royce. I wonder what he'd make of me leaving Newcastle for Luton in a private plane?'

When we finally got down to brass tacks, Terry said, 'Look, the two clubs have agreed a fee, but Newcastle are as slippery as eels. For the moment, the agreed fee stands at £275,000.' He also told me that he was aware of my knowledge of the situation through Mee, and of the fact that I did not get on with Gordon Lee. He reassured me, too, that as a former player with the club he was Arsenal through and through. 'Spurs was just a stepping-stone,' he said. 'This is my ultimate job. I want nothing else. It is my aim to bring back the glory days to Highbury, and you are the first big signing I intend to bring in.' Terry also talked about how he saw things developing at Arsenal. He enthused about the kids coming through and the experience that was there to help them. I knew all of this, of course. I had thought about it very carefully. His thinking was more or less the same as mine had been for the previous five or six months, so what I was hearing from him was music to my ears. It was just an absolute confirmation of every thought that had gone through my head.

Then, as we arrived in Luton, Terry said, 'I don't want the press to get to you. They've already got a bit from Newcastle. Will you stay at my house?' So I stayed with the Arsenal manager, expecting to talk terms. 'As soon as I get the go-ahead from my chairman, we'll talk contracts,' he assured me.

But after a couple of days nothing had happened. I asked why and was told there seemed to be a hitch at the Newcastle end of the deal. I needed to go back to Tyneside to sort out our removals and tie up other loose ends, but Terry insisted that I stayed down south until the deal was done. When I pleaded for a bit of freedom, Arsenal put me up in the West Lodge Park Hotel in Hadley Wood, which was familiar to me because England had stayed there when Alf Ramsey was manager.

I had retained my links with the *Sun*, so perhaps it was no surprise when Bob Cass tracked me down. 'What the hell's going on?' he asked. 'You've gone missing. What are you doing here?' I explained the situation to him, but asked that he keep it confidential until the deal was resolved. The next day, though, Cassie and Keith Perry, the *Sun* photographer, booked into the West Lodge Park. They were sitting on me, as it were, but we were old mates and there was no strain in the situation. In fact, they kept me sane as I had to hang around this hotel for about six days. If I wasn't playing bar billiards with Bob, it was dominoes with both of them. All the time, too, I was phoning Arsenal Football

Club to find out what the hell was going on. I had been given the right by Gordon Lee to talk to Arsenal, yet Arsenal were now denied the right to speak to me!

Finally, Terry Neill turned up and said his chairman, Sir Denis Hill-Wood, wanted to see us at his house at Hartley Wintney in Hampshire. Terry drove me down there, and we arrived late afternoon. There was a long drive from the road up to the house, then a circular arrangement around a fountain in front of it. Strangely enough, the house was exactly the same as one I had looked at with a view to buying some fifteen months earlier in Northumberland. We went in, introduced ourselves to Lady Hill-Wood, then exited through patio doors that led out on to a garden I can only describe as being the size of Lord's. Right in the middle of this huge lawn, instead of a wicket, there was a table with a portly figure sitting at it. Terry and I started to walk out towards this gentleman like a pair of batsmen going to the crease to open the innings.

When we finally reached Sir Denis, for it was he, he greeted us warmly in a very jolly fashion before putting on a stern face and saying, 'Right, I am going to get down to business immediately. We have been messed about terribly by Newcastle United and I must apologise for all the hanging about you, Malcolm, have had to do. I'm going to ask you one question, and I would like a frank answer. What do you want in your life and career?'

I answered by saying, 'Well, I've had a very long time – and not just the time I've spent in the hotel – to think about this, and I can tell you, Sir Denis, that either I sign for Arsenal Football Club or I'm going to play my football abroad.'

'Thank you for your candour,' replied Sir Denis. 'Right, I'm going to take action now.'

At that, he waved to the house for a butler, who brought out one of those old black Bakelite telephones on a lead that was about a hundred metres long. The butler put the phone down on the table and asked what we'd like to drink.

'Oh, just make it gin and tonics all round,' Sir Denis said. 'You don't mind a gin and tonic, do you?' he added, turning to us.

'No, that's fine,' we replied.

Then the Arsenal chairman picked up the phone and dialled a

number. 'My lord,' he said, obviously addressing Lord Westwood, the Newcastle chairman, 'Denis Hill-Wood here. Now, upon our little matter – here are my comments. First, I offered you £275,000. You accepted that, but three days later reneged upon that acceptance. I followed that with an offer, in all good faith, of £300,000, and you accepted that yet again. But you hummed and you hawed and you prevented us from talking to the player until, in the end, you reneged for a second time. Now I'm getting a bit fed up with this, so here is my final offer. If you accept it, I want from you an assurance that its acceptance is binding on the whole of Newcastle United Football Club and its board, so that we can get on and conclude business with the player. I am making you an offer of exactly one third of a million pounds. Now, is that acceptable or not?' There was silence for a few seconds, then Sir Denis said, 'Thank you, my lord. I think our business is now concluded, apart from the secretaries doing the necessary. Thank you, and good afternoon to you.'

And he put the phone down.

'Right,' he said, turning to us, 'we have an agreement. The two of you can get down to business sorting out terms and getting a contract signed. Let's get on with the signing-on fee, too. I hope that you two can come to an amicable arrangement, and providing that you do, I would like to welcome you, Malcolm, most sincerely to Arsenal Football Club.' Then, lifting his gin and tonic, he added, 'I think you will enjoy it here.'

But how wrong, in some important ways, he proved to be.

# CHAPTER SIX

# ARSENAL: BLARNEY TIME

Having clinked glasses with Sir Denis Hill-Wood, drained them and shaken hands, Terry Neill and I left Hartley Wintney with a view to talking terms the following morning. Time was short because the first-team squad was due to depart for a pre-season trip to Switzerland and Yugoslavia. I had phoned my accountant in the meantime, and he came up to sit in on the meeting, which took place on a Saturday, if memory serves. I'd asked him to attend the meeting in case he could advise me on any advantageous ways of negotiating terms, because, as I've said, the tax factor at the time was absolutely crippling, so much so that the 1970s had seen a mass exodus of pop stars, actors and other big earners from Britain to less severely taxed parts of the world. Footballers couldn't join them, of course, because they had to be in England to play. There was no escape for us, and there wasn't much that could be done to avoid paying all that tax. At the time, all an accountant was allowed to do during wage negotiations was advise. The rules stated that the player had to conduct the negotiations himself; he could not have a third party doing it on his behalf. How times have changed!

Once the negotiations had started, I said to Terry Neill, 'Look, this is my current situation at Newcastle. What I want is the bonuses I negotiated with Newcastle to be put on my basic wage, but to remain as a separate part of the contract.' That was my angle, and I wasn't going to budge on it. The next thing to thrash out was the length of the contract. At Newcastle, I'd always been on a one-and-one, but Arsenal did things differently and we agreed in principle on a four-year contract in which the bonuses would go on top of my basic but still remain as part of the contract. That meant that, in addition to Arsenal's usual bonus structure for wins and draws, for progress in cup competitions, for winning the championship and so on, I would be paid a lump sum each time I scored ten, twenty, 30 competitive goals. 'I want the contract structured like that,' I told Terry, 'because I am here to score 30 goals a season for you. That's why you're paying all that money for me.' Incidentally, I only got five per cent of the £333,333 as a signing-on fee, and that was split into equal payments over the four years of the contract. They always used to say a player got ten per cent of his transfer fee, but he never did; the other five per cent was paid direct to the PFA.

After I had set out everything in very precise terms, I said, 'That's what I want: take it or leave it.' Terry, though, obviously wasn't quite sure whether he should meet my demands. He kept saying 'Well, I don't know about this' and 'I don't know about that'. But I cut him short by saying, 'It's not up for discussion, Terry. We shake hands on the contract or we shake hands and say goodbye.' Faced with that sort of ultimatum, he agreed and we shook hands on it. I had got what I wanted – or so it seemed.

Having completed the negotiations, Terry was anxious to get on with the pre-season trip to Yugoslavia and Switzerland. 'I want you to go, and we're leaving pronto,' he said. 'Unfortunately, as it's the weekend and there are no staff around, I can't get the contracts and everything else typed out for you to be able to play on the tour, so will you sign blank forms?'

I was prepared to take that risk because I knew my accountant had taken down a detailed account of what had just been agreed between us. 'Yes,' I said, 'provided they are filled in later with the terms as written down by my accountant.'

There's a whole host of paperwork involved in a football transfer, all sorts of different registration forms you have to sign. At that time, I had to put pen to paper for the Football Association, the Football League and the Football Combination. There's a registration form for just about every competition you are likely to play in. Then there are three copies of the contract – one for the player, one for the club and one for the League. All those documents having been signed, I left them to be filled in while I was away on tour with the first team. But before I went I had lunch with my accountant, who handed me a copy of the terms he had written out in preparation for filling in the blank forms.

Our first stop was Zurich, where we played Grasshoppers. It wasn't the best of starts for me because my bloody bag went missing and I had to go out into town to replace the missing clothing and toiletries. But Alan Ball cheered me up before the game by gathering all the players together in the dressing-room before we went out and saying, 'Right, listen up you lot. There's a new man in the team.' Then, turning to me, Bally continued, 'Malcolm, tell us how you want it played into the area.'

To which I said, quite simply, 'You get it in there early. Then it's my job to do everything possible to get on the end of it.'

Bally just rubbed his hands together at that and said, 'Don't you just love it? Doesn't he make the game easy for us? That's all you have to do, lads. Get it in early and he'll do the rest!'

Thankfully, I was as good as my word. During the game, a cross came in from the right and I headed it high into the corner of the net from the edge of the penalty area to put us ahead. During the interval, Bally raved, 'Mal said he wanted it in early, and he gets it early, and what does he do? Sticks it in the net! Come on, we've got to keep feeding him!'

Gunther Netzer, the great German international midfielder, was playing for Grasshoppers then, towards the end of his career, as a defensive 'libero'. He had the biggest feet I've ever seen on a football field. Never mind getting boots to fit him, you'd have had trouble finding boxes to accommodate those feet! He still had a marvellously deft touch though, so it was a big surprise when, in the second half, he half tripped over the ball. Spotting Netzer's rare mistake, I sprinted towards him as he tried to regain his balance. I played the ball, ran it through his legs and gave him a nudge at the same time. Over he went, and I was free about 35 yards from goal. I hit the ball straight away, drove it with a bit of backspin, and it sort of went over and around the keeper before dropping in the corner of the net. Thank you very much!

It was a lovely introduction to my Arsenal career. In my first appearance for them I had scored two very different types of goals, the kind they hadn't had scored for them for years. By that, I mean a header from the edge of the box from a nothing cross and then a shot from 35 yards out. As they do today, Arsenal played the game intricately then; they tended to score their goals from the edge of the six-yard area. All of a sudden there was this new dimension opening up for them; the players began to realise that I could provide them with goals from anywhere on the field. So I suppose I made an impact in my first game for Arsenal, just as I had done with that hat-trick on my debut for Newcastle. The difference in Zurich was that the impact had been made on the players, not on the supporters, very few of whom had made the trip to Switzerland.

We went on to Yugoslavia and played a couple of games, both of which we won, so it was a hugely successful tour. Even so, I was beginning to detect some disquiet among the players over Terry Neill and his assistant Wilf Dixon. He was a nice kind of guy, Wilf, but there was some history between him and Bally. They'd been together at Everton, and Bally had made up his mind there that Dixon was no good as a coach. The little feller was very extreme in his opinions: he either loved you or hated you; there was no middle ground with Bally. Not only that, but it seems the Arsenal players had adored Bobby Campbell, the coach Terry Neill had booted out to make way for Wilf. All this had happened before I arrived, but I quickly realised how highly the players had rated the young, tracksuited Campbell, who had been replaced by the middle-aged, balding and uncharismatic Dixon. 'We will not move forward with that man in the camp!' declared Bally to anyone who would listen. His views were very forthright, very obvious and very loud. Terry Neill had a problem here, because it was not just Alan Ball who was anti-Dixon. Other senior players like Peter Storey, Peter Simpson and George Armstrong had begun to question Neill's ability simply because of who he had chosen as his assistant.

The animosity, and I can call it nothing less, was most obvious on the training field. When it came to coaching, Bally just ridiculed whatever Wilf said or did and would say, quite openly, that he typified the phrase 'jobs for the boys'. He would challenge him to his face, too. 'You cannot teach me anything!' Bally would snarl at Wilf. 'You, tell me what I can do to become a better player? You had ample opportunity at Everton and you failed miserably to improve any player there. What makes you so confident you can come to the Arsenal, the mighty Arsenal, and, second time around, make me a better player? I want to hear it!' Bally had this ability to completely shame an individual, and poor Wilf had no reply. Bally felt no remorse about doing it because he was, I suppose, the ultimate professional in that he would only give the time of day to somebody who had something to offer, whether it be as a player, a coach or a manager. If you didn't have something to offer Bally, you were dead and didn't exist as far as he was concerned. And he killed Wilf Dixon; he killed him stone dead.

It quickly got to the stage where Wilf was restricted to warm-ups only, and Terry realised there was a void in his set-up. He desperately needed another coach. Full of Irish blarney, Terry could chatter away and convince anybody of anything, but in this case push had come to shove and the manager was obliged to move to the fore on the training ground. I'm well aware that Terry was essentially a manager and not a coach, but it became obvious as early as that pre-season tour that something was going to have to give somewhere.

When we returned to London, I got my first wage slip. At Newcastle, the club paid the players fortnightly, but I wasn't sure of Arsenal's methods. And when I looked at my wage slip, I couldn't work it out. Nothing made sense to me at all. The gross earnings didn't relate to anything really, and the total seemed horrendously low. No matter how I looked at them, the figures simply didn't add up. So I asked Ken Friar, the club secretary, if he would see me, and the answer came back, 'Gladly, gladly!' Equally encouraging was his greeting when I went up to his office to see him. 'Welcome, dear boy, welcome!' he said. 'What can I do for you? I've got a number of things I was putting together to talk to you about, but now you're here to see me, tell me first what it is you want to see me about, then I'll talk to you about other matters.'

'Well, Ken,' I said, 'it's my wage slip. For the life of me I can't work out any of the figures on it. It doesn't make sense.'

'Let's have a look,' he said.

'Are you paying weekly or fortnightly?' I asked.

'Fortnightly.'

'Well, it's even worse than I thought.'

'Why?'

'Well, if this is a fortnight's wages, it seems you are paying me £200 a week.'

'Yes, that's right,' replied Ken.

'No,' I said, 'that's very, very wrong.'

'Ah, is it now?' he said. 'Right, let me tell you something. When you left for Switzerland and Yugoslavia, I was passed all the blank signed contracts and registration forms accompanied by a note from Terry Neill with regard to your negotiations.'

'In Terry Neill's handwriting?' I asked.

'Yes.'

'Not my accountant's?'

'Ah, you had an accountant with you, did you?'

'Yes, I did, and he recorded everything down to the last penny. When I last saw the contract and registration forms, it was a copy of his record that was put with them. That's how we were to proceed.'

'I've never seen that,' Ken admitted.

'Fortunately, he's kept the original,' I said. 'So, what are you telling me?'

'Well, I'll be brutally honest with you,' he replied. 'We have a wages policy here whereby the maximum is £200 a week.'

'You *are* joking?'

'No, I'm not. This was one of the things I was going to see you about, because when your previous employers sent us your P45 to pick up on where you are in the tax year, I saw your earnings so far this season and realised there was something terribly, terribly wrong.'

'So why did you complete those contracts when you knew there was something "terribly, terribly wrong"?'

'I had to fill them in because you were about to play, and I had to get the contract registered first before all the other registrations could go in. And if I hadn't got those registrations in, you couldn't have played over in Switzerland.'

'So, what you're telling me, Ken, is that the copy of the contract you're going to give me has me down as earning £200 a week?'

'Yes.'

'You really do have to be joking! This isn't just a mistake, is it? This is something else. I'm actually here under false pretences. I'm not even going to tell you what I finished up agreeing with Terry Neill, but it was a lot more than £200 a week. My witness is my accountant; he has got it all down on paper. There's his name and number – you ask him. And when he's told you it all, I'll come back and tell you what he said. I won't talk to him in the meantime, and I'll bet our figures concur. That way you'll get it from two sources.'

'We've got a problem here, haven't we?' Ken conceded.

'Too right,' I said. 'I am livid. This was my big move financially, and I'd hate to think I'd been cheated or swindled. In fact, Ken, I won't stand for it.'

'I understand that, I understand that,' he replied consolingly, 'but don't let's go losing our cool. We will have to get it sorted out. We are committed to you as you have committed to us. Trust me, we will sort it out. I will not be able to do it at the drop of a hat, it's going to take time, but just bear with me for the moment.'

'All right,' I replied. 'But if this wage slip were only for a week I'd still be horrified by the total. That's how major the problem is.'

Then Ken said, 'Look, I've got another matter I want to talk to you about. Do you feel calm enough to discuss it?'

'I am not one to get aerated over things,' I informed him. 'I can boil inside over one thing but be as cold as ice on the exterior over another. This is not your fault and I am not mad at you. You and I can talk all day long, calmly and civilly.'

'Fine,' he said. 'Right, Newcastle have this method of paying an awful lot of the bonuses for the season at the end of the season. There's a payment in there for a thousand pounds.'

When I told him what it was for – that Newcastle paid their players a bonus to avoid relegation – he laughed.

'Good heavens,' he remarked, 'I've never heard of anything like that! But you got various other bonuses as well. You got to the League Cup final too, so that pushed the total up. You are aware that in May you received in excess of £16,000 in one payday and paid nearly £14,000 in tax on that amount?'

'Yes.'

'Right, would you like that money to go on to your pension?'

'Of course I would. But Newcastle told me there was no way it could be done.'

'Yes, there is. I don't know who was advising you at Newcastle, but of course it can be done.'

'Well, they told me it couldn't.'

'One of the things that we ensure we do,' Ken confirmed, 'is maximise to the ultimate the players' pensions. That is part of the service here at Arsenal Football Club, and we are duty bound to offer you every assistance we can. Quite legally, I can get that money back from the taxman. All it requires is for somebody at Newcastle United to take five minutes to fill in a form, sign it and post it off to the Inland Revenue. From there, we'll do the rest.'

'You'll be very lucky to get anybody at Newcastle to do that,' I said doubtfully.

'Can you pull any strings?'

'I doubt it very much. I've got the feeling that they decided we parted on bad terms.'

'Oh, well. Let's see. What you might have to do is write me a cheque for the two thousand and odd quid you actually did receive. You give me back the net that you got, and I shall get you back the remainder that was paid to the taxman.'

'Ken,' I said, 'I'd be delighted to do that. Thank you.'

'OK. I'll speak to your accountant, and I promise you we shall get everything put right.'

At that, I left Ken Friar's office feeling I could truly rely on him – something I have to admit I could not say about Terry Neill. The wages disagreement apart, I could not believe it when the teamsheet went up for Arsenal's first game of the season, at home to Bristol City, and I found myself partnered in attack with John Radford. I was disappointed on two counts: first, because our styles of play did not complement each other; and second, because I'd begun to build a bit of a partnership in Switzerland and Yugoslavia with a promising youngster by the name of Frank Stapleton.

Frank was exceedingly raw, but I was working on him. I had detected a huge talent in this young Irishman, but he had to work hard at his game and he had to listen. He had the appetite, without any shadow of a doubt, to learn quickly and to do massive amounts of hard work. At the end of every training session, Frank would come over to me and say, 'OK, I want to do what you do.' Every day, at the end of the session, I did a minimum of an hour's practice at finishing. It was just second nature to me. I never missed. No matter what, I did that extra hour at least. Sometimes it would go on for two. So when Frank came and joined me, I thought, 'Good for you, son! You're the first who's ever done that!' I started to give him all sorts of tips on how to strike the ball. The one thing I didn't have to help Frank with was his heading. Although he sometimes mistimed his jump, he learnt fast. We were spending so much time together and developing such a good understanding that, as I said, I couldn't believe my eyes when that first teamsheet went up. Nor, to be fair, could Raddy. 'What the f★★★ing hell's that?' he said. 'The f★★★ing idiot! He's put the wrong f★★★ing name on!'

At that time, of course, John was coming towards the end of a distinguished career with Arsenal. Ray Kennedy's senior attacking partner in the side that in 1970/71 had become the first at Arsenal to win the League and FA Cup double, he was one of the Highbury immortals. Now, though, he was just looking to get away before he was too old and make some money on one last big move. A typical Yorkshireman, Raddy was dour and outspoken. Everything was 'f★★★ing this' and 'f★★★ing that', and he'd moan and groan about anything and everything. Terry Neill's team selection was the perfect excuse.

'Look,' Raddy said to me, 'you and I knew when you came here that we were never going to be able to play together. I've got other clubs interested in me and it's time for me to get on my bike and move. I don't need to play with you because I know it won't work, and you know it won't work. Away, lad, you come with me! We're going to see that ruddy idiot Neill!'

So Raddy and I marched up the corridor, knocked on Terry Neill's door and went in. Raddy immediately got down to the nub of the matter by saying, 'What the bloody hell do you think you're doing, putting me in the team? I can't play with him. He plays a different game entirely. I'm not the man for you. Get my bloody name off that teamsheet and put young Stapleton in!'

'No,' said Terry, 'I think we need to go for a bit of experience.'

'Experience, my arse!' replied Raddy. 'Me and him,' he continued, pointing at me, 'will not make it together. I go this way, he goes that way. All hell will break loose. It'll be bloody chaos!' At the same time, Raddy made it clear to Terry that he wasn't ducking the issue. 'If you really insist,' he added, 'I'll play. I always have done and always will do, but I'm telling you it's a mistake putting him and me together. You'll find out tomorrow how wrong you've been and you'll have to correct it afterwards.' Since Raddy was known to have a hugely intelligent football mind, I just let him speak. It didn't need anything from me other than a nod of the head.

The following day, Raddy and I tried our level best to make it work, but we were just diametrically opposed to each other in the way we went about our game. I found myself having to go back into midfield to allow Raddy to do what he always did up front; with me there, I was just getting in his way. We finished up getting beaten 1–0 at home by newly promoted Bristol City. They were on a high, and good for them, but we were completely punchless.

Raddy, diplomatic as ever, came in at the end of the game and said to Terry Neill, 'See, I told you, you stupid, stubborn Irishman! You wouldn't listen. You're a bloody centre-half! What the f★★k do you know about forwards? You've got two experienced players like him and me telling you it's wrong, but would you listen? Would you bloody hell! Now listen here, and listen well. Blackburn Rovers are interested in me, so get the bloody deal through because my time's up at this club. I accept it, so don't try and make something work that won't. Just get me bloody shifted to Blackburn!'

The following week, Raddy left for Ewood Park, and I was looking forward to renewing my promising partnership with Frank Stapleton. But then I got a phone call from Harry Haslam who told me he'd been talking to Terry Neill and that he seemed very keen to get rid of Frank.

'Harry,' I said, 'you *are* joking?'

'No, I'm not,' he replied, 'and I'm phoning you, really, to get some first-hand information about the boy.'

I told him about playing and working with Frank on the pre-season tour, and all the pluses that had come out of it. 'If you see through the rawness of the kid,' I added, 'he's going to be a phenomenal player. He's big-boned, and he's going to develop further physically. When he hits people, he hits them hard and hurts them. Centre-halves hate playing against him, he works all day, and if Terry Neill is stupid enough to think about selling him, you take him. I won't kid you though, Harry. If Terry asks my opinion, I'm going to have to tell him.'

'Well,' said Harry, 'I'm asking my board to see if they can muster £60,000, because I think that is what it'll take to get him.'

'You'll make it over and over again, you really will,' I assured him through gritted teeth, disappointed to hear that Frank might not after all be around to replace Raddy as my attacking partner.

Not long afterwards, Terry Neill approached me and said, 'OK, I've thought long and hard about that Saturday, and you and Raddy were right. So, who do you want to play with?'

'Like I told you last week, Frank Stapleton,' I replied.

Terry launched into a list of Frank's shortcomings.

'Don't tell me what he can't do,' I interjected, 'tell me what he can do. You're looking at him negatively. Look at the positives. He's young and he wants to learn, plus he learns quickly. I've seen a big change in him in the past few weeks. Surely you must have seen it?'

'I have,' Terry admitted, 'but I just can't see him somehow actually having the touch that is necessary at this top level.'

'Don't worry about that,' I argued, 'it'll all come. He's eighteen years of age, and at the moment he's struggling to come to terms with the bulk he's putting on. How tall was he six months back? I bet he's put on three or four inches in that short space of time. That takes time to adjust to, and once the growing has finished – and it'll finish any day now – then you'll have a hell of a player. All right, he's not quick, but he covers the ground. He's big, raw and bony too, so when he hits people, they stay hit. That means they always think twice the next time he's got the ball or it's on its way to him. I know you've got somebody interested in him, and that doesn't surprise me.' I was half inclined to bite my tongue because I knew Frank would be a wonderful signing for Harry Haslam at Luton, but at the same time I had to look after my own patch first. I told Terry Neill outright that he'd be daft to take the money. 'Stick him in the team with me on Saturday and give me three months with him. I know I'll change your mind about Frank Stapleton.'

To my great relief, Terry agreed to go along with that.

My first step was to go and talk to Frank. I didn't tell him about Luton's interest because there was a certain insecurity about him and that news would only have unsettled him. I wanted him to know that there was somebody who thought the world of him and was prepared to fight his corner with him. So I went right through what Raddy and I had said when we went to see Terry Neill and told him how Raddy had pleaded with the manager to pick him, Frank, instead of himself as my partner. 'That's how highly Raddy thought of you,' I said. 'He thought you were the guy to do it, and so do I.' I also told Frank that I had asked Terry to give him three months in the team with me. 'Now, don't let me down,' I concluded. 'You have got to graft harder than you have ever grafted in your life. You've got to learn three times quicker than you've ever learnt before. You make yourself a career in these three months, or sod you. It's as simple as that. I'll give you every bit of encouragement, every bit of help, but it's up to you. I can't do it for you.'

Frank wasn't one to say very much, but I saw a little bit of a strut creep into his stride as he walked away from my little pep talk. It wasn't a cocky strut; it was the determined, confident strut of somebody who knew that somebody else believed in them and was out to prove how right he was.

What happened in the next three months was phenomenal. Frank grew from boy to man and became a major talking point in the game. His development was so impressive that he was elevated to the Republic of Ireland squad, and all manner of other good things were happening to him. But I was determined he would not let it all go to his head. 'Feet on the ground, old son!' I kept saying to him. 'It doesn't matter what comes along, at the end of each training session, you and me, we do our hour. You never take a day off in your life. You don't take a minute off even when you're relaxing. Sitting at home or having a beer, you think about how to improve your game.' He went for it hook, line and sinker, and the rest is history.

But how Frank hated me for it at the time! That's because I gave him no quarter. I treated him worse than a poacher treats his dog. During games, I'd get on at him. 'You didn't run hard enough for that! You didn't do this, you didn't do that!' I kept on at him almost as if he was a whipping boy; I made him push himself beyond the limit. I drove him hard. At the same time, I encouraged him to go through the old routine that I found so valuable: get it, turn and shoot. That is the key to it all, I told Frank. On top of everything, on top of all your hard work, you get it, you turn and you shoot. Echoing my old teacher Harry Haslam, I advised him, 'Learn to say it very quickly, then do it quicker than you can say it.' In training, Frank would want to do crosses, but I wouldn't let him. 'No, you're going to do this,' I'd tell him. 'Get it, turn, shoot! Come on, do it quicker!' And he'd keep going until he was almost fainting with fatigue. He kept on doing it, and I kept on insulting him. Oh, how I insulted the poor lad! There I was, short and square, with a very low centre of gravity that made my balance just about perfect, almost impossible to knock off the ball. All the time I was trying to make Frank get low, to take his body low, so that he made himself a mass between the ball and the centre-half. From there you're able to spring like a cat, and as the ball comes to you you half-turn automatically.

'I can't do that,' Frank would say.

'Yes you can,' I'd reply. 'Come on, do it, do it!'

All of this chivvying paid off handsomely when we came to our home game against Newcastle at the beginning of December 1976. There was all sorts of stuff coming out of Newcastle, and press guys were coming up to me quietly and asking if I'd heard what Gordon Lee had been saying. Apparently, he'd been shouting the odds and predicting I wouldn't score against them. Not only that, he was claiming I had been holding Newcastle back, and the best thing he ever did was get rid of me. To be fair, they were going fairly well at the time. As I've said, they actually qualified for the UEFA Cup by finishing fifth in the First Division, so even the London press lads were saying that Newcastle were going to stuff us. 'Oh, really?' I thought to myself. 'We'll see.' When asked for a quote on what was going to happen, for once I declined. 'You guys know me well enough,' I said. 'Just watch on Saturday.'

I wasn't the only ex-Newcastle player playing for Arsenal that day.

Paddy Howard had followed me down to Highbury, and he lined up alongside David O'Leary in central defence. Having the two of us there was manna from heaven for Alan Ball, who would find any excuse he could to gee everybody up before the game. Bally had been at it all week in the dressing-room. 'Come on, this is a special day for these two!' he'd say. 'We can't let them down! We've got to give them every support!' He went on and on about it until, come the game, we were well and truly geed up.

I don't include myself in that. I was, as usual, very quiet. In the dressing-room, I used to go almost stone cold. I didn't experience nerves; I just worked on my own mind and didn't want to talk to others. There were those who needed to hear a loud boost coming from somebody else, but I never did.

When the Newcastle teamsheet came in half an hour before kick-off, I took one look at it and said to my team-mates, 'OK, let me tell you something. Alan Kennedy, their left-back, has got two major faults. One is that he will dive in and give you a chance to skin him. He plays the game too much on his arse. But, even worse, he has a tendency to get underneath free-kicks and crosses that come from the other side of the field. So, if we get anything on our left-hand side, stick it above Kennedy's head and I'll make my run accordingly.'

Arsenal v. Newcastle was one of only three games played that day because most of the country was snowbound. It went ahead because Arsenal was one of the very few clubs with undersoil heating at the time. Even so, the pitch was hard and quite icy in places, though soft elsewhere, so we were going to have to tread carefully. Every step was going to be recorded for posterity too. Because this was one ground where they knew they were not going to be wasting their time, BBC TV had sent the *Match of the Day* cameras straight to Highbury that Saturday.

The game didn't start too well for us. Micky Burns had a tremendous game for Newcastle that day, and he put them ahead. Trevor Ross equalised with a shot from the edge of the box, then we got a free-kick for a foul on Frank Stapleton after about half an hour. It was just outside the corner of the Newcastle penalty area on our left-hand side, so Bally gave me a nod and a wink because he knew it was the ideal position for what we'd been talking about before the game. When Liam Brady rolled the free-kick short to him, Bally had a little look before flighting the ball beautifully above Alan Kennedy, who promptly ran underneath it. I, as promised, had made my run in behind him; I got my head to it and knocked it in at the far post.

We led 2–1 until just before half-time, when Frank Stapleton made yet another unselfish run and seemed to do the impossible by rescuing a ball from going out for a goal-kick at the very last second. It took the Newcastle keeper, Mick Mahoney, by surprise and caught him out of position, and Frank somehow managed to squeeze the ball along the byline and over the goal-line to send us in at half-time 3–1 up.

But it was early in the second half when all the hard work we had put in together really paid off. When, with Frank in the inside-right position some five yards outside the box, the ball was played into him, he trapped it, turned and shot. But, as he often did in training, he pulled the shot across the face of goal. Anticipating this, I whipped in and popped the ball into the net from about five yards. 'Thank you very much,' I was thinking, 'isn't life easy!' Frank was livid. He turned round and threw his arms in the air in disgust because I'd gained from all his hard work. It didn't improve his mood any when I said, 'Don't you worry, old son. You keep getting it, turning and shooting and I'll just keep knocking it in the net for you.' He was getting madder and madder by the minute, but the madder he got, the better he played. I knew exactly how to press his buttons, and it was good to see him worked up. It was a bit how I used to be when I was younger, because I'd get angry with myself for not putting shots on target. I'd think to myself, 'I've been working at that all week, and I thought I'd just about overcome the mishitting.' And here was Frank going through the same thing.

Three goals behind now, Newcastle staged a massive fightback. They didn't half show some character by pulling things back to 4–3. All of a sudden it became a real knife-edge job, and the pitch was getting icier and icier as the temperature dropped and the dying minutes approached. Newcastle had just had one point-blank shot saved and another kicked off the line when the ball was cleared to Bally. He did a great little bit of magic, then knocked it across to George Armstrong, who played it in to Trevor Ross on the overlap. He was a lovely striker of the ball, Trevor, and now he offered me this wonderful far-post cross. I'd hit the bar a couple of times already, and Mick Mahoney had made a couple of saves from me, but there was no mistake this time as, wumph!, I completed a hat-trick in my first game against my old club. For me, it was a bit like Roy of the Rovers all over again. Better still, it had shut Gordon Lee right up. Not only that, but it was one of the best games of football I can recall playing in, and it provided wonderful excitement for the crowd despite the very dodgy, and sometimes dangerous, conditions underfoot.

Typically, Lee said not a word to me before or after the game, but the Newcastle fans let me know how they felt. There were up to 10,000 of them crammed in at the Clock End at Highbury and there wasn't a single derogatory sound from them. This was my first time playing against Newcastle after five wonderful years at St James's Park, and yet there was no booing or anything like that. I thought to myself, 'Well done, you lot! You knew what was going on, you understood. You could have just looked at the surface of the situation and thought I'd walked out on you.' But they hadn't; they'd looked a little bit deeper than that. They are an intelligent crowd, and I thought they did themselves proud on that particular day. The only sound they made towards me was one of appreciation. I have to say it was a very strange but very fulfilling afternoon, in as much as you never quite know what the reaction is going to be when you play against a former club. You just have to wait and see what it brings. To have both sets of supporters cheering me at the end of a very tense and intense 90 minutes was a very satisfying and emotional experience.

Another thing that game reminds me of was the difficulty I experienced identifying team-mates when I first started playing for Arsenal at home. All through my career I'd been a member of teams – Fulham, Luton and Newcastle – whose colours were a combination of black and white. When I played for Luton, orange was unheard of; that came later, after Alec Stock. In those days at Kenilworth Road it was just white shirts, black shorts and white socks. At Highbury, it took me a while to switch my mentality from negative to positive and get used to those coloured shirts.

When we played the return game against Newcastle towards the end of the season, the animosity again coming in my direction from you-know-who was brought to my attention by the press lads in London. It just made me all the more determined to do well, of course. So, when the ball was played back from the kick-off to Irving Nattrass, I have to admit I just made a bee-line for him and kicked him and the ball up in the air. I had the greatest respect for Irving, he was quick and strong and a very good player, but I was eager to establish total physical dominance from the word go, and it worked. The referee awarded Newcastle a free-kick, but Irving needed treatment from the trainer and that was the job done for the whole game. Newcastle couldn't string two passes together from then on. They had been rocked on to the back foot and couldn't get off it for the rest of the game. With the likes of Peter Storey snarling in the middle of the park alongside Bally, who could be as brutal as anybody when he wanted to be, Newcastle showed their nerves whenever the ball went anywhere near them. Meanwhile, up front, Frank and I were giving them a physical battering too, and they just never came to terms with it. All it took was about ten minutes of the rough stuff, then we started playing our football. Newcastle never mustered an attack, and we ran out comfortable winners with goals from me and John Matthews.

By this time, the spring of 1977, I was earning something like the wages I'd been promised originally by Terry Neill. But there had still been a bit of a shock in store when Ken Friar had finally called me up to his office.

'Right,' he said, 'I've sorted things out and I'm going to explain to you everything that has happened. But first, let me make it clear that if the board had known the money you were on at Newcastle, they would never have made a move for you.'

'I find that rather strange, Ken,' I replied, 'because, normally, it's one of the first questions asked if terms are going to be an issue. This was a record transfer, too [I think the record had stood at a quarter of a million at the time], so surely Sir Denis Hill-Wood would have asked Lord Westwood what kind of money I was on?'

'No, he's not that kind of man,' said Ken.

'Well, what's going on here then?'

That was when Ken first told me all about the wage structure at Arsenal.

'Look, don't let anybody know that you're aware of this,' he said, 'but I can tell you nobody at this club is earning more than £200 a week. That's why, while you were away in Switzerland and Yugoslavia and I saw Terry Neill's notes about your signed contracts, I found it very difficult to believe all of it was accurate. However, Arsenal's word is their bond, and the chairman has instructed me to put the matter right to your satisfaction, so I have contacted your accountant and asked him for the figures. But it's got to stay between the chairman, you and me. Nobody else is supposed to know.'

Ken went on to explain that, since Football League rules did not allow my existing contract to be updated, a new, improved one had to be prepared and signed. But, again to comply with the rules, that necessitated adding a year to the length of the contract, making it five instead of four. Then, he added, the contract would allow for an additional payment by the club to make up for the money I had lost since signing the original agreement. Not only that, but Ken reminded me that his offer to get back all the tax I had paid at Newcastle still stood. He asked me to write out a cheque for £2,300 and said he would send it to Newcastle right away with the necessary forms. 'It'll take somebody only five minutes to go back into the records,' he said, 'and all they have to do is put it in the post to the Inland Revenue before the end of this tax year.'

While mightily relieved to hear all this, I was still puzzled by what had happened after I'd left those blank signed forms with Terry Neill.

'Ken,' I said, 'I was very specific about what I wanted and the manager was very specific about writing it down and saying, "OK, agreed." I trusted him on all that, and hands were shaken on it. So why did it not happen?'

'I'm not sure,' replied Ken. 'All I can tell you is that we were supplied with a completely different set of figures.'

'If that's the case,' I persisted, 'it was always going to be found out. So what the hell's gone on?'

'That's a matter for the board to deal with,' said Ken. 'All I can say to you is that the board of directors and the chairman – particularly the chairman – have sought to put right the whole situation, and I would ask you to forget it, to let it pass as one of those things. We'll put it right.'

'All right, Ken,' I said, 'but you've got to understand that I simply can't forget it. I can't look that feller in the eye ever again and trust what he says to me.'

'Well, only you can deal with that. Providing you keep your end of the bargain and keep it just between us, how you feel inside is totally a matter for you.'

'OK, but I hope you're careful with any future dealings.'

'Oh, steps have been taken already,' he assured me.

And that was the end of that particular episode. It reflected a lot of credit on Arsenal Football Club for putting the situation right without a quibble, but it did leave me in a peculiar situation with regard to the manager. I wasn't going to let it affect me in any way, but I was going to be very interested to know how Terry Neill dealt with contractual situations in the future. The crunch moment between us personally, I knew, would come when we met at training the following day.

When I arrived at Arsenal's old London Colney training ground the next morning, I saw Terry, said hello and looked at him long and hard. Returning my greeting, he sidled up to me and said, 'Everything's sorted, then? Now you can get on with things.'

'You've got to be joking!' I said.

To this day, I don't know whether he felt he really could get away with tricking me, or whether he had just used me as a weapon to break the wage structure at Arsenal. He had been at the club as a player for many years, don't forget, and he knew the chairman, Sir Denis Hill-Wood, as well as anybody apart from Ken Friar. What is certainly true is that from then on Terry had far more leverage when negotiating transfers because my revised contract had not just broken the Highbury wage structure, it had smashed it to smithereens. I'd been on £300 a week at Newcastle, plus all the bonuses I'd negotiated into my contract, but at Arsenal I was on £500 a week with all the same bonuses. It meant I was earning two and a half times more than Alan Ball, the Arsenal and England captain, and a World Cup winner. Even so, because the Labour government had pitched the top rate of tax at 85.5 per cent, only £90 a week was going into my bank account. There I was at 26 going on 27, the most expensive and certainly one of the best-paid players in Britain at the peak of my career and earning power, and I was taking home

£90 a week! No wonder so many film and rock stars just upped and left the country.

Although Arsenal were now paying me what Terry Neill had promised me they would, I no longer had much faith in the manager's word. In view of the John Radford–Frank Stapleton business, I wasn't too keen on his judgement either. My opinion of him didn't improve a great deal when in the summer of 1977 I spent my first close season with Arsenal playing for St Hellas, an Australian club run by the Greek community in Melbourne. As I've said, I never enjoyed long spells of inactivity, and as it had become more than obvious I was not going to be included in the England set-up under new manager Ron Greenwood (of which more soon), I got Terry's permission to go Down Under for the summer. I was grateful for that, at least, but while the manager was giving me the go-ahead, he told me that, funnily enough, he was considering taking Arsenal to Australia for a pre-season tour.

'Well,' I said, 'if I'm over there and keep myself fit by playing all the way through, then I could link up with you.'

'Let's see how things pan out,' he replied noncommittally, 'but that's always an option to consider.'

He was not quite so accommodating when it came to the crunch, though. That arrived when I was contacted by Arsenal Football Club and told that, yes, there would be a pre-season tour of the Far East and Australia. It would take the form of a tournament involving ourselves, Red Star Belgrade, Celtic and the national teams of Singapore and Australia. The tour was due to start in Singapore, then move on to Australia. This all seemed ideal for me, well and truly over the jet lag by now and bursting with life and energy Australian style. I phoned Arsenal and spoke to Terry Neill. I suggested to him that, rather than come all the way back to England only to make the long return journey to the Far East, it would be more sensible if I were to join the party in Singapore. He seemed to agree at first, but then rang back to say I had to return to England, do three days' training, then fly out to Singapore.

'Terry,' I said, 'three days' training will be worthless to me. If I fly back, I'll be jet-lagged and not fit to train for three days. It's far, far better for me to stay in this time zone. I'm training here, I'm playing here, and I'm as fit as a fiddle. I'll join you in Singapore.'

'No,' he said, 'I want you back for three days' training.'

'Terry, have you ever been to Australia yourself?'

'No, I've never been.'

'Well, unless you've experienced it, the jet lag is almost beyond description. It's an absolute killer. But what you're asking me to do involves a double dose of it. While I'm recovering from one, you're going to immediately subject me to another.'

'I don't care,' he said, 'I want you back here.'

I've no idea why Terry was so stubborn on this matter. All I could do was put his behaviour down to Irish logic. So I returned home, via Singapore. Unfortunately, engine trouble caused an unscheduled stopover in Singapore that virtually wiped out the extra two days I had allowed myself before the three days' training with Arsenal. What I discovered, too, was that the jet lag coming back from Australia is even worse, so I practically sleepwalked my way through those three days of training at London Colney before packing my bag again and boarding a plane for Singapore.

I was hardly in the greatest nick, then, when we played our first game in the National Stadium, which seats 50,000 and was packed to the rafters. The heat and humidity were something none of us had ever experienced before, and we had been told by the club doctors to drink only bottled water. However, there was a limit to the amount of water we could consume, they added, and they recommended bottled beer or orange juice as the best way to replace liquid lost from the body.

By this time, my Arsenal room-mate was Alan Hudson. Terry Neill had bought Huddy from Stoke to replace Alan Ball, who had been sold to Southampton, and I have to say that, on the ball, he was as good a player as any I've ever seen. So Huddy and I decided we had to plan for this loss of fluid. As the mini-bar in our hotel room was empty, we went out to a local supermarket and bought pint bottles of Carlsberg lager, which we then crammed into the mini-bar.

Our first game was against Red Star Belgrade, who were one hell of a side in those days, and it kicked off at nine o'clock at night. Just before we went out to play, the club doctors weighed each of us with the intention of seeing what 90 minutes of football in those conditions took out of your body. Unfortunately, we were locked at 1–1 after 90 minutes, so extra time had to be played because there had to be a result. During the first fifteen minutes of it, Red Star went 2–1 up.

Even at that hour of night in Singapore, the temperature was in the 90s and the humidity 98 per cent. The only way I can describe what it was like to play in such overwhelming conditions is to say it was similar to having an invisible roof constantly pressing down on your head. We could have been accused of letting the grass grow under our feet, although the pitch wasn't actually covered in grass, but something more like a flat weed across which the ball passed quite nicely. Even so, the humidity was such that you could almost feel the plant life pushing up underneath your feet, so you had this strange double sensation of being pushed up from below and pressed down from above.

Long before the end of the game we were all suffering from dehydration. My socks had lost all their elasticity and had basically rotted with all the sweat they had had to soak up. All we wanted to do was drink, but we were told we mustn't swallow, only wet our lips and mouths. We kept battling away in this game against Red Star, though, and at one point the ball was knocked beyond their centre-half, just the way I liked it. I set off, I got my shoulder across the centre-half, and I was heading goalwards. Then, as I was in full flight, the elastic in my shorts rotted and they worked their way down over my knees, sending me flat on my face. I could have levelled it at 2–2, but instead I had to change my shorts.

Red Star went on to win 3–1, and we came in complaining bitterly about goalkeeper Jimmy Rimmer, who the players felt had been responsible for one of the goals and who did not take kindly to the plentiful dressing-room criticism of his general form. But such arguments were forgotten when we were asked to step back on the doctors' scales. Look in the record books, and you'll see that they always had me down as being 5ft 8in tall and eleven and a half stone; during my playing days, though, I was 5ft 10½in tall and exactly thirteen and a half stone. I was a lot heavier than I looked, which is why I think centre-halves were often caught out. When I hit them, I did so with a far greater force than they were expecting. Anyway, I got on the scales and discovered that I'd lost twelve and a half pounds, nearly a stone, in one game! Like everybody else, the inside of my cheeks felt as if they were stuck together, and my tongue was glued to the roof of my mouth to the point where I couldn't talk properly. Huddy and I were so parched that when we got back to the hotel, whoosh!, three pints of Carlsberg went down each of our necks without touching the sides.

In our hotel, the Singaporeans had laid on the most fantastic buffet – it was wonderful, wonderful food – but none of us could eat a thing; all we wanted to do was get liquid inside us. In the end, we found a bar in the red light area where American GIs used to hang out at the end of the Second World War. We sat at a table outside, and as more and more players drifted down from the hotel, we pushed the tables together. In the end, there was a party about twenty strong that included Tony Donnelly, the kitman, as well as the club doctors. We were drinking either Tiger beer or Lion beer, I can't remember which, and I decided to keep count because I wanted to know just how many bottles I needed to consume until I felt I'd replenished the lost liquid. My personal count, when we arrived back at the hotel at about seven o'clock the following morning, was 22, in addition to the Carlsbergs – and I hadn't had to use the toilet once! Not only that, but Huddy and I were stone cold sober. In fact, we remarked that it was the soberest we had ever been, and we'd just had an all-night drinking session. It was as if the body had just dispersed the liquid to wherever it was required without letting any of the alcohol into the bloodstream, and therefore into the brain.

What with one thing and another, that was not a happy pre-season tour. Still feeling the effects of the double dose of jet lag Terry Neill had subjected me to so unnecessarily, I was seething over the non-appearance of the extra payment of about £250 a man the manager had promised us for playing a friendly in Norway at the end of the previous season. So were the other players, and the mood in the squad was soured further by the fact that we were not getting the spending money we were entitled to, under FA rules, while we were on tour. On top of these and other niggles, I was still hugely mistrustful of Terry Neill after the contract dealings a year earlier. As a result, I felt I couldn't believe a word he said.

I was so fed up, I said as much to Ken Friar when I bumped into him in Singapore. 'Ken,' I told him, 'if you had my passport and plane ticket in your pocket now, I'd take them and go back home to England. I am sick of everything that's going on. The manager has had me traipsing halfway round the world for three day's training, only for me to go back almost to where I'd started from in the first place. On top of that, he's had me and the rest of the team parading around a heaving department store here for no apparent reason. It wasn't as though the store appeared to be direct sponsors, or anything, of the tournament. So why were we obliged to make that kind of arduous personal appearance? For money?'

My outburst came as a bit of a shock to Ken, who said, 'Look, why don't you just get playing and see this out? Let's finish what we've got to do here in Singapore, let's go to Australia and get done what needs to be done over there, and then, when we get back to England, we'll talk again.'

Our second and last match in Singapore was against the Singapore national team, and we beat them 5–0, with me scoring a hat-trick. Crazily, we were then booked on a five o'clock flight to Australia the following morning. It meant that, because of the late-evening kick-off and the complete dehydration you suffer playing for 90 minutes in that kind of humidity, we went without a night's sleep. Having got away from the stadium at about 11.15, we spent the next three or four hours just replacing lost liquid. Then we went back to the hotel, packed our bags and got on the bus to go to the airport. After flying through more time zones, we arrived in Sydney at breakfast time, starving hungry. All we wanted was steak, but we couldn't get it at the bog-standard motel we were taken to from the airport. They kept telling us we could have egg and this, egg and that, but not egg and steak. Terry Neill told us to stop complaining, which hardly helped to quell the growing dissatisfaction with him among the players.

The result of our first game in Australia did not improve the general mood: Celtic deservedly beat us 3–2 and we didn't play well at all. After that, it was another early flight to Adelaide the following morning. Again, after more time changes, we arrived at the hotel hungry. Looking for an early lunch, Huddy and I dropped our bags in the room and went straight down to the restaurant, which was due to open twenty minutes later. We thought we'd have a drink while we were waiting, and went into the bar. There, we found the Arsenal chairman, Sir Denis Hill-Wood, sitting all alone. He welcomed us at once, and we began to chat to him about football. It was really the first time either of us had had a chance to talk to him at length, but we soon discovered that he liked nothing more than to sit and converse with his players. It emerged, too, that Sir Denis thought the sun shone out of Peter Storey's backside because he loved a hard man. Apparently, Arsenal's upper-crust chairman had been a bit of a hard case himself when he'd been at Eton, where he'd played more rugby than football.

'Come on, boys, let me get you a drink,' he said to us. We responded by asking for a large gin and tonic each, because our plan was to have an alcoholic drink, take a sleeping tablet, eat a large steak, go back to our room and crash out. We'd found that was the best way to overcome the combined effects of jet lag and tiredness after playing matches in those exhausting conditions. 'Good idea,' said Sir Denis when we'd explained it to him. 'Three large ones, please.'

Shortly afterwards, the restaurant opened and we said our goodbyes to Sir Denis, who was waiting for the rest of the Arsenal officials to join him. Our steaks duly arrived, and we were tucking into them when Terry Neill came into the restaurant and made a beeline for us. The drinks Sir Denis had bought us were standing on the table, and Terry picked one up and said, 'Is this what I think it is?'

'Yes, it is,' we replied.

'You two are a disgrace!' he said.

'Terry, to be honest, we don't give a shit what you think,' we said.

Having sent him away with a flea in his ear, we ate as quickly as we could, zoomed up to our rooms before the sleeping tablets could take effect, got into bed and crashed out. The next thing we knew, all hell was breaking loose in our room. The door crashed open and Terry Neill stormed in screaming and shouting. We were desperately trying to recover consciousness, so not a word he was saying was registering until we thought we heard him say, 'I'm sending the pair of you home!'

'Mmm,' we went. 'F***ing good job!' And rolled over back to sleep.

When we woke up several hours later – and by now it's about eleven o'clock at night – I said to Huddy, 'Did I have a bad dream, or did it really happen?'

'I think I must have had the same dream as you,' he said. 'Terry Neill came into the room and said we're going home, yes?'

In no time at all, Tony Donnelly, the kitman, was knocking on our door and saying, 'I've been told to pack your gear up. I'm sorry about this.'

'We're not,' we said. 'What the hell is all this nonsense about anyway?'

It turned out that not only had we transgressed in Terry's eyes by having an alcoholic drink with our meal, we had missed the training session he had arranged for that afternoon. Unfortunately, the manager had neglected to tell Huddy and me about it. We'd been on a plane with the man for five hours, but he hadn't said a word about training, nor had he mentioned anything about it at the hotel. In any case, who in their right mind organises a training session the day after a game played in gruelling conditions and a five-hour flight? Huddy and I suspected it was all part of a vendetta by Terry Neill against the players who were kicking up a fuss about him.

We had a couple of callers in the next few hours. The first was Geordie Armstrong. 'Is it right you're both being sent home?' he asked. When we told him it was, and that we were going first thing in the morning, Geordie exploded in a way that typified the unhappiness in the camp. 'The f★★★ing bastard!' he said. 'I've been every bit as bad as you, and I want to go home as well. I'm going to see the bastard.'

That came to nothing, of course, as did a visit by Ken Friar. 'Ken,' I said, 'we're happy to go. I told you something like this was going to happen. But let me tell you this: woe betide the club if anything comes out publicly because the main reason we are being sent home, so we hear, is that we were having a drink with our meal. That drink was bought for us by the chairman.' Ken's face fell a million miles when he heard that. It did not climb back up much when we went on to explain that the club doctors had recommended the combination of gin and tonic and a sleeping tablet as a recipe for a good twelve hours' sleep. Besides, the sleeping tablets had come from the doctors, who would not have given them to us had they known we were due to train. Nobody knew what was going on, we told Ken, and this was just a ruse by Terry Neill to put us in a bad light.

'Look,' he said, 'I'm just doing my job. No doubt it'll all come out in the wash when we're back in England.'

We got there first, of course, and were met at Heathrow by hordes of cameramen and journalists. Until then we had managed to fend off most of the media, who had clearly been tipped off about what was happening (no prizes for guessing who might have spilt the beans). The tabloids had flown reporters out to try to meet our plane halfway at places like Abu Dhabi, but the captain had been brilliant and had radioed ahead to warn the ticket clerks about reporters trying to buy their way on to the flight. One or two might have sneaked aboard, but we dealt with them.

I had an expert in the field to call on, of course. I'd phoned ahead to speak to Reg Hayter, who met us at the airport and told us that Terry Neill had sold his side of the story to the *News of the World* for thousands of pounds. We decided not to say a thing at Heathrow. Instead, we posed for a few photographs before going off to meet up later at a pub nobody knew about, where we planned our counter campaign over a couple of pints of beer. Reg did a deal for Huddy with the *Sunday Mirror* and for me with the *People*. I confined my version of events purely to the facts: the Arsenal chairman had bought us the gin and tonics, and neither he nor we knew there was going to be a training session that afternoon. Huddy, on the other hand, launched into a somewhat personal attack on Terry Neill. That didn't do him a lot of good, because Terry was soon looking to offload him to another club. I, on the other hand, was suspended for two weeks without pay. It didn't matter much because we were still doing pre-season training and I was earning good money as a columnist with the *Sun*, who sent a photographer to take a picture of me training on my own, running with the dog.

Things did not get a great deal better during the 1977/78 season. At the end of February we played West Ham at Upton Park, and went in at half-time 2–0 up, both goals having been scored by me. In the second half, with the ball at our end of the ground, I was just walking across the pitch when my studs caught in the grass and I tore the cartilage in my right knee. I went across to Fred Street, the Arsenal physiotherapist, and said, 'You're not going to believe this, but I've torn my cartilage just walking! I know what I've done, so don't say I haven't done it. I know exactly what it is, and I'm just starting to feel it swell, but let me carry on.'

After the game, I was sent off for various X-rays that confirmed I had torn the cartilage. Then it was a question of talking it over with the doctor, the physio and Terry Neill to decide what action to take. My preference was to undergo surgery right away because I'd had the same problem in my left knee at Newcastle and had been back playing within six and a half weeks of tearing it. But Terry didn't like that idea at all. 'That means you'll miss the sixth round and semi-finals of the FA Cup,' he said. 'We're struggling to be among the serious challengers for the League title, but we're going well in the cup, so I need you for that, I really do.' Reluctantly, then, I agreed to delay the op and played against Wrexham, one of several giantkillers that year, at the Racecourse Ground in the sixth round of the FA Cup a couple of weeks later. We beat them 3–2 and I got one of the goals, but my knee was getting worse and worse all the time. I was playing in all the games, League as well as Cup, but hardly doing any training. Most of my time was spent doing remedial work on the knee.

'It's getting bad,' I told Terry Neill.

'Yes,' he said, 'but it's not showing on the field.'

It wasn't showing because I wouldn't let it show, but I knew it was having a debilitating effect on me and that my performances were suffering as a result. The manager, however, was deaf to all my pleas. 'Let's keep it going,' he insisted. So, at the beginning of April, I played against Orient at Stamford Bridge in the semi-final and scored twice in a 3–0 victory. The tear, though, was now so bad that the bit of cartilage hanging loose was actually getting trapped in the joint and the knee was locking on me. At times, I couldn't even straighten my leg.

Even so, I was picked to play against Ipswich in the final. Bobby Robson, their manager, came out with all sorts of sob stories about the injuries they had, but there was a whole host of Arsenal players – Liam Brady and Pat Rice, as well as me – carrying injuries that either needed time to heal properly or an operation. In the second half, my knee kept locking up and I couldn't move it. I'd have to stand like a stork on one leg waggling the other one just to free it up so I could get running again. A couple of times I was in mid-flight when the knee locked up, and there was just nothing I could do. It was either hop at high speed or allow myself to crash to the ground, which I did on both occasions.

But to be fair to Ipswich, they were absolutely brilliant that day. They beat us 1–0 with a goal from Roger Osborne, but we couldn't have had any complaints had it been 5–0. They hit the woodwork a couple of times, and Pat Jennings made a couple of great saves. David O'Leary had a scoring opportunity for us from a set piece in the first few minutes, but he got underneath the ball and headed it over the bar. It was unlike David to do that, and I think a few heads went down as a result. Whatever the reason, it became a real uphill task for us. Ipswich, on the other hand, absolutely romped it, and well done to them. It was the first time Bobby Robson had won the FA Cup, and, gutted as I was at losing at Wembley yet again, I was really very pleased for him.

From there, it was straight into hospital to have the cartilage sorted out. Then I spent most of the summer recuperating and working hard on the rehabilitation. I got myself into absolutely peak condition for pre-season training, and the spirit in the camp was good, too. Everybody was keen to make up for the Wembley defeat by Ipswich, and 1978/79 didn't start too badly. But then we played an early League Cup match at Rotherham, and damn me if I didn't go and do the cartilage in my other knee – this time on the outside! Although I completed the game, there was no messing about this time. Having consulted the surgeon, Nigel Harris, I was taken straight into hospital to have the cartilage removed.

In those days, long before the advent of keyhole surgery, they used to put your knee in plaster after the operation, and when the plaster came off, the joint was very tender. You had to move very gingerly, wondering whether you could put weight on your leg, because up to that point the plastercast had been taking all the strain and the leg muscles had wasted away. Anyway, very gently, you worked on increasing the bend of the knee. This was very important because it was put into the plaster slightly crooked and you had to work on getting it absolutely straight. And that was where I was having the problem. I just couldn't do it. After three weeks of trying, I told Fred Street I'd got a problem. 'I can't straighten it,' I said. 'Not only that, but I can feel something in there. It's like a door wedge and I can't free it.' I was sent back to the specialist, who took a whole load of X-rays that revealed… precisely nothing. Do this, do that, he suggested, and I followed his instructions to the letter, but still I couldn't straighten my leg fully and the knee kept swelling up. More X-rays, but nothing showed up. I was walking around with a major limp and I had the whole of Arsenal's medical team plus surgeon Nigel Harris completely baffled. Every three days I had to go to see a doctor who had this bloody great needle the length of a pencil and the thickness of a pencil lead, which he stuck into my knee in order to draw off all this yellow fluid. There was so much of it that I began to think there was something seriously wrong with me.

Finally, Nigel Harris told me he was sending me to see a specialist who had this machine that was the only one of its kind in the country. It was called an arthrogram, and it took detailed pictures of knees. 'It's the next step on from X-rays,' Nigel explained. I'd have felt a bit more confident about the consultation if the specialist hadn't been called Bram Stoker. Yes, that was actually his name! When I rang the bell at his Harley Street consulting rooms, I half expected to hear the howling of hounds. The worst that happened, though, was that he fished out another bloody big needle and stuck it into the side of my knee. Then he attached the end of it to the equivalent of a bicycle pump, and pumped my knee up. This went on for a quarter of an hour or twenty minutes, by which time my knee was the size of a football. When he was satisfied that enough pumping had been done, old Bram positioned the cone of an X-ray-type camera on my knee, which transmitted images of the inside of my knee on to a little television screen. He could manoeuvre the camera to look wherever he wanted, and in the end he took 150 pictures. 'If there's anything there,' he said, 'it will show in at least one of them.' He manipulated and examined my knee from every conceivable angle, and still he couldn't find a bloody thing. In fact, the medical men were clearly beginning to think I was telling porkies.

Then, eureka! One of them was looking at the pictures and suddenly said, 'What's that?' It was nothing more than a tiny white speck, and they were not sure at first whether it was a spot on the film or something in the knee. 'Right,' said Nigel Harris when they'd decided it must be internal, 'I want to talk with you. You've now had two operations on your knee, one on the inside to remove the meniscus and one on the outside to do exactly the same. That is all the knee will cope with. If a surgeon goes into the knee a third time, it sets up so much trauma in the joint that it can never recover. If I open it up again to take out whatever is in there, I have to tell you there is every likelihood you will never play football again. So, what do you want me to do?'

I tend to look at things in life in a very basic way, so I said to Nigel, 'The first thing I would say is that I cannot continue to walk like this. I'm not really walking, I'm shuffling and limping because there's something in there. I need to get that out just for me to walk. If I can then start running again, fine.'

'Well,' he replied, 'it's not as easy as that. The trauma is something that the knee never recovers from. It will be almost a miracle if you ever play again.'

'But,' I insisted, 'I can't carry on as I am. Get it out, then we'll see.'

When Nigel came to see me after I had come round from the anaesthetic, he could scarcely conceal his astonishment. 'You should see what we've taken out of your knee!' he said. 'How on earth it never showed itself on the arthogram and all the X-rays we shall never know, but it didn't. Here it is.' With that, he produced a sample bottle containing liquid and a piece of gristle growth about fourteen inches long. 'I really had to rip open your knee joint to find it,' he revealed.

What Nigel discovered was that the problem had started when my interior cartilage had been removed while I was at Newcastle. Essentially, the cartilage is a crescent-shaped cushion that goes in either side of the knee joint and acts as a buffer. It's free standing, other than at the ends, where the blood flows in and out. What had happened during the Newcastle operation was that they'd cut off the cartilage at the attachment where the blood flows in and not sealed it off, so the blood had continued to pump into the knee. But, having nowhere to go and no access to air, it did not form a scab. It sort of calcified and turned itself into gristle, which just kept growing and growing wherever it could in the knee joint. In effect, it had zigzagged right through the inside of my knee joint.

Now came the real test. When the plaster was removed, the rehab took months rather than weeks. It was a long, long process. I worked and I grafted. I was in the weights room and the treatment room, and I ran up and down the terraces. I would run up the stairs in the stands just to give myself a change of scenery and a different surface underfoot. On and on it went like this. I was seeking to rehabilitate a knee that was so swollen it didn't look like mine. They were still having to take liquid out of it every other day. But I worked so hard to get things back to normal that by the spring of 1979, with two or three weeks of the season left, they reckoned it would be all right for me to get back into full training. The joy I felt at just having a ball at my feet again and being in the fresh air playing small-sided games was indescribable. It was still uphill progress, though, until I had played two or three reserve games, by which time I was 100 per cent fit. This, too, at the start of the week Arsenal were back at Wembley and playing Manchester United in the FA Cup final.

Terry Neill talked to me every day. Arsenal were going through a period where they were struggling to score goals, so one day he'd have me in the team and the next day I was out. This went on all the way through the week, and still I was none the wiser. I didn't know if I was going to be in or if the attacking partnership was going to be Frank Stapleton and Alan Sunderland. They hadn't got a clue either. In fact, everything was so up in the air that I remember walking up to Don Howe, the chief coach, on the Friday and asking him point-blank whether I was playing or not.

'If I'm not,' I said to Don, 'please let Frank and Alan know. People have to know now what task they have to prepare themselves for.'

And Don, loyal as ever, said, 'Well, the team for the final is the manager's choice.' So it was obvious to me he didn't know either.

That Saturday morning, all was revealed. I wasn't playing, but I thought I'd be sub at least since I'd been in and out of the team all week. But, damn me, Terry Neill didn't even make me sub, he made me thirteenth man, which meant I was right out of things, because in those days an FA Cup final's thirteenth man was like a spare prick at a wedding. 'Not to worry,' I said to myself, 'I'll do my best to jolly the lads along, particularly Frank and Alan.' So I did, and, of course, they proved Terry Neill's team selection absolutely right by scoring a goal apiece in a 3–2 victory, Alan getting the winner in the last minute of a dramatic Liam Brady-inspired finale.

My only thought then was to graft through the summer to get myself right for the following season. I got Terry Neill's permission to go and play for Djurgaarden in Stockholm during the close season. I knew their manager well, because he was Alan Ball senior, but no sooner had I begun to play for Djurgaarden than he was sacked. A Swedish coach took his place, and the players' union was so strong over there that I was excluded from one meeting while they discussed whether or not they wanted to have me around. Fortunately, they voted for me to remain, and I played over there for a good two months. In fact, I was in Sweden watching on television when Nottingham Forest beat Malmö in the 1979 European Cup final.

What I found out playing over there was that at first all would go well with my knee; only in the last fifteen minutes was it a struggle. Unfortunately, the pain began to set in earlier and earlier with each game I played, so I felt duty bound to tell Djurgaarden about the deterioration. Well aware of the reason I had gone there in the first place, they introduced me to a wonderful Swedish knee doctor who specialised in braces for various parts of the body that had been weakened. He fitted me with one, I went training in it, and it was marvellous. It took all the strain off my knee. It was a metal contraption that came down either side of my knee and followed the contours of the leg; then there was a brace around the knee that had very clever circular, ratchet-type hinges that allowed totally free movement. I played a game in it and it was bliss. It fitted snugly and it gave me such wonderful freedom again. Better still, the Swedish specialist made me a gift of this hugely expensive brace. 'That will prolong your career for a very long time,' he said.

When I came back to England and showed the brace to Fred Street, he was hugely impressed, but then he pointed out that I had to get Football Association approval for it. We had pictures taken of me in this brace, but the FA said I couldn't wear it. If the reason was that it constituted a danger to other players, it was a load of tosh. The thing was made of ultra-light aluminium alloy; even I didn't know I had it on. All I could put it down to was excessive caution on the part of the FA – scared of change and all that. That's how they worked then, and there was no appeal against their decision.

When Arsenal started pre-season training, I said to Terry Neill, 'Look, if I can't wear that brace, I'm a goner. I'm sorry, but I can't do 90 minutes. I can do you 45, but I can't do 90 any more.' My pessimistic assessment was underlined when Don Howe set up a 400-metre running track and every player was given twelve minutes to run round it as many times as possible. I ran it without the brace, got to eight minutes and stopped. It was like running barefoot on broken glass. The pain was intense and the tears were streaming down my face. That twelve-minute run, flat-out, was the equivalent of the running you would do during a 90-minute game, and I couldn't get beyond eight minutes.

Terry Neill thought that perhaps we could find an answer by talking to the club's medical staff, but I knew better. I knew that if I couldn't wear the brace, in three months' time I'd be unable to play for more than ten minutes. The knee was in such a terrible state, too, all big and misshapen. I went to see Nigel Harris again, who had the final say not just on behalf of Arsenal but the Football League as well.

'Well,' he said, 'I'm not one to say "I told you so", but I did tell you so, didn't I?'

'Yes,' I replied, 'but I had to give it a try, didn't I? If I was allowed to wear this brace, it would be fine because it's a brilliant piece of kit.'

'Yes, it is,' he said, 'but you can't. Unofficially, I have the forms that state you are over and done with. You are finished.'

And that was it, playing career over at 29. Arsenal were very good, bless them, in that they made a payment on the rest of my contract. Having been forced to retire early, though, I have to say I was disappointed not to get a benefit game. At that time, unfortunately for me, the club had decided they were going to keep testimonials and benefits to a minimum.

So off I limped into the sunset.

# CHAPTER SEVEN
# ENGLAND: A MATTER OF RECORD

My 14-cap England career had ended four years before that knee injury finally curtailed my playing days. I'd like to think it would have gone on a lot longer had Sir Alf Ramsey not been sacked in 1974. I'm proud to think that the manager who won the World Cup with England gave me my first five caps and obviously thought highly of me as a player. Unfortunately, Alf's successor, Don Revie, was much less enthusiastic about what I could do, and Ron Greenwood, the man who stepped in when Revie did a flit to the Middle East in 1977, clearly did not rate me at all.

As I explained in an earlier chapter, I first realised Alf was an admirer of my goalscoring ability when I was still at Luton and he called me up, via a policeman, as a late replacement in the squad for an under-23 match against Scotland in Glasgow. I have to say I loved being a part of it. Here were all the young hopefuls of the English game, and I, a player from a club that wasn't big, fashionable or in the top division, was being regarded as their equal. I suppose I could have felt a bit of an interloper, but I didn't look at it that way. I was just chuffed to bits that Alf Ramsey had recognised my goalscoring talent so quickly.

I didn't actually win my first under-23 cap until January 1972, by which time I had been transferred from Luton to Newcastle. It was against Wales at Swindon, and I managed to score one of the goals in a 2–0 win. The other came from Mick Channon, who was my partner up front in that game and several others at that level. Mick was a hugely gifted footballer; everything seemed to come naturally to him. He would sort of float about here, there and everywhere. I, on the other hand, was focused, as always, on everything from the halfway line to the opposing goal, so I suppose our different styles made us good for each other. In addition to his ability as a footballer, Mick was a great lad to have in any squad. He had a wonderfully gregarious personality that allowed him to get on with anybody and everybody. He only saw the best in people, and I'm delighted he has become such a success as a trainer of racehorses, his other great love.

Later that year, we went down to Swansea to play Wales again. This time we won 3–0, and I scored all the goals. I got the third seconds before half-time by pouncing on a bad back-pass, so I came off feeling quite pleased with myself. Back in the dressing-room, Alf, meticulous as always, was waiting for us. He allowed us all to get a cup of tea and sit down before saying, 'It's going very well.' Then he picked up on one or two little defensive things we needed to work on, suggested we could look to get a bit more width in midfield, and topped it all off by saying, 'Malcolm, what you are doing is wonderful, it's great!' He then proceeded to impress on the side the importance of giving me the ball. 'You've got a man here who's on a hat-trick,' he said. 'You've got to be feeding him in the box – he's going to be so hungry!' And he went on and on about my being on a hat-trick, to the embarrassment of everybody else in the room.

Mick Channon, Tony Currie and I were looking at one another wondering whether we should say something. Finally, I plucked up the courage to say, 'Alf, I'm sorry to tell you this, but I'm not on a hat-trick. I actually got the third just before the half-time whistle.'

'Did you really?' he replied, genuinely surprised. 'Well, forgive me for not congratulating you! We came into the dressing-room a minute before the whistle, so I must have missed that one. You've got your hat-trick, then, so there's nothing more to say. Wonderful, wonderful! Just get out there and get some more! Now you can go out and enjoy it, can't you?'

Alf was always a great supporter of me as a player for exactly what I did at club level. That message came through loud and clear at team meetings and during half-time talks. He was always urging people to get their heads up to look for my runs and knock me in, so it was obvious for me not to stop doing that. In fact, Joe Harvey, Newcastle's manager, had advised me strongly to keep doing it. Chuffed to bits when I first played for the England under-23s, Joe said to me, 'You are only there for exactly what you do here. Don't listen to the clever dicks. You keep doing for England exactly what you do for us. Don't change!' When I joined up with England, I listened very carefully to Alf and found the same message coming through. At international level, you have to work much harder on your first touch to ensure you get yourself solidly between the defender and the ball. At League level you can, perhaps, not be 100 per cent right all the time and get away with it, but against international defenders you can't show a fraction of the ball to the guy behind you because he'll just go and nick it. That was perhaps the weakest part of my game, and yes, Alf would say, 'Come on, you've got to work harder at making sure you get your body fully between the defender and the ball.' But all the time it was accompanied by encouragement. Alf would pick players not to change them, but to enhance what they did at club level; he put them in the side for exactly the qualities they showed on the pitch week in, week out with their clubs. So he was well aware of the runs I liked to make and would get upset with players who failed to notice them. 'When somebody's through on goal, you've got to knock it in there!' he would say. 'We've got to look to kill teams at international level, so if you see the opportunity for an incisive pass, play it. If you're not seeing it, it's not worth his while running.'

By the time I got that hat-trick for the under-23s at Swansea, I had already made my senior debut for England, on 20 May 1972. Again it was against Wales – we seemed to have some kind of magnetic attraction for each other – and England started off the Home International Championship, now defunct, by winning 3–0 in Cardiff. I didn't score on that occasion, the goals coming from Emlyn Hughes, Colin Bell and Rodney Marsh.

I was playing up front with Marsh, whose ball control skills were quite incredible. A big man with big thighs, he was so nimble that he just danced with the ball. He could control it and hold on to it effortlessly, no matter how big the opponent or how much they tried to kick him. Time and again he would turn with the ball, and I'd be flying through the inside-left channel screaming, 'Marshy, knock it, knock it to me!' But every time I made these runs he'd knock the ball out to his Manchester City team-mate Mike Summerbee on the right wing, so I'd have to backtrack, wait for a cross from Summerbee and look to come into the penalty area again. I'd been through on goal so many times it wasn't true, yet Marshy had not given me the ball once. Needless to say, soon I was absolutely fuming with him. When we got back to the dressing-room at half-time leading 1–0 – Emlyn Hughes had scored the first – I said, 'What a f★★★ing idiot you are, Marshy! I'm through inside left over and over again with just the keeper to beat. Just knock me in! Every time you bob it out to your Man City team-mate. Talk about looking after your own! I might as well not be out there!'

'You're shouting on my deaf side,' he said dismissively.

'What?'

'I'm deaf in my left ear.'

It was no excuse, of course. Marshy still had two good eyes and should have been able to see the runs I was making. But he'd played under Alec Stock at Queens Park Rangers, hadn't he? I realised he was doing to me what I'd seen Alec do to others for two years – cocking a deaf 'un. My outburst changed nothing, of course. In fact, I ended up making his goal for him. I got to the dead-ball line and clipped the ball back for him to volley it in.

'Cheers!' he said.

'Now will you knock me in?' I asked.

'Not if you keep running on my deaf side, son,' he replied.

I have to say that Rodney Marsh was the only player I ever saw upset Alf so much that he said something derogatory. It was during the game against Scotland at Hampden Park in that same Home International Championship. I was a substitute that day, and I could see Alf fuming on the bench. He was getting madder and madder until you could practically see the steam coming out of his ears. In the end, he couldn't contain himself. 'Harold, get that f★★★ing clown off!' he said to the trainer, Harold Shepherdson. So off came Marshy early in the second half, and on I went in his place with England leading 1–0.

Now, for the benefit of those who never experienced those annual clashes between England and Scotland, let me describe what it was like for English footballers to play at Hampden Park. As the coach inched its way off the main road and through the car parks that surround the stadium, you'd see all these Scottish supporters lining our route. There they were, in their Boy Scout socks, kilts and blue shirts with tam o'shanters on their heads and saltires around their shoulders. They would have been on the piss since Wednesday, and probably not been for a pee in all that time. The England bus used to get sprayed with urine all the way down to the stadium, the kilts going up one after another. At Wembley, as I've said before, it got warmer and warmer as you went up the tunnel, and what hit you, apart from the noise, was the smell of fried onions. At the old Hampden Park, there was this smell of stale beer that hit you straight in the face. It was like playing a game in a brewery! Plus, of course, you had 120,000 Scotsmen booing you. I always had the feeling they were there not so much to support Scotland as to hate the English.

So this was the sort of atmosphere I went into when I replaced Marshy alongside big Martin Chivers. The Scots put us under more and more pressure in a bid to get the goal back, but we got to the last five minutes without cracking. At that point, we started to play the ball down the line towards the corner to see time out, and Alan Ball ran it right down to the corner flag. He then looked back upfield at the Scots, who were miles away but desperately trying to get back to close him down, and he only went and sat on the bloody ball! Now it's pretty common knowledge that Alf did not like the Scots, but his dislike was nothing compared to Bally's hatred of them. 'Look at these skirt-wearing tossers!' he'd said contemptuously as our bus had made its way to Hampden. 'We're going to get out there and we're going to stuff them!' As he sat on the ball, he was also giving the Scots the V-sign with both hands. I shouted to him to calm down, and I heard Martin Chivers saying, 'Oh, f★★k! We'll never get out of here alive!'

Not surprisingly, when the Scots defenders reached Bally they kicked him up in the air and we got a free-kick. But that didn't satisfy the little feller. A few moments later, Martin and I took the defenders away again and the ball was played down the channel for Bally to chase. And what did he do? You've guessed it – he took the ball down towards the corner flag once more, turned round to look upfield and sat on it. The 120,000 Scots in the crowd went berserk, and we were shouting, 'Bally, no, no, don't!' In the end, he sort of threw his arms up in the air as if to say, 'Oh well, you won't let me have my fun!' and stood up. But then he put his foot on the ball, got hold of the flag of St Andrew that was flying on the corner flag and wiped his nose with it. 'Oh, shit!' I heard Martin say from a few yards behind me as Hampden exploded. The Scottish players wanted to kill us, the Scottish supporters wanted to kill us, and I, being a young, go-for-it novice at the time, showed my inexperience by getting caught on the far side of the pitch as we moved into the final seconds of the game. All the other England players had worked their way towards the tunnel so that they only had ten yards or so to run when the final whistle blew. Me, I had a 40-yard dash to safety, and I only just made it.

'F★★★ing cheers, Bally!' we were all going in the dressing-room. 'How are we going to get out of this stadium now? The bus'll have no windows when we get to it!'

Just then, Alf walked in, and with a big grin on his face he said, 'Alan, Alan, you really are a naughty boy. You should control yourself a lot more!' That was Alf, and that was the nearest I ever heard him come to rebuking Bally. They shared an absolute hatred of the Scots, and I think that was one reason they got on so well together.

I don't know if anything happened to the England bus because I got a taxi to Glasgow's Central Station to catch a train across to Edinburgh and down to Newcastle. It didn't dawn on me until after the game that I would have to travel alone through Scottish territory like that, and I bought a paper to hide behind. I had never been so fearful. Fortunately, at that time my face was not well known; if I'd been recognised, I hate to think what might have befallen me.

In between the wins in Wales and Scotland, we lost 1–0 at home to

Northern Ireland, and I had an absolute stinker. That's why I was on the bench at the start of the game against the Scots, and rightly so. It was my first ever appearance at Wembley, and I found it frighteningly awesome. If things weren't going right for you, Wembley was a terrible place to be. There was nowhere to hide; you were just out there and exposed in all that space. In fact, it was all very false playing at Wembley, because the conditions were totally different from anything you'd experienced before. I couldn't gauge distances, for instance. I found that very, very difficult. You did get used to it over time, but Wembley did come as a bit of a shock when you first played there, particularly at night. Maybe that's just me recollecting it that way because my first game there was at night and I played badly, but it was never again quite as fearsome a place as it had been that first time.

And I had been so looking forward to that game against Northern Ireland, one we had been expected to win. The whole England team had a bit of a nightmare, but being the new boy, I didn't know how to cover myself, so the worse I got, the more I exposed myself and the harder I tried to put things right. I remember coming out to the outside-left position and having the ball played out to me. My mind was racing ahead so much to how I was going to take the centre-half on that the pass went underneath my foot and out of play. Alf promptly took me off, and I don't blame him.

But I was in almost all of his senior squads from then on. The only game I missed was the one where we went out of the World Cup so disastrously against Poland, in October 1973. I think that was when I was having my cartilage out at Newcastle. When I was fully fit, he always included me, and he seemed to be making it very clear that I had an international future under him. I was certainly in the squad in November 1973 when Bobby Moore played his last game for England, though we didn't know that at the time. All we knew was that he was going to win his 108th cap against Italy at Wembley, thereby increasing his lead over the previous record holder, Bobby Charlton, to two.

What I remember most about that occasion was the time, before the game, when there were 22 of us sitting in this huge room with big French windows and long velvet drapes at the West Lodge Park Hotel in Hadley Wood, having a team meeting. It was very sunny outside, so much so that the curtains had been drawn to darken the room. But one pair of curtains wasn't quite on the hooks properly and had parted in the middle, so there was just this one beam of sunlight coming through and slowly making its way around the room as Alf was giving his team talk. He was oblivious to this, because once Alf got going there was no stopping him. He was so thorough that his talks could last as long as two hours. He would go through every position in the England team, every player in every position in the opposing team, how generally he expected us to play against them, what we had to watch out for them doing to us, and where their strengths and weaknesses lay. He would then go through corner kicks, free-kicks, and who went in our wall, even to the extent of establishing who would be at one end and who would be at the other, who would charge the ball down, etc. He was absolutely meticulous in his planning. Everybody knew his role exactly because he covered the lot. He never referred to any notes, either. It all just came out of his head.

Anyway, this shaft of sunlight was making its way around the room as Alf was talking. People began to sit in funny positions to get out of its way, but finally it descended on Mooro, who was sitting in the very centre of the room on an upright chair with nowhere to go either side of him. The sun was beating down on the side of the England captain's face, and he started to nod off. Soon he was fast asleep with his chin on his chest. Still Alf, deep in his tactical talk, did not notice. But all of a sudden there was a little choking cough from Mooro and Alf looked up. Bobby woke himself up, looked around and went, 'Sorry, Alf. Sorry about that.' And Alf, to his eternal credit, remarked, 'Robert, I know you've heard all this 107 times before, but, just this once, would you mind listening for the 108th?' I thought that was a lovely way of dealing with the situation.

And that was it so far as those two, the manager and captain of England's World Cup-winning team, were concerned. Mooro never played for his country again after that game against Italy, and we younger players were given the distinct impression that the old guard was slowly departing after the failure to qualify for the 1974 World Cup. The youthfulness of the squad Alf picked for the next game, away to Portugal in April 1974, was evidence of that. The only remaining members of the 1966 and '70 teams were Alan Ball and Martin Peters, who was named skipper. Alf actually spelt it out to us after a training session at a little local football ground in Estoril, near Lisbon, a couple of days before we were due to play at the original Stadium of Light. He called us all together and said, 'You can see, gentlemen, just by looking around you that we are embarking on a whole new road now. Apart from Alan and Martin, hands up those who are over 24.' I think one or two hands went up. Peter Shilton's was one, Trevor Brooking's might have been another. 'It's a very young side,' Alf continued, 'but you are all such wonderful and gifted players, and you are England's future. We have got to set the next World Cup as our target, and that's precisely where I'm starting from, as of today. We are going to put together a side from this squad that's going to win the next World Cup.'

The side he started with in Lisbon that night read as follows: Phil Parkes; David Nish, Dave Watson, Colin Todd, Mike Pejic; Mick Channon, Martin Dobson, Trevor Brooking, Martin Peters; Stan Bowles, Malcolm Macdonald. Of those eleven, six – Parkes, Pejic, Watson, Dobson, Bowles and Brooking – were previously uncapped, and the rest of us, Martin Peters excepted, could only scratch together sixteen caps between us. It was a revolutionary team, and we should have won. The game finished goalless, but we could have scored ten. We hit the post, we hit the bar, and their goalkeeper was inspired.

As a result, Alf got absolutely slaughtered; the tabloids pilloried him and the FA sacked him. I think it was the most foul, cowardly act that has ever taken place in English football, and I don't say that from any selfish point of view. Whether Alf had picked me or not, it would not change my opinion of him as a man or a football manager. He'd done right by everybody. The time for change on the field had arrived and he'd had the courage to put out his new side against a bloody good Portuguese team. We should have won, but we didn't lose, and you can't look on that as failure. Unfortunately, nobody at the FA liked Alf because he didn't suffer fools gladly, and there were plenty of fools around him who resented the power he had taken away from them in terms of team selection. I remember one member of the FA's England under-23 committee calling me 'Ted' repeatedly. I couldn't work out why until Mick Channon twigged. 'He thinks you're Ted MacDougall!'

laughed Mick, referring to the Scottish striker then playing for Bournemouth. And these were the sort of people who sacked Alf Ramsey, the only England manager ever to have won the World Cup. I thought it was the most self-defeating decision ever made by the FA. If they wanted an experienced international manager, who better than the man who'd won the World Cup? What else had he got to do to prove he was the best?

I have to admit his sacking shook me as a person and as a footballer. It shook me to the core that English football could pick up a gun, so to speak, and go 'Bang! Oh, no, let's not be happy with just one foot, let's make it two!' In fact, I was so bewildered by the decision that I went to see Joe Harvey and asked him to explain it to me.

'I've spent an awful lot of time with the man over the last three years or so,' I told Joe, 'and he's absolutely brilliant. Could talk you into total unconsciousness in the team meetings, but, by heavens, he knows the game.'

'I agree with you wholeheartedly,' said Joe.

I discussed it with other England players, too, when Newcastle were playing teams containing people I'd got to know on international duty. Within two or three weeks the feelings of the players had spread throughout the country, and I didn't hear one opinion that differed from mine. I loved Alf, I make no bones about it. He was an absolute gentleman and very much a players' manager. He was very deep in his team talks, very deep and too laborious at times, but they made you go out and be so thorough when you played, so you didn't love him any the less for them.

I would add that, after Alf was sacked, a dinner was held in his honour. If I remember rightly, it was at the Grosvenor House Hotel in London's swanky Park Lane, and all the 127 or so pros he had selected during his eleven years as England manager were invited. Of those, 115 turned up. That said everything anyone needed to know about the affection and respect he generated among his players. There were times when I looked at him and he was so wrapped up in his own thoughts that he kept very distant from the press and aloof from the FA people, whom you could sense he detested and regarded as just a necessary evil. At times, I felt as if I wanted to put my arm around him and say, 'Do you want to chat? Would you like a hug, just to let you know somebody loves you?' Why I felt like that, I'm really not sure. It was just that he was so totally insular and took all the pressure on himself, passing none of it on to his players.

And do you know what Alf Ramsey was earning in 1974, the year he was sacked? A paltry £7,500 a year! I was only 24 at that point and earning nearly £300 a week, or about £15,000 a year, at Newcastle. Worse still, he didn't even get a bonus for winning the World Cup, an achievement that ought to have guaranteed him a job of some sort for life with the FA. Since his salary was so small, his pension can't have amounted to much. The whole thing was an absolute disgrace. I think it was shameful that the FA never sought to correct the situation financially, even when he was in ill health towards the end of his life. For it to have happened in the first place was bad enough. Those involved should be ashamed of themselves.

But international life had to go on, even without Alf. In the summer of 1974 there were home internationals to be played, followed by a tour of Eastern Europe. (Eastern Europe! How many times did I go there? I don't like to think about it. It goes in cycles, doesn't it? There were guys in the game who did nothing but go to South America, but where did I go? Moscow, Leipzig, and all sorts of other grim places behind the Iron Curtain.) As everyone knows, the guy they got in to hold the fort after Alf had been sacked was Joe Mercer, who, with Malcolm Allison as his assistant, had enjoyed a lot of success as manager of Manchester City. Joe was a lovely old feller and not a bad choice really. He was a good old soul everybody knew and trusted, including the players, but the last thing he needed was a two-week tour involving cramped airline seats. He had such a problem with his back that he would sit up most nights in a hard chair and just nod a bit. He drank to numb the pain, and I remember him doing a bit of a talk after naming his team and flinching as he spoke. In fact, tears were rolling down his cheeks at one stage. There was no way, then, that Joe wanted the England manager's job full time.

He included me in his squad, but I didn't even make the bench for the first two home internationals. I came on for Frank Worthington, who had taken my place alongside Mick Channon, in the 2–0 defeat by Scotland, but that was it. Joe didn't have Alf's sense of adventure at that

185

level, and I think he brought back some of the old hands. I didn't get a look in, either, when we drew 2–2 with Argentina at Wembley before going off on tour, or when we drew 1–1 with East Germany and then beat Bulgaria 1–0 in Sofia.

Our last game, on 5 June, was against Yugoslavia in Belgrade, and on the plane from Sofia Mick Channon, Martin Peters, Monte Fresco (the former *Daily Mirror* photographer) and I made up our usual cribbage foursome. As far as I was aware, it was a perfectly normal flight. Had anything untoward happened it would have gone around the squad like wildfire. The significance of this will become apparent later.

When we got to Belgrade airport, the four of us immediately found somewhere to carry on with our card game. Out came Monte's photographer's case again to make a table, and we sat on the luggage carousel, which wasn't moving. I'd seen Kevin Keegan, Emlyn Hughes and one or two others also sitting on a stationary carousel. Then Kevin, I think, sort of stretched out on it with his head on a bag. Then, all of a sudden, all hell broke loose on the other side of the carousel, and we saw Kevin being hauled off by two guys who took him into a sort of Portakabin office in the baggage area. I asked Emlyn Hughes what was going on, but he didn't know. 'We were just sitting there,' he said, 'and I thought Kevin was asleep.' So we all sort of pushed across to the carousel and started shouting towards the Portakabin. We were also looking around for people from the FA, but we couldn't see them anywhere. Then we heard Kevin yelling and screaming, and somewhere in the middle of it we heard a couple of thuds. With that, the lot of us piled over the carousel to the rescue, but then the door of the Portakabin opened and a policeman appeared carrying a little machine gun, which he pointed right at us. He motioned to us to get back, and I'm afraid you don't argue with a sub-machine gun. But the door was open now and we could hear for sure that Kevin was getting a belting. That put us in a real quandary: we couldn't go to Kevin's aid, there was still nobody from the FA around to sort the situation out, and we still had to wait for our bags to arrive.

At last, someone went through customs to search for one of the FA people. When he came back, he said, 'Would you be surprised? They ain't interested!' What we couldn't understand was why nobody from the FA was in the same baggage hall as us anyway. Normally, we were forever moaning about them always being there. Had they had their bags taken through a separate VIP way? That's all we could think. Finally, however, one of the FA bods did come in. It was Alan Odell, the international secretary.

'Right, lads,' he said. 'Get your bags and come through because we have got a situation here that we are going to have to resolve.'

'What the hell's going on?' we chorused. 'Where's everybody been? Why hasn't something been done already?'

'Well, we've got to find out ourselves just what's going on. Is there anything you can tell us?'

'No. Kevin was just lying on a carousel, that's all.'

When we got outside the airport, the coach was waiting for us, but we said we'd rather stay and try to put pressure on the Yugoslavian authorities by not walking away from our team-mate. Safety in numbers, and all that. But Alan Odell pleaded with us to get on the bus and go to the hotel. 'There are reasons Kevin's being held,' he said. 'Certain allegations have been made, and the police have acted accordingly.'

'Allegations of what?' we asked straight away.

'I don't know, but they are acting on allegations. From whom, we don't know; what about, we don't know. But we have an incident that we need to deal with, so it's best that everybody gets on the bus and gets booked in at the hotel.'

We were not very happy about it, but we got on the bus and went to the hotel. There, it was arranged that we would come down for the evening meal at about seven o'clock, but then we were told somebody from the British Embassy was coming and we were to congregate in the meeting room. After a while, Alan Odell, one or two other FA officials and a haughty chap from the embassy came in. Then this consular attaché, or whatever he was, dropped a bombshell.

'Allegations have been made by the Bulgarian stewardesses,' he told us.

Bulgarian stewardesses claiming that Kevin had been touching them up on the plane? We thought that very unlikely, not least because Kevin had been up all night playing cards and he was a dozy little bastard in the mornings. As far as we all knew, he'd been fast asleep all the way from Sofia to Belgrade. In fact, the only members of the party who had been awake were our cribbage foursome of Monte Fresco, Martin Peters, Mick Channon and me.

When we asked what was going to happen next, we were assured that Kevin's release was being sought. Not satisfied with that, we made it clear, on a point of principle, that there was no way we were going to play the game against Yugoslavia if he had been badly treated. The guy from the embassy responded to that with sympathetic noises and a promise to do everything in his power to get Kevin released as soon as possible.

That happened quicker than we expected. We were just finishing our meal in the dining room when Kevin walked in. He was battered black and blue. Split lip, bruised eyes, bruised forehead, bruised cheek. They'd given him a few in the body as well. Bloody hell! Though everybody was pleased to see him released, they were livid at his physical state. 'I don't feel like anything to eat,' he said, to nobody's surprise. 'To be honest, all I want to do is go straight to bed.' And off he went.

We chuntered over the remains of our meal and decided en masse in favour of telling the Yugoslavs to stick the game right up their collective arse. We were definitely not interested in playing them after seeing the state of Kevin. We had been flown out to East Germany and on from there to Sofia on the usual FA charter plane. For some reason that was never explained to us it had not come out again to fly us from Sofia to Belgrade, hence the flight on a Bulgarian plane, but now we demanded that it take us home first thing the following morning.

After the meal, though, the guy from the embassy returned to implore us to play the game. 'The Bulgarian air stewardesses have withdrawn their allegations,' he said, 'but I've still got a really critical situation here.'

'But what about our allegations against the Yugoslavian police?' we asked.

He told us that the matter had been referred to 10 Downing Street, but we were still determined not to play the game. We went to bed agreeing only to discuss the situation again the following day.

The next morning, the FA bods and the guy from the embassy continued to beg us to play, and Kevin was asked to write a letter of apology to the Bulgarian stewardesses. Quite rightly, he refused absolutely to do that. 'No,' he said, 'that would be implying I'm guilty.' It was a real ding-dong battle, because we countered with a demand for an apology from the Yugoslavian police for what they'd done to Kevin. If they apologised, we said, we'd play. Whether that apology ever reached Kevin, I don't know. The embassy guy told us that if it ever did arrive it would be many months in the future. 'Believe me,' he added, 'these are difficult times between Great Britain and Yugoslavia and Eastern Europe in general. I just implore you, and greater powers than me in London implore you, to go and play the game!'

So we did. If you can play a game of football through gritted teeth, we did it. Kevin played too – he had to, as a show of bravado. It was a way of displaying his scars and bruises to the world. In fact, he saw out the whole game, and it was Frank Worthington who was again taken off to make way for me. The score was 2–2 when I went through, the keeper came out and I steered the ball past his foot. I thought it was in, but it just clipped the outside of a post. That miss, above all, sticks in my mind. If I had stuck that chance away, my whole international future might well have changed. It's millimetres that make the difference between success and failure at the top, you know, and I was absolutely gutted to have missed.

We returned to England and never heard another word, as far as I know, about that incident at Belgrade airport. I thought the FA might have had the courtesy to tell everybody who was involved what the outcome was, but I think it was a real 'sweep it under the carpet' job. And there was a real master–servant feeling between the FA and the players in those days. It used to make me laugh when, at the end of every trip with England, you had to complete the expenses form that was included with your little FA handbook containing the squad and the itinerary. You'd have to fill in your name, the name of your club and then either your car mileage or train expenses for travel between home and London. And after train fares it would have 'third class only'. That just about sums up how England footballers were regarded then by the FA.

I can give you another example of that 'them and us' attitude. After we'd played the game against East Germany in Leipzig, we went back to the hotel to get changed and showered before coming down for the evening meal. Having eaten, the whole squad just sat in the hotel lobby twiddling their thumbs because we weren't allowed out. But those who had played were desperate for a drink to replace the liquid lost from their bodies during the match. This may sound just like a good excuse for a binge, but, as I've already explained, the best way of making up a liquid deficiency is to drink a couple of beers. Coke's not a good way of doing it, and you certainly couldn't drink from the taps in East Germany back in 1974. But we couldn't buy Coke, bottled water, beer or anything else because we didn't have any local currency. We had been promised some spending money by the FA, whose own rules stated it had to be so much per day; but it hadn't materialised. In addition, we weren't allowed to put anything on our room bills, or to exchange our own money for marks. In those days, changing money behind the Iron Curtain could be a tricky business. In fact, we had been told never to change sterling into the local currency because there were all sorts of conmen dealing on the black market. 'Don't get involved,' was the message.

There was a nightclub in the hotel, but we were banned from there as well. Still, everyone was getting so cheesed off that four of us decided to defy the order. The sight that met our eyes hardly improved our mood, because there seemed to be FA committee men enjoying themselves all over the place. One of them was Michael Gliksten, then the chairman of Charlton Athletic. He was with a group of people swigging champagne. There were ice buckets filled with bottles of the bubbly stuff, and he was filling glass upon glass with it.

In a cold fury now, I went over to Gliksten and said, 'Are you enjoying yourself? You've got a party of footballers out there who are still waiting for their spending money. They cannot move from the lobby and they cannot get a beer, a Coke or an orange juice because you lot won't get the thing organised properly!'

'Nothing to do with me,' he replied. 'Now, get out of here.'

'I will,' I said, 'but, don't worry, it's noted. All of this – it's noted.'

I suppose the real point of the story is that, once Alf was sacked, there was this huge vacuum that couldn't be filled unless his successor was someone really special. It was our first trip abroad without him, and he would never have allowed his players to be left high and dry – quite literally – like that. Joe Mercer clearly wasn't that special person. Loved as he was by his own players at Manchester City, and by others from many other clubs, he couldn't sort out the fine detail in the way Alf could.

Fine details were almost an obsession with Don Revie, but that didn't mean he was the right man to take over as England manager, as he did later that year. He certainly didn't turn out to be the right one as far as I was concerned. My first contact with the former Leeds manager was at the massive gathering of potential England candidates he organised in Manchester as a first step towards putting a squad together. There must have been nearly a hundred of us from as many as twenty clubs, all staying at a city centre hotel. It was a new and interesting way of approaching the job, and we went along with open minds to see what happened. There were five of us from Newcastle – me, John Tudor, Terry Hibbitt, Terry McDermott and, I think, Irving Nattrass – and my club colleagues found it inspirational because they had never been considered at international level before and were now getting some recognition.

We all arrived in Manchester on the Saturday after our games and were told there would be a meeting on the Sunday morning. Most of the players saw that as an excuse to enjoy their Saturday night in the usual way, but I played it very cagey. I decided to keep my head down, because international football was hugely important to me and I didn't know this guy Revie. I only knew what had been passed on by the Leeds players, and they thought the world of the man. Even so, I reckoned I faced some fierce competition in Mick Jones and Allan Clarke, the strikers who had served Leeds and Don Revie brilliantly. So I thought to myself, 'Tread very carefully, don't give this feller an inch.' I did go out, but I made very sure I was back a good fifteen minutes before the midnight curfew. I also made sure that everybody in Revie's managerial party saw me in that hotel at a quarter to twelve. There were always a few who went well overboard, but I decided on this occasion to keep my nose clean and look after my own interests. John Tudor was with me, and we had a couple of beers in the hotel before going off to bed.

The two of us felt very virtuous the next morning, then, when we saw how many sore heads and bleary eyes there were at the meeting with Revie. We listened to him outline his thinking, had some lunch, then departed. We, the Newcastle contingent, had come from London, where we'd been playing Queens Park Rangers, to Manchester by train, but it was difficult in those days to get from Manchester to Newcastle by the same means, so we decided to hire a car.

On the way back, John said, 'Well, what did you think, then?'

At that, everybody turned to me because I'd been a regular in England's international squads. 'Well, I'm sitting here, driving this car, and I can't remember what he said,' I replied. And there really was nothing in what Revie had said that stuck with me at all. It had been a case of 'do this, but don't do that', and I had found it very basic. It was almost as if I was being talked to as a new kid in the game, a sixteen-year-old apprentice. But I didn't want to pour too much cold water on the experience for the others, so I just added, 'What did you get out of it?'

They seemed to be fascinated by what they had heard.

'I thought he had a lot to impart,' said John.

'Like what?' I responded.

'Well, the playing of the game,' he said.

'But what did he really say about the playing of the game?' I insisted. 'All he said you know anyway just from watching Leeds United. You only have to play against Leeds once to know what his thinking is about the playing of the game.'

John disagreed with me; he was an eager beaver who thought a new era was dawning. He also thought that, having been included in the call-up, he might have a chance of playing for England.

Terry Hibbitt saw it very differently, however. He had worked with Revie at Leeds and took a more pessimistic view. 'All he's doing,' said Hibby, 'is setting out the ground rules and warning you not to break them. The stick he will beat you with will follow.'

Revie excluded me from two squads, those for the European Championship qualifiers against Czechoslovakia and Portugal in the autumn of 1974, before public opinion forced him to change his mind. After a goalless draw with the Portuguese at Wembley, there was a huge clamour in the papers for him to include a recognised goalscorer in the side. It was more or less a straight choice between me and Francis Lee, because early in 1975 we were neck and neck at the top of the First Division scoring charts, and he chose me.

It was quite a game to come in for, too: West Germany at Wembley.

The Germans had been crowned world champions only the summer before, and now they were coming to England to play one of their first matches – it may even have been the first – after winning the World Cup. Full of the joys of spring, I drove down to the West Lodge Park Hotel and walked into the reception area. Don Revie was there with Les Cocker, his sidekick from Leeds whom he'd taken with him into the England set-up, and a few other bods.

When we'd had that get-together in Manchester, Revie had made it abundantly clear that every player was to call him 'Boss', so I went across and said, 'Afternoon, Boss. No injuries from yesterday. I'm fine.'

At which he looked up at me and said, 'You do realise that I don't want you here?'

I was used to the banter of Alec Stock and Joe Harvey, so I expected a joke to follow, but no such luck on this occasion. With Revie, there was no humour – none whatsoever.

'I've been under immense pressure to bring you in,' he added, 'and it's against my better judgement.'

I just stayed silent, wondering what on earth was coming next.

'Right,' he said, 'you're playing on Wednesday, and if you don't score I'll never pick you again.'

'Oh, OK,' I said. 'Thanks for the welcome.'

Having checked in and gone up to my room, I reflected on what Revie had said. There was good and bad in it, and the optimist and the pessimist were fighting for supremacy within me. The bad was that it placed me under enormous pressure, because you could always play bloody well and not score. Nobody, and especially the manager, should put any player under that kind of pressure. On the other hand, I knew I was playing and was probably one step ahead of everybody else. Playing, too, against the world champions.

I have to confess I couldn't keep it a secret. After training, I was sitting next to Alan Ball on the bus, and he remarked that I had been a bit quiet the previous night. I told him I'd had a lot to think about, and explained why. 'Bastard!' exclaimed Bally when I related what Revie had said. 'That is so out of order!' During training on the Monday and Tuesday, Bally, who'd been appointed England captain for that game and kept the job for the next five, had a little word here and there with

Mick Channon, Colin Bell and a few of the other players. 'Don't you worry,' he told me afterwards. 'You just keep making your runs and leave the rest to us.'

In the match, Colin put us ahead in the first half, and said to me, 'I wish it had hit you and gone in, then you could have stuck your arm up.' Bally, too, did his best to get me a goal, laying on a terrific ball in the second half that left me one on one with the great Franz Beckenbauer. I was away and starting to motor when Beckenbauer rugby-tackled me. Today, he would have got sent off; then, the referee just gave a free-kick. I was so angry I wanted to punch the distinguished German captain. That had been my golden opportunity, that was just what I had been waiting for, and he had robbed me of it. 'You bastard!' I thought. A bit later in the second half, though, Mick Channon was clattered while chasing a pass down the right-hand side of the box. He had gone down on top of the ball, and without rising to his feet he tapped a quick free-kick short with his knee. Bally came in and lofted the ball into the goalmouth, where I lost Beckenbauer and another West German defender, and came round them to nod the ball between goalkeeper Sepp Maier and the far post. It was my first goal at Wembley, my first senior goal for England, and I didn't even realise it at the time. All I was thinking was, 'Go on, Don Revie, f★★★ing pick the bones out of that! Now what are you going to do?' Bally was not a Revie lover – there was past history of some sort between them – and he came running over to me full of joy. Mick and Colin were also delighted for me. 'Just you relax!' they all said. 'The problem's over there now.'

Before that game against West Germany in March 1975, I had also told Joe Harvey what Revie had said to me on arrival at West Lodge Park, and he'd been shocked rigid by it. 'You know what you've got to do, sunshine,' he said. 'You don't need me to tell you. And, to be quite honest, you're the worst person in the world to throw a challenge like that to, aren't you?'

Not that Joe let the matter rest himself. Quite a long while afterwards, a good friend of Joe's, Bobby Cowans, told me a tale that Joe himself had never mentioned. Bobby, a businessman who had played at full-back in that great Newcastle team with Joe and who acted almost as his unpaid assistant manager at St James's Park, said Joe had bumped into

Revie at a midweek game.

'Did they talk?' I asked.

'Talk?' said Bobby. 'Joe ripped him off in front of everybody in the room for what he said to you. He absolutely slaughtered him in front of all those football people, and quite a few have wanted to talk to him like that for a long time. He said, "Never mind the fact that he is my player, you don't do that to any player! I'd be saying this to you if you'd said the same to a player from any other club."'

My goal was the last of a match we won 2–0. It had been a wonderful game, and England had got the better of the world champions with an emphatic performance that had everybody enthusing over it. We were in the mood to celebrate, and Bally provided the opportunity by arranging to meet the German players at La Valbonne, a nightclub just off Regent Street. Because of 1966 and all that, Alan knew the Germans better than he knew some of the England players, and they held him in utter reverence.

Under Alf, we'd always been put up in London on the night of the game and could travel back to our clubs the following day. Revie changed all that and made us go back right after the game. But, by the time everything's done, you're talking about it being eleven o'clock when you're ready to go. In my case, that then meant a four-hour drive back to Newcastle through the night, but only after catching the team bus back to the West Lodge Park Hotel to pick up my car. Nobody needs that after playing for England in an international match! So I'd organised myself a hotel in London. I stayed at the Holiday Inn, Swiss Cottage, in a suite of rooms booked by Roy Santos, a Portuguese restaurant owner from Newcastle who always went to England matches with a few friends. Roy was a fabulous guy and a very funny man. What a sense of humour he had! He'd have everybody in fits at times, but he didn't realise he was being funny; it was just his disposition.

Anyway, I took him and his friends along with me to La Valbonne, where we joined Bally, Mick Channon and the other southern-based players. They were there with Franz Beckenbauer, Berti Vogts, Sepp Maier and Gerd Müller. 'Right,' said Bally, 'give us fifty quid!' He took £50 from each of the England players and told the waiter, 'I want champagne. Just keep bringing champagne!' He also insisted that the Germans did not buy a drink all night. 'No, no,' he said to them, 'you always look after us when we come to play you. This is our treat.' In the end, that night out probably cost me more than I had earned. At that time, we got £200 for winning but nothing at all for playing. I also had the hotel to pay for. I couldn't get that on expenses because it was after the game and I was supposed to be on my way back to Newcastle. So it really cost me some money that night, but who cares? It was wonderful. We just sat there and talked football. To be with people like Beckenbauer and Bally, and to listen to them talking through the 1966 World Cup final again, was like being in some kind of seventh heaven. I felt honoured to be in such illustrious company. La Valbonne was open until about three o'clock in the morning, and we stayed until they kicked us out.

Roy Santos was bowled over because these great players had not dismissed him and his friends in any way. It had been a case of, 'If they are friends of yours, then they are friends of ours.' They welcomed them fully. Roy and his mates were all prepared to put their £50 in. In fact, Roy would have been quite happy to pay for the lot himself, but I wouldn't hear of it. 'No,' I said, 'this is down to us England players. If we need more money, we'll let you know.' Roy was as chuffed as anybody I've ever seen to be regarded as one of the boys in this company. He was even more chuffed when, addressing Beckenbauer as 'Mr Beckenbauer', he was told by the great German captain to call him 'Franz'.

During that magical night, we had some deep conversations comparing the way the game was played in Germany and England. The Germans were critical of the way the English resorted to booting the ball upfield. They argued that with four or five good passes you could easily get from one penalty area in full control of the ball; if you booted it, it might take half the time, but you weren't necessarily in control of the ball when you got there. All the different philosophies on the game were coming out, and I loved it.

Incidentally, Don Revie later changed the way England players were paid. One day he came in and he had a smile like the Cheshire Cat's on his face. He couldn't contain his excitement, and was clearly expecting a pat on the back. 'Right,' he said, 'gather round everybody. I've got some very important news for all of you. I have negotiated on your behalf with the FA and changed the whole financial structure for you.

I have got you a £200 match fee plus your win and draw bonuses (£200 and £100). You are professionals and you have the right to be paid for playing, whatever the result.'

Revie, however, did not get quite the response he had hoped for.

'Boss,' Alan Ball piped up, 'when it comes to playing for England, the fact that I've got three lions over my heart is all the payment I need.'

That shut Revie right up, but I saw the look in his eyes and I thought to myself, 'Bally, you will live to regret that. He will make you suffer.' And, sure enough, Alan remained in the squad for just another game or two, and then he was gone.

It was Revie, too, who brought in Admiral as the first sponsors and suppliers of England's kit, their version of which, with its collars and garish stripes, I thought was horrible. It seemed everything was money, money, money to the former Leeds manager, so much so that it was easy to understand why he was nicknamed 'Don Readies'. By the same token, I suppose, people could argue that he had great foresight and was merely laying the foundations of the commercial enterprise the England squad has now become.

The victory over West Germany gave the whole country a huge lift. It was a fabulous feeling to have beaten the world champions, and from what other people were saying to me, the mood of the nation was reminiscent of 1966. Then, just a month later, we went from one extreme, West Germany, to another: the arrival at Wembley of little Cyprus for a European Championship qualifying match.

After the emphatic victory over the world champions, it was always going to be interesting to see what squad Revie would pick. It seemed to me it would be crazy to change anything, so I was not surprised to be included. Joe Harvey was chuffed to bits at the news and wondered what Revie would say to me this time. 'I don't know, Joe,' I said. 'I'll let you know. Let's just see.'

Newcastle played, as usual, on the Saturday, and the next day I drove down to the West Lodge Park Hotel. I went through the door with my bag, and there was Don Revie, sitting with Les Cocker and the rest of his entourage. 'Hello, Boss,' I said. 'There are no injuries at all from yesterday. I'm fine.'

Revie looked at me and said, 'I'm still not happy about you being in the squad. I still feel you've been foisted on me by the press. The same rule applies as before: if you don't score, I'll never pick you again.'

As you can imagine, I was absolutely flabbergasted. The words had been almost spat at me, and I wondered what on earth I had to do to win this guy over. His demeanour told me that this wasn't just a footballing decision; there was something else to it all. This second time, certainly, I felt it was more of a personal thing, but I couldn't understand it because our paths had never really crossed before. Whenever I'd played against Leeds United I had always been polite and respectful to the manager, as I was at all opposing grounds. So I had no idea what the problem was, and I never did find out.

During training, Bally asked me if everything was all right, so again I told him what had happened. 'Bally,' I said, 'I can't believe it! He's done exactly the same thing to me. If I don't score, I'll never get picked again.'

'What a bastard!' said Bally. 'Right, we'll get it sorted.'

After the team meeting on the Wednesday afternoon, he called Mick Channon and a few of the others over and told them to do the same thing as before. 'Let's go for it against Cyprus,' he said. 'Do you know, Mal, that nobody has ever scored six goals in one game for England? That's what you're aiming for tonight, and it's our job, guys, to help him get them.' Now, given what later transpired, people reading this will probably think I've made it all up, but I haven't. It was a totally audacious plan, I'll grant you, but it was nothing more than a typical Alan Ball reaction to a pressure situation. Extreme action was called for, and that action was going to be carried out in the terms he knew best – footballing terms. Bally had even gone to the record books to discover that nobody had ever scored six for England in a professional game. Vivian Woodward had done it against Holland in 1909, but that was only an amateur international. 'Willie Hall scored five against Ireland in 1938,' he told us, 'but nobody's got six. That's our target for Mal tonight. Make sure that ball gets in there for him.'

The evening didn't start promisingly at all, I have to say. On the way to Wembley, the police outriders accompanying the team coach took us into Hadley Wood, which is a vast area near Barnet full of narrow roads. One road was so narrow that the bus couldn't take a corner as easily as the police motorbikes. The driver tried to rectify the situation by reversing, but only succeeded in getting stuck on a grass verge. So we all had to pile out to help push the bus clear. Most of us jockeyed for position at the back to avoid the spinning rear wheels, and we were laughing and joking among ourselves as to who was going to be the idiot to get behind one of them. Step forward the hulking Peter Shilton, who was clearly determined to push the bus clear all by himself. He put his massive hands on the back of it and, sure enough, it started to claw its way clear of the soft ground. Unfortunately for Shilts, at the same time the wheels sprayed out mud and covered him from head to toe. Since he was all dressed up in his England uniform of blazer and slacks, Shilts was not at all pleased, I can tell you. In fact, as he was trying to clean himself up he was threatening to sue the FA, the bus company, the police and anybody else he could think of. But at least it gave the rest of us a bit of a giggle and put us in a good mood for the game.

The first of my five goals came early in the first half from a free-kick awarded to us about ten yards in from the left touchline, and level with the penalty area. Alan Hudson took the kick and flighted it into the goalmouth. Dave Watson, our big centre-half from Sunderland, looked like getting to the ball first, but I sprinted past him and headed it into the corner of the net. Bally came running up to me and said, 'Right, that's the first. Come on, five more to go!' Then, late in the first half, Kevin Keegan performed a little bit of dribbling magic to the left of goal, but as everybody was going into the congested six-yard area, I withdrew. I went the opposite way to create the angle for a pull-back, and Kevin duly obliged. It was a bobbly old ball that came up almost to waist height, but, by getting right over the top of it as I had practised so hard at Luton, I volleyed the pass into the ground and into the far corner. That made it 2–0 to England at half-time.

The feeling in the dressing-room during the interval was that we'd got the game sewn up; they were not going to cause us a problem as long as we just played it sensibly. But here was an opportunity, we decided, to make goal difference count in the qualifying group, so we went out for the second half and Kevin again did some super work on the left-hand side of the Cyprus goal. I was unmarked when he played the ball into the middle, so all I had to do to complete my hat-trick was duck and nod the ball over the line as the goalkeeper came out. After the second goal, Bally had run up to me again and said, 'Come on, only four to go now!' This time, though, he changed his tune slightly. After the other players had finished congratulating me on my third goal, our little captain said, 'You're halfway there now. Come on, get yourself a second hat-trick!' As we're running back to the centre circle to restart the game, Kevin Keegan sidled up to me. He'd congratulated me on the third goal, but now he said, 'All right, you greedy bastard, you've got your hat-trick, how about making one for somebody else?' Grimly determined to make a scoring statement to Don Revie, however, and with Bally's exhortations about a second hat-trick ringing in my ears, all I could think of by way of a reply was, 'Kevin, f★★k off and get your own!' I was a man on a mission.

The next development saw Mick Channon replaced halfway through the second half by Dave Thomas, the Queens Park Rangers winger. He played outside-right, which suited me enormously because he was a great crosser of the ball on the run. He would whip it in, crossbar height. Bally understood this, and moved to a sort of inside-right position with the intention of just feeding Dave in behind the full-back, which he did. When Dave whipped in his first cross, I reached a hell of a height to get to the ball and powered it into the top corner with my head. Sure enough, Bally came running over again and said, 'Come on, you're on your way now! That's four – only two more to go!' He helped me get my fifth by sending Dave Thomas to the byline in the dying minutes, then immediately geed me up again by saying, 'Come on! One more and you've got the all-time scoring record for England!' I tried hard to respond, but hit the post with a volley and also had a goal disallowed for offside against somebody else, so in the end it wasn't to be. Cyprus, admittedly, were no great shakes in international terms, but 5–0 is a convincing win no matter who it's against, particularly when you're playing in the European Championship.

When the final whistle blew, I was in the Cypriot six-yard box at the far end from the tunnel. I knew I'd set a Wembley record, and that I'd equalled Willie Hall's record for England, so I was delighted to see what flashed up on the scoreboard above the tunnel. Whoever was operating it had changed the usual scoreline and replaced it with CONGRATULATIONS! SUPERMAC 5 CYPRUS 0. In fact, that whole evening was a boyhood dream come true. It was the kind of dream everybody connected with football has had as a schoolkid, and I had just made it a reality. The crowd were going daft, but I just looked at that scoreboard, looked across at Don Revie as, head down, he made his way round the running track, and thought, 'Read that and weep! What are you going to say about that, you bastard?'

As it turned out, he said bugger all. In the dressing-room, Revie went round shaking hands with every player in turn, saying, 'Well done!' But when he got to me, he blanked me like he'd done after the West Germany game. I'd just equalled the individual scoring record for England, and the manager never said a word! Bally and Mick Channon just looked at me and said, 'Don't worry, we saw it. We won't forget. The man is impossible.' Revie then left the dressing-room. We all got ourselves into the bath, but while we were in there he returned. Among all the other reasons I had for despising him, he never, ever called me by name. He would just look at me and start talking, or he'd say 'You'. Now, he looked down into the deep plunge baths they used to have in the Wembley dressing-rooms and said, 'You, the press want to talk to you, and BBC Television want to interview you. Get yourself out of the bath and get changed.'

When I'd got dressed and packed my bag, I followed Revie through the maze of corridors at Wembley to the BBC's whitewashed interview room. Normally, the television people are always bubbly so that they create a good, warm atmosphere for the interviewee and the viewer, no matter how dank and gloomy the surroundings might be, but when I walked in, I was greeted by a cold, frosty atmosphere. Normally there was lots of banter and people fawning over you, but this time everybody seemed distant and unfriendly. Tony Gubba was the interviewer, and I tried to engage him in conversation before going on air, but he made out he was reading his notes. Having got the signal we were now live to the nation, Tony said, 'Welcome back to Wembley Stadium. I have with me tonight's goalscorer, Malcolm Macdonald.' Then, turning to me, he said, 'Malcolm, you might have scored five, but tell us about the two you missed.' Well, I was gobsmacked. I thought to myself, 'What kind of a question is that?' I blustered my way through it and got on to other things, but it felt like a put-down interview.

Still wondering what the hell was going on, I moved on from there to face the press. As we were walking from one place to the other, Revie said to me, 'I've got it all sorted out. I've got it all organised,' and I remembered that he'd said the same thing on the way to the television interview. Puzzled by what he meant, I walked into the press conference room straight into another strange atmosphere. Things were definitely not as they normally were, but I couldn't quite put my finger on what was wrong.

It wasn't until the following season that I discovered what had actually happened. Having scored the most goals for Newcastle in a big home win against (I think) Coventry, I was surprised not to be asked for interview for *Match of the Day* afterwards, as was the custom. They interviewed another Newcastle player instead. Then, when I bumped into the *Match of the Day* crew by accident that evening as they were leaving their hotel, I was even more surprised to be snubbed by big John McGonagle, the programme's producer. Usually such a lovely, affable man, John snarled, 'I don't know how you've got the cheek to try to shake me by the hand after what you did to me at Wembley.'

Taken aback, I said, 'I beg your pardon, John?'

'You know what you did to me at Wembley,' he insisted, 'and you offer me your hand. How dare you!'

'John,' I replied, 'I haven't got the foggiest idea what you're talking about. If it's to do with the Cyprus match, all I can say is that the atmosphere in your interview room was very strange and I was feeling uncomfortable. By the way, Reg Hayter says he has never received the standard payment of £25 for the interview.'

That sent John into apoplexy. 'I've already paid you!' he spluttered.

'No you haven't,' I retorted.

'Yes, I have,' he insisted. 'I gave Don Revie £200 in cash for that interview.'

'John, I don't know what you're talking about.'

'Don Revie came to us at the end of the game and said that you wouldn't come for an interview unless you were paid £200 in cash.'

'You're joking, aren't you, John?'

'I am not. You demanded...'

'Wait a minute, *I* didn't demand, Revie demanded. Apart from anything else, the guy never spoke to me and would never listen to anything I might have to say.'

All of a sudden, John lost the puffed-up look of an irate man. 'Do you know,' he said, 'I had to have a whip-round to raise that £200. I emptied my wallet of the £40 I had in it, I got £30 off the sound man, I got £25 off the lighting engineer and so on. We all chipped in to get that £200 together because we don't carry that kind of money to pay out on fees. And now you're telling me you never saw any of that money?'

'That's exactly what I'm telling you. I never saw a penny of it, and neither did I ask for it.'

'Well, I never!' he said.

And to this day I've never been paid for that interview. So, to add insult to injury, Revie not only refused to congratulate me for scoring those five goals against Cyprus, he seemed to have made a few quid out of my achievement himself. Worse still, as a result I have not had as good a relationship with the BBC since then as I once had. And then, to cap it all, after scoring a total of six goals in those two games – an England record even today – Revie still saw fit, after an end-of-season training get-together, to send a scathing report about me to my club manager, Joe Harvey. Joe called me into his office and said, 'I don't know why I bought you!'

'How do you mean?' I said.

'Well,' he explained, 'according to Don Revie, there's an awful lot you can't do. You can't do this, you can't do that; you're no good at this, you're no good at that. I take it, then, that when you were down at the training get-together you didn't do any shooting, or anything like that. Any work around the goal?'

'Nothing at all,' I assured him. 'It was completely without targets of any kind. It was just control and pass, sometimes under pressure, sometimes not.'

'Well, yes,' Joe conceded, 'your touch is not the best under those circumstances, but you're not that type of player. Revie has said in his letter that he expects me, as your club manager, to work unceasingly on correcting your faults. But I'm not sure that's the best way for a manager to proceed. It's more sensible, I think, to decide what a player can do before working on what he can't. Don's got the cart before the horse on this one, so I'll tell you what I'm going to do. I'm going to file this in a special file.' And with that, he threw the report straight into the bin.

All along, Joe had urged me not to change my style of play in an attempt to get into or stay in the England side. He reminded me that Alf Ramsey had called me up regularly and been quite happy with the way I played. Never once had Alf asked Joe to work on my control or any other aspect of my game. Joe told me that all Alf had ever said was that he was delighted I could run like the wind and wanted to take centre-halves on all the time. 'Alf recognised what your strengths are,' said Joe, 'and if we are happy with you, why can't this guy be?'

Ironically, my last game for Revie and for England was the European Championship qualifier away to Portugal in November 1975, in Lisbon, where only eighteen months earlier Alf Ramsey, before his last game as manager, had indicated to me and others that we were the future of English football. Because that friendly was so recent, about half a dozen of us in Revie's squad had played in it, and we knew that we should have won it easily. So we couldn't believe it, just a year and a half later, when we got this dossier from Revie which made the Portuguese out to be the best side in the world. In fact, every time we played under his management, we seemed to play the best side in the world. Strange, that. Even before the first Cyprus game we had these bulky brown envelopes pushed across the table to us. They contained detailed descriptions of 35 players, only about three of whom actually played, and made a country that had only ever won about three games in their history sound like Brazil. (The brown envelopes, incidentally, made us players feel like spies getting our orders. All that was missing was the cyanide pill!) I was left with the impression that these player profiles were a figment of somebody's imagination, put together in an effort to stir us up psychologically. The trouble was that one or two of the players had taken the dossier really seriously, so Alan Ball, Mick Channon, Alan Hudson and I had tried to impress on them that it was only Cyprus we were facing and that what really mattered was how *we* played. But it was causing a rift in the camp. On the one side, you had those who had the self-belief to go out and play the game and do what they did best; on the other were those who believed every word of the dossiers and, if not quite full of fear, went out on the back foot, as it were, in readiness for a Brazil-like attack.

We were fed the same kind of dispiriting information before the game against Portugal in Lisbon in November 1975. During training, and in meetings to discuss the opposition, I'd be hearing how great and strong and powerful and quick and fluent the Portuguese were, but that didn't square with what I'd discovered for myself only eighteen months earlier, when England drew 0–0 in Lisbon but should have beaten the Portuguese backsides. From what I could see, it was pretty much the same Portugal side we'd be playing, and I couldn't imagine they'd suddenly become supermen in a year and a half.

I found myself getting into a ruck with Les Cocker over this, and realised I was really getting into a ruck with Don Revie, who was looking daggers at me. It cost me dear, too, given that he subbed me about five minutes into the second half. I couldn't believe it, because I had been the only England player threatening the Portugal goal. Their keeper had made three brilliant saves off me, and I was growing in confidence all the time. I knew that the chance would come and I'd bury it, but he took me off. I think he sensed I was going to notch that night, and he decided to get me off before I could. As I was walking off, I thought, 'That's it. I'll never see an England shirt again as long as Revie's manager.'

Two years later, of course, he departed for the United Arab Emirates, and I was rubbing my hands in anticipation of a return to the England squad. I was only 27 when Revie went, I was now playing for Arsenal, I was absolutely on top of my game and I was playing the best football of my life. But the FA did the worst thing possible for me personally by appointing Ron Greenwood as Revie's successor. I had nothing at all against Ron as a person; in fact, we got on quite well. Unfortunately, to the way his footballing mind worked, I was the complete antithesis of his ideal centre forward. That's when I knew for sure that I'd never pull on an England shirt again.

# CHAPTER EIGHT
# FULHAM: FEET OF CLAY

L ike a lot of footballers, I wasn't quite sure what to do with myself
when injury forced me into retirement at 29. Unlike the players of
today, those of my era did not earn enough to set themselves up for life,
and it was necessary to look for some other way of making a living
when we stopped playing.

My future began to look a lot rosier when I was approached by Sam
Leitch, head of sport at Thames Television, the company that used to
provide ITV's weekday coverage in the London area. Sam, a real football
man, had become famous as a football writer for the *People* and was a
good friend of my agent, Reg Hayter. It was through Reg that Sam and
I met for lunch. When he asked me if I was interested in a career in
television, I jumped at the chance. I had never had any inclination at all
to be a football manager. I had thoroughly enjoyed playing the game, but
managing it I saw as nothing but absolute frustration. The thought of
trying to get people to do what you know you could do better were you
young and fit again did not appeal to me at all. I did enjoy my media
work, though. I still had my column with the *Sun*, for instance.

Sam told me that he wanted to revamp Thames' sports coverage completely. Above all, he was aiming to get rid of the old stiff collars who basically did everything out of the studio. 'I want to get in amongst it,' he said, 'and that would be ideal for you. Let's get out among the players, the managers and the coaches. You can interview them knowledgeably because you know them and know what to say to them. You know how to get the right kind of conversation flowing. That's what I'm after!' It all sounded just fine to me, and I told him so. His plan was for me to do this big preview of the weekend football on a Friday evening between about 5.30 and six o'clock, just before Thames handed over coverage to London Weekend. He told me that his producer, another Sam, would be getting in touch with me at the start of the following season, 1979/80, and that he wanted me to get used to studio work in the meantime. Better still, the money I would be earning was far in excess of what I'd been getting at Arsenal.

Sure enough, Sam the producer made contact with me in advance of the new season and we decided my first assignment should be a feature on Crystal Palace. Terry Venables was their manager for the first time then, and his talented young 'Team of the Eighties' had climbed from the old Third Division into the First. It seemed a good place to start. I went home from my meeting with young Sam feeling really chuffed, but knowing I had a major task on my hands. That TV work ain't as easy as it looks, you know.

It was then that I received a mysterious telephone call from somebody at Thames. 'Please don't ask my name,' the male voice said, 'because if I'm ever identified I will be in very serious trouble. No calls are supposed to be made out of the building, but this is just to let you know that all the unions have gone on strike, so don't bother turning up at the Crystal Palace training ground. At the moment, we are trying to avert a closing down and going off air, but Sam (which of the two, I don't know) has asked me to ask you to just sit tight. As soon as this thing's blown over in a few days' time, we'll be in touch and get everything going again.'

Sure enough, there were huge headlines about the strike the following day. All the technicians had walked out and ITV was blacked out, not for just one or two nights, but for six weeks. That meant I was

*Newcastle goalkeeper Mick Mahoney, an old mate, and I exchange pleasantries during my first game against my former club as an Arsenal player.*

*Just to prove my goalscoring wasn't all about power and pace, I lob Leeds goalkeeper David Harvey and Gordon McQueen (on the line) with a touch of finesse.*

*The 1978 FA Cup semi-final against Leyton Orient that we won 3-0. I claimed two of the three, even though ITV commentator Brian Moore argued they were own goals.*

*Terry Yorath heads the ball away as I jump for it between him and Mike England during my full England debut against Wales in 1972.*

*In that same game, I show what I can do on the ground.*

*Sinister-looking sightseers Emlyn Hughes, Larry Lloyd and I peer over the Berlin Wall before England's goalless draw with West Germany in May, 1972.*

*Bang! In goes the fourth of the five goals I scored against Cyprus at Wembley in 1975. The Cypriot on his heels is Greg Savva, who was a pro with Fulham at the time.*

*A stunted picture at Checkpoint Charlie. We didn't want to go over into East Berlin, and the American border guard is just pretending to examine our passports.*

*More frustration for me on my full England debut as Wales goalkeeper Gary Sprake gathers the ball before I can get to it.*

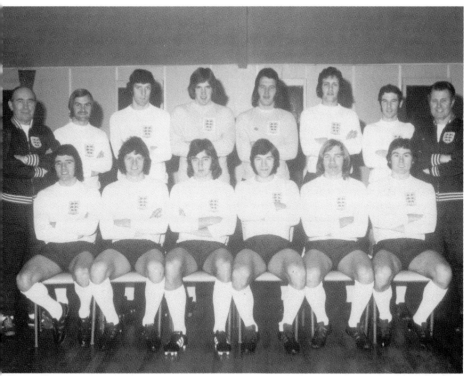

An England Under-23 team that never played together. Many of us were already in the senior side, but Sir Alf Ramsey wanted a picture showing the up and coming talent.

With two of my favourite people. Luton's chief scout Harry Haslam (left), Newcastle manager Joe Harvey and I celebrate my transfer from Luton to Newcastle with a cup of tea.

*Preparing for my second career. Wearing an unmistakable 1970s shirt, I do my Thursday afternoon programme for BBC Radio Newcastle.*

*Managing Huddersfield was not the happiest time of my life, and the strain shows as I make my feelings known on the touchline.*

*Carol, my wife, and I had just met for the first time when this picture was taken 30 years ago. We did not meet again until 25 years later.*

I competed three times in BBC TV's multi-sport series, 'Superstars'. I won the one in Mälmo, Sweden, clocking a very respectable 10.4 secs for the 100 metres.

When we were young – or a lot younger. Bobby Robson and I suck a half-time orange during a charity match in Co. Durham about 20 years ago.

One of the proudest moments of my life. Lining up at the Park Lane Hilton in 1999 with the other surviving players named among the best 100 in the Football League's long history. I am second from the right in the front row, with Bryan Robson to my left, Alan Shearer and Geoff Hurst to my right and Len Shackleton directly behind me.

*Back on Tyneside after all my post-career trials and tribulations, I host the radio 'phone-in programme I did for Century before they were bought out by Capital.*

*A fantastic and moving experience. I get a standing ovation from the Toon Army when filling the guest player spot at half-time in the game against Liverpool last season.*

left in limbo at a time when I was raring to go. I'd even gone out and bought a whole range of clothing for television purposes. I was mightily relieved, then, when the strike ended and all the ITV people went back to work. The clubs had begun pre-season training by then, too, but there was still no contact from either of the Sams at Thames.

Anxious about this, I phoned Reg. 'Are they going to call me or what?' I asked him.

'I've got some bad news for you, I'm afraid,' he said. 'I just heard about it late last night and I've been trying to get it verified. It affects you badly.'

'What's the news?'

'Sam Leitch has died.'

'I'm sorry to hear that, Reg.'

'Yes, it came as a bit of a shock. But that's not all the bad news. I've heard that Sam, his young producer, has died as well.'

'You're kidding, aren't you?' I said, scarcely able to believe what I was hearing. 'The fellow was only in his late twenties!'

'It seems he died from a rare condition, some obstruction. The two of them have gone within the space of a few hours.'

Naturally, after receiving this astonishing news, I wanted to know what happened next. Reg suggested we might have to wait until a new head of sport was appointed because there had been a glitch over my contract. I had signed it, but the strike had intervened before Sam Leitch had been able to countersign it and send me a copy. So I was left waiting again, with Reg unable to get any sense out of anybody.

'It seems they are in utter turmoil,' he told me later. 'All the money they've had to give to the unions has created such a huge financial levy on them that they're having to reschedule budgets. The whole place is in uproar, so don't hold out too much hope.'

When there was no further contact, I felt that, since I had signed the contract in good faith, I might have a legal claim against Thames. When we sought advice from my solicitor friend Alan Hurd, he thought we would probably win the case, but he also pointed out that my two primary witnesses were dead and that Thames could drag out the legal proceedings for years. 'What would you get out of it?' he asked, thinking not only of the time and cost but the danger of prejudicing any future television work. After talking the situation over, Reg and I decided to walk away, forget it and go on to something else. But what?

Another option seemed to have been provided by Ernie Clay, the Fulham chairman, who had contacted me while I was in limbo waiting to hear from Thames. I knew Ernie because he and Eric Miller, then a Fulham director and not yet knighted, had tried unsuccessfully to persuade me to challenge the retain and transfer system further when I was having problems with Newcastle. Ernie, of course, had backed George Eastham in his successful legal action against the system in 1963. Now, he appeared to be offering me a job. I had been trying to hold him at arm's length, not really wanting to get involved, but when Thames did next to nothing on football after getting back on air, I agreed to listen to him more closely.

The trouble with Ernie was that you could never have a straight conversation with him; he would go all round the houses rather than get to the point. First, you had to discover the riddle in the maze of words; then you had to work out the solution to it. It could be a bit tiring talking to Ernie, believe me! I used to find it funny whenever I saw him described in the papers as a blunt, straight-talking Yorkshireman. He was anything but that! I found his conversational manner particularly irritating because I have a habit of being somewhat direct. I'm not rude, but I do like to see the head of the hammer put to the head of the nail. So, getting to the point, I said to Ernie, 'I'm taking it that you're offering me the commercial manager's job at Fulham Football Club?'

'No, no, no,' he replied. 'You don't understand.'

'Well, I will do, Ernie, if you speak clearly about what you want.'

'Well, you see, it's like this...' and off we went around the houses again, but by a different route.

'Look, Ernie,' I said, 'what you're basically after is a commercial manager for Fulham, isn't it?'

After a lot of humming and hawing, he conceded that that was indeed what he wanted, and that is what I became.

I soon saw why a commercial manager was needed, because there was next to no commercialisation at all at Fulham. They ran a little bit of a lottery and they sold a few advertisements around the ground and in the programme, and that, basically, was it. There was nothing else going on; it was a completely neglected area. I began by setting out to find a sponsor and started talking to business people I knew, through Reg, who were looking for that kind of investment opportunity. What I discovered, though, was that nobody was interested in doing a deal with Fulham; if I'd been representing Arsenal, I was told time and again, well, that's another matter. When I reported this to Ernie and suggested an entirely different approach, he asked me to draw up a plan of attack, so I took on somebody with a bit of oomph to revamp the lottery and all sorts of other things. Wherever I went, too, I promoted the idea that Fulham Football Club was open to all sorts of commercial ideas and had a progressive chairman. But what I found – and this happened several times – was that people would say, 'Oh, yes, I've heard of him', then change the subject very quickly. 'Hmm, problems here,' I thought.

To be honest, I did not enjoy the year I spent as Fulham's commercial manager. I felt I was capable of an awful lot more. 'Nobody is interested in Fulham because the team isn't doing anything,' I told Ernie Clay. 'It's a complete waste of time!' It was certainly very hard to raise any commercial interest in a side that was languishing in the old Third Division at the end of that season and which began the next one dreadfully. I had to rethink my position, apart from anything else because the job was so time-consuming.

All that time I had stayed well away from the playing side of the club, but word had got back to me that the manager, Bobby Campbell, wasn't happy about my association with Ernie Clay. That annoyed me a little bit because, having heard Alan Ball speak in glowing terms about Bobby as a coach when he was at Arsenal before I arrived, when I became commercial manager I'd gone out of my way to meet the Fulham manager and set out my position. 'Look, Bob,' I'd said, 'it might seem highly suspicious if I'm around the place, but I'm purely and simply looking for commercial business. I'm not looking for involvement in your side of things in any shape or form.' That was the only time we ever spoke. Although our paths crossed several times over the ensuing months, Bobby Campbell did not utter another word to me. His assistant, Mike Kelly, displayed the same sort of attitude, and I have to say I found that a rather blinkered approach. I never once got involved with the players, and I only ever went into the boardroom on the odd occasion after a game. I never discussed the team's form or football with Ernie either. 'I will not do it,' I told the chairman. 'It's hard enough being a football manager without somebody else putting their oar in behind your back. I will never do that!'

Having said that, by the time Bobby Campbell and Mike Kelly were sacked, in October 1980, I have to admit I had developed a huge yearning to become involved with the actual playing of the game itself. Thoroughly frustrated in my job as commercial manager, I often found myself thinking when driving home, 'Yes, I could do that!' I can also put my hand on my heart and say that I played no part in the dismissal of either Campbell or Kelly. Ernie did not consult me about the decision and it was as big a shock to me as it was to anybody else. But after they'd gone, I thought 'What the hell!' and rang Ernie up.

'I've thought about this,' I said, 'and there is something powerful building up inside me. If you want somebody to take over as manager, are you willing to talk to me, or should I forget it?'

Ernie ducked and dived, as usual.

'Look,' I continued, 'I've asked you a straight question – are you going to talk to me or not? If you say no, fine. All I'm saying is that the position is there and I feel I could do it, and do it well.'

Still he vacillated and remained unclear, so I said I would speak to Brian Dalton, the financial director, the following morning. I told Brian that since Ernie had not said no, I could only assume he was interested in my proposal.

'Well, you know,' said Brian, 'you haven't got any experience as a manager.'

'You're the financial director of a football club,' I replied. 'What experience of that job did you have before you came here?'

'Well, my work has been in finance.'

'Yes, but not connected with a football club. It's different to anything else, you know that. But I've been involved with football all my life, from the grass roots all the way through to the very top. If you look through my record, you'll see that I've got more experience than Bobby Campbell. Take it or leave it, it's up to you.'

That seemed to do the trick. Next thing, they invited me to go and talk to them, which I did.

'You know,' I said when we'd all sat down together, 'this is a bit daft. You're sitting there trying to decide whether I am the right man to manage Fulham Football Club when – and forgive me if I appear presumptuous, or even rude – the two of you don't know very much about football. I don't think, for instance, that you could explain to me how I could go from playing for Tonbridge in the Southern League to playing for the full England team within four and a half years. That's the kind of experience I'd be bringing in, and I'd be looking for youngsters at this club to make the same sort of progress. You get youngsters making progress, and the club itself progresses. Get the right blend of youth and experience and you will always be moving upwards.'

Though taken aback a bit by this outburst, Ernie and Brian seemed to like what I had to say and offered me the job. The salary they proposed seems awful now, and on first hearing it didn't strike me as great then, but football managers were pretty poorly paid in those days. When I left Newcastle in 1976, Gordon Lee was on £7,500 a year, and here I was, over four years later, being offered a take-it-or-leave-it £15,000. But that really wasn't bad at all considering that Fulham were five or so places from the bottom of the old Third Division with gates of just over 3,000. I accepted.

My appointment completed the circle. Whatever I did in life, I always seemed to do it first at Fulham Football Club. It was the club I always supported as a kid, it was my first club as a professional footballer, and now it was to be my first club as a manager. Everything, it appeared, had to go through Craven Cottage first.

What I found when I started the job wasn't very encouraging. The dressing-room was depressed, the offices were depressed, and the people who worked in them were depressed. There was hardly any laughter; the sound of people enjoying themselves at work was noticeable only by its absence. I decided there was a fear factor at work and concluded that I would have to find its source. My first step was to make training a light-hearted affair without allowing it to become frivolous. I wanted to get people working with a smile on their faces, but the initial response was sluggish. As in every football club, there were one or two piss-takers, but the leg-pulling was done in a cruel way I didn't like. That sort of cruel streak doesn't express itself naturally, I thought, it has to come from somewhere else. Then I discovered that there had been a bit of a reign of terror under Bobby Campbell and Mike Kelly during which the players had been subjected to shouting, threats and punishment. Staff had been brusquely treated, and there'd been no genuine feeling of team spirit, with everybody pulling in the same direction.

Realising I had taken on one hell of a job just to raise morale, I seized on the opportunity provided by my first game in charge at the beginning of November 1980, away to Carlisle. During that long coach journey from London to Cumbria on the Friday afternoon, I got in among the players and got them talking about themselves, about football and about their careers. I wanted to see how they saw themselves, how they saw the game. There was a certain reticence, but the five-hour journey allowed me to delve a lot deeper than if it had been a trip to Reading, say. We lost 3–2 at Brunton Park, which wasn't a bad result considering that Carlisle were a half-decent side at that time. Encouragingly, I realised there had already been a vast improvement just in the way each player had gone out and performed. A team spirit had been shown that had not been there before. These guys had gone out and given their all; they could not help it if some of them were just not good enough, and anyway, that could be tackled over the coming weeks and months. The important thing at that point was to praise them. They came into the dressing-room at the end almost cowering in anticipation of a lambasting for losing, so there was a look of shock on their faces when I said, 'Well done!' I shall never forget that look, or the way their shoulders lifted and their heads came up. 'Yes,' I thought, 'these are genuine guys who want to do it, but they've become frightened of failure.'

I laugh when I hear about teacups being thrown across dressing-rooms by managers. That's no way to be managing a football team, because you're not giving reasonable credit to the intelligence of people. Throwing teacups and raging all the time is not going to work with human beings. If you have to rant and rave, then make it such a rare occurrence that when it happens everybody knows you mean it, and make sure you have every reason to do it.

The next step, I decided, was to bring in somebody with a big, jovial personality, and I immediately thought of Roger Thompson. Roger was the youth-team coach at Arsenal and I had got on with him very well throughout my time at Highbury. He wasn't the greatest coach in the world, but he was hard-working and, most importantly, had a wonderful, mischievous sense of fun about him. He had the sort of face that could light up any room he was in, and I thought I needed that kind of character more than I needed a master tactician. The whole place needed brightening and lifting. I had an awful lot of work on my plate, so while I was otherwise engaged he could be making the sun shine and showing people the positive ways in life.

I rang Terry Neill, the Arsenal manager, to enquire about Roger. Terry told me he had decided to go and live in the United States at the end of the season and was being employed on a week-to-week basis by Arsenal until they found a replacement, so I suggested it would make little difference if he were to come and work for Fulham for a few months instead. Terry agreed and gave me permission to speak to Roger, who told me he'd love to have a go at working with the senior players at Fulham.

He had a remarkable effect on them, too. In no time at all he was the darling of the players, who thought the world of him. He might have had coaching limitations, but he was certainly getting the best out of people. As a result, we started to win games and climb the table. But though I felt this was exactly what was required in the short term, I had to start thinking long-term. Ernie Clay and Brian Dalton were happy, but there was a whole host of other things that needed sorting out.

One of them was a ticket scam that was siphoning off money – money we could ill afford to lose – from our gate receipts. My suspicions that something untoward was going on were aroused when, sitting in the dugout at Craven Cottage, I looked around the ground and estimated that there must be a crowd of about 5,000 for one home match. Don't forget that I knew that old stadium like the back of my hand. The only change there had been since I was a lad was the building of the Sir Eric Miller stand on the river side. If you know a ground well, you can get to estimate numbers pretty accurately. At St James's Park, for instance, you could quickly scan the stands and terraces and tell whether there were

40,000 present or maybe only 37,000. Similarly, at Highbury, you would know whether the crowd was 36,000 strong or just 33,000. That day at Craven Cottage, I took a second opinion from Roger Thompson, and he estimated the crowd at 4,800. When the attendant came round with an official attendance figure of 3,215, we started to laugh. Both Roger and I believed that was well short of the true figure.

I gave myself the weekend to think the matter over, then went to see the club secretary, George Noyce, on the Monday morning to ask how many complimentary tickets had been issued for the game. He passed me on to Dave Barnard, the ticket office manager, who estimated that there had been only a couple of hundred comps, and explained that they were not included in the attendance figure. When this evidence was laid before George Noyce, he began to sit up and take notice instead of trying to dismiss me as some kind of simpleton. Even then, he challenged me to prove that the crowd was actually 5,000 strong, as I'd claimed. In reply, I suggested we examine the way the operation worked. We started by calculating how many season-ticket holders we had – just a few hundred – then went on to all the 'bunking-in' spots I knew from childhood, which were still there. I took George and Dave round the ground to point out the spots, and advised them to get them closed up.

Finally, we looked at the way the turnstiles were operated. I was told that the turnstile keepers came in on the day and were paid a match fee of something like £8; then they were free to watch the game. I took a look at the book in which the turnstile keepers had to sign in and give their addresses every matchday. What surprised me was that there were people travelling from the Midlands to man the turnstiles at Craven Cottage for just £8. They were very good supporters, I was told. If they were good supporters, I retorted, they would be watching the game, not sitting in the turnstiles for at least the first twenty minutes of it. We then took a close look at what happened to the money taken at the turnstiles, and we found a dodgy operation going on; it appeared that some people were getting into the ground without going through the turnstile 'clickometer', the machine that records each entry, and some of the turnstile operators must have been pocketing those admission fees. It prompted a complete reorganisation of all the gate staff and turnstile operators for the next home game, at which we recorded a crowd of 4,750, and the takings were much higher. I had had to work hard to overcome the apathy; 'Oh, but you don't know how hard it is to get people to go on the gates' was the sort of attitude I had to deal with. But there had been thousands of pounds going missing every game! I warned everybody that they had to keep on top of the situation.

I had been proved right, and that gave me the licence to poke my nose in wherever I wanted from then on. I thought I'd get George Noyce to work out for me exactly how much it cost Fulham Football Club to function. Having had Ernie Clay on at me constantly about cutting costs, I just had to find out for myself what he was talking about and put it into figures I could understand. I don't think enough football managers consider the general financial aspects; like supporters, they always believe there's a fortune in the kitty. Sure enough, when all the calculations were done, I was horrified to discover that, just to break even on gate receipts only, we had to draw an average attendance of 25,000.

Having established the gravity of the situation, I realised I was going to have to make some very difficult decisions in terms of cutting the size of the playing staff. To be quite frank, the wage bill for a club like Fulham in the position they were in at that time was exorbitant. The highest-paid player on the books was Dave Clement, the England international full-back and father of the present West Bromwich Albion wing-back Ian Clement. I knew Dave already because we'd been in the England squad together, and he was a highly experienced guy. He'd spent many years at Queens Park Rangers before going to Bolton, and Fulham had bought him from the Lancashire club before I arrived. I'd hardly seen him play, though, because he'd been in the treatment room ever since I'd taken over as manager at Craven Cottage. This is difficult to explain, but I would have to describe Dave as an athlete who trained so hard it actually took him beyond fitness. It took him to the point where his muscles were at breaking point in everything he did. As soon as he got fit, he would play for five minutes before pulling yet another muscle. So I had this guy who was just occupying the treatment room but all the while costing me a load of money. Since he was also 34 or 35 by then, I thought it was time for us to have a chat.

I decided the opportunity was right on one of the very rare days he was at the training ground while I was manager. It was a nice early spring day in 1981, and we sat outside on a grassy knoll, talking.

'Dave,' I said as diplomatically as I could, 'it's not that long ago I had to suffer retirement from the game. Do you feel that perhaps you're close to approaching that stage in your life?'

His response was to point out that he kept himself super-fit, but I countered by saying that I had been at Fulham for several months and hadn't yet seen him play a full game. I told him I didn't doubt his ability as a footballer, but I was questioning – and in a major way – his physical capacity to fulfil his end of the bargain in terms of the contract he had with the football club. I added that I needed fit players who were ready to go out Saturday after Saturday, match after match.

'Now,' I concluded, 'it's time for you to have a think about yourself and your future, because this isn't a holiday camp. I've got a tough job and I've got to make some very tough decisions, and this is one. I can come at you from a number of angles in a number of ways, but what I'm trying to do here is give you an opportunity to decide your own future, to have some control over your own destiny, because only you know what you want for your future. But the bottom line here is that I don't think you're physically capable any longer. Have you given any thought to what you're going to do when your playing days are over?'

I'm looking for some feedback from him, but he just looked at me blankly. 'He must have something to say to me,' I thought, but he just continued with the blank stare. Even when I asked him again if he'd thought beyond his playing days, I got no reaction. I began to wonder what sort of person I had in front of me. Dave was certainly not unintelligent, so the only conclusion I could reach was that he simply didn't want to face the reality that comes to all footballers, usually in their thirties, that physically they can't do it any more. In the end, I suggested he should have a think about what I'd said and go home and discuss it with his wife. During our conversation, I'd asked him whether he wanted to take up coaching or had a business interest he'd like to pursue when he stopped playing, but he had replied in the negative. Well, the ball was in his court.

He came back to see me the following afternoon and knocked on my door. When I asked how I could help, he said, 'Following on from yesterday, I've had a think. Make me your youth-team coach.'

I looked at him and said, 'I beg your pardon?'

He repeated his request, and I replied, 'I've got a youth-team coach. You want me to sack somebody to give you a job?'

'Well, put me on the coaching staff, then.'

'Dave,' I said, 'it doesn't work like that. You decide for yourself what it is you want to do, and I'll give you all the help I can, but all the positions are taken here. I'm sorry, but I think you have completely misunderstood me, and I don't know where that misunderstanding could have come from. I was not talking about this football club at all, I was talking about you, your future, and deciding where it is you want to move on to.'

'Oh,' he said, 'it's like that, is it?'

'Yes, Dave, it's like that.'

He then insisted that, despite what I had said, he wanted to carry on playing, and that he believed he could do it. I told him I would see what I could do.

As promised, I started mentioning his availability around the football circuit. Managers meet up at reserve games and the like, and Dave Bassett, who was just starting out as manager of Wimbledon then, was the first to ask me what the score was with Dave Clement. I explained that the player felt he still had a bit of playing left in him and would be interested in doing a bit of coaching after that. I also made it clear to Bassett that there would be no transfer fee involved. It seemed a move to Wimbledon would be a good thing for both Daves. 'If he's fit to play, I could do with him until the end of the season,' said Bassett. 'I'm a right-back short, and there's a vacancy coming up on the coaching staff.'

Having given the Wimbledon manager permission to speak to Dave Clement, I broke the news to the player the next day. Explaining that he was wanted as a player for the rest of the season with a view to becoming a coach, I said, 'It sounds ideal for you. Do you want to go and talk to Dave Bassett?'

'Yes,' said Dave, 'because I'm obviously not wanted here!'

'Dave,' I replied, 'don't be like that. We've all got to move on at some point in our lives, and don't you feel you've reached that time yourself? Don't go from here harbouring grudges or anything. Look on it as a sort of release for you to make your future a better one.'

He mumbled some sort of response, then left. He and Dave Bassett soon reached an agreement, and Dave Clement duly signed for Wimbledon. Everything seemed fine, but not for long. The sad news we heard next was that Dave had gone out in his first game for his new club, stretched for a tackle in the first few minutes and broken his leg. It was a terrible blow for the guy, the sort you would not wish on your worst enemy, never mind a player I had been trying to ease gently into retirement. When I met Dave Bassett again at a reserve game shortly afterwards, I asked him how it had happened. 'I don't know what Dave thought he was doing,' he said. 'He went for something that just wasn't on for him at all. You can't blame the opposing player in any way – he was put in an impossible situation. Dave just completely overstretched for a ball he was never going to reach in his life. The other player tried everything he could to get out of the way, but he ended up on Dave's boot and snapped his leg.' Having recounted the conversation that Dave Clement and I had had, I suggested that the player might have been trying to prove a point about his ability to carry on playing the game. 'It wouldn't surprise me if that was the case,' said Bassett.

Whatever the reason for the accident, when Dave Clement's broken leg was repaired and he started getting back to fitness, there seemed no cause for alarm. But then his wife came home one day to find him dead. He had committed suicide. All of us at Fulham were shocked rigid by the news. It was one of those times when you go cold to your marrow. I told the players that there would be no training on the day of the funeral and that anyone who wished to attend could go.

The message on the grapevine from Dave's wife was that there was an open invitation to the funeral, but it did not extend to me – and it came with a bit more bite than that, too. The Clement family's finger was pointing at me, but I was determined not to feel guilty about Dave's death. I didn't see why I should carry the blame for the rest of my life. After all, I had simply sought to do what was best for Fulham Football Club and the player himself. Everybody has to face reality in their lives, and if they can't handle it, they can't go round blaming others. Even so, it was a very sad and horrific end to a matter I, then the youngest manager in the Football League at 31, had had to deal with during my first year in the job. I think about it even now. You constantly go back over every conversation with the player and ask yourself, 'Did I handle that right?' At the time, Dave Bassett helped to reassure me by saying, 'Mal, you must have been as amazed and shocked as I was. None of us could ever have guessed that such a thing was inside him, so don't hold yourself responsible.' Nevertheless, it was, without doubt, an horrendous experience for Dave Clement's family because he was a young man in the prime of life when he died. But that is the cruelty of football: a young man in his prime can be an old man in the game and be finished.

It was not easy after that tragedy to carry on whittling down the playing staff at Fulham, but I persevered. One of my methods was to throw out challenges to players to see how they responded. The sort of response I liked to see was the one I got from Tony Gale, the central defender who went on to play for West Ham and who now earns a living as a media pundit. Galey was a wonderfully gifted player who could be absolutely brilliant one minute, then all over the place the next. He came to see me, and we talked about whether he was actually seeing what was most important of all. I wrote him out a list of questions about himself that was almost endless: Are you good in the air? Are you brave in the air? Are you quick in the air, and if not, how do you react?' 'Do you put yourself in positions where, if you need pace, you can get out of them if it goes wrong? It was a real jumble of questions about one guy as a footballer and what he does and doesn't do. All he had to do was give a 'yes' or 'no' answer to them and it would open or close a door for him. 'Look,' I said to him, 'it might seem a bit nonsensical, but just apply yourself to this. Take it home and answer it.'

In fairness to Galey, he took the questions home, answered them all, then came back the following day and said, 'I see what you're getting at. I'm neither one thing nor the other, am I?'

'Yes, Galey, you've got it! Now, go for it!'

He was three times better after that. For instance, he wouldn't just try to get a little flick over the shoulder of the opposing centre-forward; now he'd let the centre-forward have the ball, drop off, and get himself right to solve the problem with the abilities he had. In other words, he started playing to his strengths. He began to enjoy his game more too. He also became more dominant with regard to the players around him; in fact, he started applying to them what I'd applied to him, and they also started to improve. Some, inevitably, were failing my little test, but Galey was emerging as the shining example of how to pass it. I'd proved it could work, and I was determined to stick with it.

One benefit from all this was that by the time we reached the end of the season we were about mid-table; relegation had long ceased to be a threat. At the same time, I was steadily building a side. One player who claimed a place was the Welsh defender Jeff Hopkins, who was only seventeen when I gave him his debut in a game right at the end of the 1980/81 season. When I'd taken over six months earlier, Jeff had more or less resigned. He was a Youth Opportunities apprentice, but he'd been bullied so much by my predecessors that he'd gone home to mum. That made it look as though he didn't have the bottle for it, but our youth development officer, Del Quigley, and I made contact with him and eventually coaxed him back to the club. The claim that Jeff had bottled it couldn't have been further from the truth. I found him to be a very quiet lad, but very tough and resilient with a phenomenally strong character. It was just that he was a very proud boy and refused to be abused by people all the time. He had made his stand on a point of principle, and his reward was a first-team debut within six months. To my delight, Jeff went on from there to win sixteen caps for Wales.

The game before Jeff's debut, I'd blooded another future international defender, Paul Parker. We were playing Reading, and Kerry Dixon, the future Chelsea and England centre-forward, was playing for them then, so I told Paul, all 4ft 13in of him, to mark him. And, I tell you, he was brilliant. If he couldn't win the ball, he'd make sure Kerry didn't. 'You'll do for me, son!' I thought. Other managers came to think the same thing because Paul reached the peak of his career with Manchester United, played at just about every level for England and finished up with nineteen senior caps. Another fine prospect was the striker Dean Coney. What a player he was! I put him in the team too.

I was very fortunate, in fact, to have a very good group of kids coming through, and I encouraged them whenever I could. We regularly took the youngsters on trips with the first team to get them used to the atmosphere: the banter, the stick, the crowds – everything surrounding the playing of the game. Basically, in those first months at the helm I started to get rid of the – I want to be careful about the word I use here because there isn't one that actually describes the whole – wasters. What I mean to say is I got rid of those who weren't good enough, those who had been two-season wonders elsewhere and were now just failing to put the effort in. I was being quite brutal about it without feeling brutal in any way. I just asked the question, 'Are they good enough?' If the answer was yes, they stayed; if it was no, they were out. Simple as that. Getting them out, of course, meant the wage bill was steadily going down, and I was also able to move players on for nominal amounts here and there. Basically, I was looking for people with the right mental attitude, the right temperament. Outstanding skill was of no use to me if it didn't come with those two other attributes. By applying all these criteria and sorting the wheat from the chaff, I had pretty well sorted out my team in a 4–4–2 formation come the end of that season. In fact, I wrote the team down on a piece of paper and said, 'There it is. That's going to get us promotion!' It was a fairly young side, but it was a good mix of youth and experience.

The one position I hadn't yet been able to fill satisfactorily was the left side of midfield. I was adamant that I wanted a left-footed player who could pass and cross the ball and wasn't afraid to tackle. Having made it clear to the coaching staff that this was a key position that could make or break the team, I invited them to suggest a few names. I had earmarked Kevin Sheedy, then a youngster at Liverpool, as the ideal solution, but Everton scooped me on that one. Then Del Quigley told me Peter O'Sullivan might be getting a free at Brighton.

To cut a long story short, I persuaded Sully to join us. I did that by impressing him with the way I wanted Fulham to play and by promising to give him another free transfer – and the chance to make some more money – at the end of the following season if he helped us to win promotion. The latter was an important consideration for Sully, a shrewd old beggar with a mischievous sparkle in his eye, who was then 32. His wages – he had been earning big money, by our standards, at Brighton – and a large signing-on fee were potential problems, but I persuaded Ernie Clay to sanction them by convincing him that this was the signing that would win us promotion to the Second Division. Ernie was desperate for us to go up because of the Football League's voting structure. The 48 Third and Fourth Division clubs had something like eight votes between them, but the 44 in the First and Second Divisions were entitled to a vote each. Our chairman wanted his own vote. He wanted to be able to stand up and have his say rather than have to go through the committee that controlled the eight votes of the Third and Fourth Divisions.

As I said, Peter O'Sullivan was the last piece of the jigsaw. With Les Strong playing at full-back behind him – well, if there has been a scarier, dirtier, stop-them-at-all-costs left side in any team, I've yet to see it! Les, strong by nature as well as by name, was not the greatest of players, but his intelligence made him a good one. He could psyche out anybody in football, and he used to play on it. When there was that hush as the teams lined up for the kick-off, Strongy would shout to Sully loud enough for the opposing winger to hear, 'When you've finished with the little bastard, throw him over to me. I'll finish him off.'

I was so certain we were going to go up at the end of the 1981/82 season that I went to see financial director Brian Dalton in the summer of 1981 and suggested that we take out an insurance policy against all the bonuses promotion would cost us. A friend of mine in the insurance business had told me he had a syndicate at Lloyd's that would give us £50,000 if we were promoted, provided we were willing to pay a premium of £3,200. That kind of thing had never been done before, and Brian took a bit of persuading, but he eventually managed to talk the chairman into sanctioning it. Maybe Ernie realised that, since the bookies were offering twelve or fourteen to one against us going up, these were far better odds.

Roger Thompson having emigrated, as arranged, to the United States, I strengthened the coaching staff by recruiting my old Arsenal team-mate Geordie Armstrong to look after the first team, Terry Mancini the reserve team and Ray Harford the youth team. Ray, as everyone knows now, is a wonderful coach; he helped Kenny Dalglish win the Premiership title at Blackburn in 1994/95, and he did a brilliant job with the fabulous group of youngsters we had at Fulham. They started to come through to such an extent that, later that season, half the first team were playing for the club in the FA Youth Cup. I was more than happy with this. While the current first team was going for promotion, I already had the next one ready to take over from them. Ray's influence was such, in fact, that I asked him for his input on the first-team bench, whenever possible, after he'd overseen the youth team match on Saturday mornings. That put Geordie's nose out of joint a bit, but what I found was that although the players would listen to what Geordie had to say, it was Ray they really responded to. In fact, it began to dawn on me that I had got the two men the wrong way round in terms of the teams they were coaching. Still, everything was working – the first team was pushing for promotion and the youth side was coming on in leaps and bounds – so I decided to leave things well alone for the time being.

Promotion to the Second Division was indeed clinched that season, in our last game at home to Lincoln. It was an incredible night because the situation was that Fulham would go up provided they didn't lose, while Lincoln had to win to go up in our place. When it came to kick-off time, which was slightly delayed, there were still nearly 15,000 people outside the ground. They came in their droves to see that game, partly because there was no other football on that night, and we finished up with a gate of about 28,500. They were still queuing to get in as we approached half-time. As for the game itself, Roger Brown, one of our centre-backs, headed us into the lead, Lincoln equalised later and then it was a backs-to-the-wall job for twenty minutes. But Lincoln gradually lost the initiative, we were able to see out the rest of the time, and a 1–1 draw was sufficient to take us up. We went on to the balcony of the Cottage at the end and were presented with one of those big publicity cheques for the £50,000 our innovative insurance policy had brought us. There was a big song and dance about that, and as it was a long time since Fulham had had any kind of success the celebrations went on long into a wonderful night.

Once the euphoria had died down, I realised I had a number of problems to resolve. Prominent among them was the Geordie Armstrong-Ray Harford situation. As the season had progressed, it had got to the stage where the players weren't listening to Geordie at all. He had proved limited in what he had to offer, whereas Ray's ability was almost limitless. I realised there was no easy way out: I could fiddle and faddle and have a lot of unhappy people around me, or I could just be decisive. Geordie was a good mate, but I had to look at the bigger picture, the long-term future. I sacked him.

It was not the proudest moment of my life, I can tell you. Geordie was shocked to the core by the news, if only because Fulham had just won promotion. 'I take no pleasure whatsoever out of this, Geordie,' I told him. 'It's been the hardest decision I've ever had to make in my life, but I've got to do what I feel is right for the good of the club. It galls me to think I'm doing it, but do it I must.' I lost a good friend that day, because I knew Geordie would never forgive me for what I'd done, but football management – any management – is about taking those very tough decisions and never seeking to fudge them in any way. I'd thought of other ways of resolving the situation, like switching Geordie and Ray around, but everybody in the club would have seen that for what it was – one promoted, the other demoted. So I decided I had to do it swiftly and cleanly, no matter how much it hurt Geordie and me to do it. I have to admit the decision did me no harm in the dressing-room. The players went, 'What? Wow! Geordie was a nice guy!' and the sacking got the message across that nobody was safe, not even best mates. You had to give it your all, and even then you couldn't be sure.

Another problem was that old one on the left side of midfield. Although Peter O'Sullivan wasn't much liked by the majority of the fans, who saw him as just an old pair of legs, he had been absolutely brilliant as far as I was concerned. He was so effective at reducing to virtually nothing any attacking threat from the opposing right side, he had a wicked left foot for whipping the ball in, and he got his fair share of goals as well. But Sully admitted that, at his age, he couldn't cope with another year of doing that. Honouring my promise to him, I said I would put the word about that he was available without sticking him on the transfer list – a stigma he wanted to avoid.

All the dreaded retain and transfer lists were being prepared by clubs at that time of year, of course, and we at Fulham got wind of the fact that Ray Houghton, a player we'd been following very closely, was being given a free by West Ham. I couldn't believe my luck; Houghton was the ideal man to replace Sully. Just to make sure I wasn't dreaming, I rang John Lyall, West Ham's manager, to check that the R. Houghton on the Hammers' transfer list was in fact Ray Houghton. He confirmed that it was, and explained that they were letting him go not because of any problem with the boy, but because he and his coaching staff believed that Alan Dickens was the player to replace Trevor Brooking in central midfield when the England veteran hung up his boots. Again I had to pinch myself. To me, Dickens was a very stiff-legged player who, when he ran, appeared to be marching in double time. In my opinion, there was just no comparison between him and Ray Houghton in terms of ability, and I think the marked difference in their subsequent careers would bear me out in that. Lyall wanted to give Ray every chance to find his place in the game and was only too happy to let me talk to him.

Ray came to see me at the Cottage, where I explained that, though he was basically right-footed, I wanted him to play on the left side of midfield as the final piece in the jigsaw. I also promised him first-team football and offered him generous terms. I was so determined to get my man that I'd already instructed the club secretary to draw up a contract, and he put his signature on the dotted line there and then.

After the formalities had been completed, I phoned down to the dressing-room for Les Strong to come up to my office. I was pleased to see Les's eyes come out on stalks when he saw Ray Houghton, of First Division West Ham, standing there. You can tell how well you're doing as a manager by the reaction of the players to the new guys you bring into the club, and I knew from Les's reaction that this signing would be an absolute winner in the dressing-room. I asked Strongy to take Ray down to meet the rest of the boys, and on the way, apparently, he said to him, 'Welcome, mate! You'll be very happy here. We're a really friendly, happy club and we like everybody to feel at home, so we're very careful to make sure the new arrivals have things to their satisfaction because we want them to stay a long time. Now, is there any sort of name you don't like and don't want to be called?' Although Ray went on, via Oxford United, Liverpool, Aston Villa, Crystal Palace and Reading, to win 73 caps for the Republic of Ireland, he was actually born in Glasgow of Irish parents. As a result, he grew up with a broad Glaswegian accent, so he confessed to Strongy that the one thing he hated was being called 'Sweaty', as in Sweaty Sock – Jock. 'Right,' said Les, 'don't you worry, Ray. Leave that to me!' They walked into the dressing-room, and Strongy said, 'Guys, I'd like to introduce you to our newest and brightest recruit, signed from West Ham this very lunchtime. Meet Sweaty!'

That was typical of the dirty tricks that would be played on the new boys. The classic one involved telling a newcomer casually that Tony Gale's sister was a concert pianist and better known than he was. When the new boy first came face to face with Galey, usually over the dinner table, and was looking for something to talk about, he'd say that he understood his sister was a concert pianist, at which Tony's face would go black as thunder, he'd look at the new player with a mixture of rage, contempt and hate, then storm from the table. When the poor lad enquired anxiously what he'd said to upset him, somebody would quietly whisper in his ear, 'Tony's sister's a thalidomide child – she hasn't got any arms.' All untrue, of course, and in the worst possible taste, but a good example of the practical jokes the players played on one another all the time. There were all sorts of initiations new players had to go through, and they came out of them very much part of the scene. That was the way it was – everybody had to stay on his toes on and off the field.

With the two Rays, Harford and Houghton, in place, I was a very happy man that summer. My happiness increased when I was able to spend the whole of the 1982 World Cup finals in Spain working for Monsanto, the manufacturers of agricultural chemicals. My job was to greet the company's staff and customers who had won competitions to attend the finals. It was idyllic. A Fulham supporter let me use his studio apartment in Marbella, and the agency working on behalf of Monsanto gave me a ticket for every single World Cup match. Occasionally, though, I'd just go along to a bar in Puerto Banus to watch games on the big television set they had there. That, by accident, became a regular meeting place for me and Alan Ball, who just happened to be out in Spain as well, and half the Scottish squad. They'd been eliminated by then, of course.

Back at Fulham for pre-season training, I was asked by the insurance people whether we wanted to take out another policy against promotion. I was all for it because I believed we could do it again, and I persuaded Brian Dalton and the chairman to agree after a lot of humming and hawing on their part. It only cost us a couple of hundred quid more this time, and I knew the side was a lot stronger than the previous season. We had Gerry Peyton, a Republic of Ireland international, in goal; Jeff Hopkins, a Welsh international, at right-back; and Kevin Lock, ex-West Ham and an England under-23 international, at left-back. In between them were Tony Gale, an England under-21 international, and big Roger Brown. In the centre of midfield, Robert Wilson had emerged from our youth scheme and created a fabulous partnership with the former Chelsea and Wimbledon player Ray Lewington. Either side of them were Shaun O'Driscoll, a Republic of Ireland international, and Ray Houghton. Up front there was a nice blend of youth and experience in Dean Coney and the Welsh international striker Gordon Davies. Plus we had the likes of Paul Parker and Dale Tempest in reserve.

It proved to be quite a remarkable season. The side was playing with such confidence and self-belief that a run started to be put together. We won four of our opening six fixtures in the late summer of 1982 and drew the other two. Then, during one notable spell in the autumn, we scored four goals away from home in each of our victories over Middlesbrough, Newcastle, Grimsby and Wolverhampton Wanderers. That last one was particularly valuable, because all season Wolves were chasing the permanent leaders of the Second Division, Queens Park Rangers, and we, in turn, were chasing Wolves.

QPR were undoubtedly the division's outstanding team. Terry Venables was in charge of them, and they had gone to the top of the table from the word go. There was no doubting their ability. I have to say, though, that they enjoyed an enormous advantage over the rest of us in that they were allowed to play on an artificial surface at Loftus Road. They were used to playing on it, and they made that count in home games. There were stories circulating that the pitch hadn't been laid correctly, and that was the reason for the extraordinary bounce of the ball. I'm not saying they wouldn't have got promotion without that pitch, I'm sure they would, but it was a nasty, nasty surface to play on.

As the season went on, our own form was good enough to create a significant gap between ourselves, in third place, and the fourth-placed team. One of our outstanding early performances was that game at Middlesbrough, where we won 4–1 despite losing our goalkeeper, Gerry Peyton, who was left with his scalp flapping on his skull after diving at the feet of David Shearer and being caught by the striker's studs. Substitute goalkeepers weren't allowed in those days, so we had to bring on Paul Parker at left-back and put Kevin Lock in goal. We won by keeping possession, by passing Boro into an hypnotic trance almost, then hitting them with quick breaks. It was a style we perfected as the season developed. We had tremendous pace in Gordon Davies up front, Shaun O'Driscoll on the right and Ray Houghton on the left. The full-backs, too, were quick. Through the middle we were slow but solid. We had good footballers there, footballers who loved the ball at their feet and had quick minds. Then there was big Roger Brown at centre-half. His running style was that of a carthorse – and I'm being unkind to carthorses, here – but he was improving all the time. There was none better in the air, that's for sure. He'd deal with any aerial threat, and anything on the ground would be left to Galey.

As we approached the old transfer deadline date in March 1983, though, I sensed that the two up front, Gordon Davies and Dean Coney, were beginning to look a bit jaded. I went to see the financial director and the chairman and told them I needed to buy a forward. 'I've not asked you for any money since I've been here,' I reminded them, 'but if you want promotion, we have got to buy. I need the impetus for everybody through a fresh pair of legs up front. So if you want First Division football next season, I need a few quid now.'

While they were thinking about it, I went off to do a piece for television with Terry Venables. It was an opportunity too good to miss, so I asked the QPR manager if he would be willing to sell me one of his strikers, Tony Sealy. He said he didn't really want to let him go and was under no pressure to sell, but I had already planted the thought in his mind that it would be good business the following season for Fulham, another west London team, to go up with Rangers. He agreed to talk to his chairman and said he thought we could do a deal for £60,000. About five days later, Venners came back to me on a Saturday night, after QPR had won again and virtually guaranteed promotion, to confirm we had a deal. Then, on the Sunday morning, Ernie Clay rang me at about six o'clock, as usual (sometimes it was even earlier!), to find out what was going on. I told him about the Sealy deal and emphasised that it was a necessity because I could feel our promotion campaign beginning to slip and wanted to act before it went too far. He complained about the price and asked me to leave the matter with him.

Ernie was always adamant that I didn't know how to do a deal, and I had a series of phone calls from him that Sunday. I knew he would have phoned Venners, Jim Gregory, the QPR chairman, and heaven knows who else as well. One day, I'd got a call from Don Howe, when he was the Arsenal manager, to tell me that Ernie had been trying to sell him Tony Gale behind my back! Now, I could tell, he was trying to hijack this Sealy deal. Sure enough, at 7.30 that Sunday evening he phoned me again.

'There you are, the deal's done,' he said.

'What do you mean, the deal's done?' I said.

'You've got Tony Sealy for £75,000.'

'What do you mean, £75,000?'

'I told you you didn't know how to do a deal. I've got him for you for £75,000.'

'Ernie' I said, barely able to contain my anger, 'I'd already agreed £60,000 with Venners and his chairman!'

'No, no, you don't know what you're talking about. Seventy-five – that's the deal. Take it or leave it.'

'Ernie, I'm not having £75,000 spent on a player I've agreed £60,000 on!'

'Oh, well, then, we'll have to leave it. That's the way to do business. If you can't get the price right, don't have them!'

I think that was the first time I sensed that Ernie Clay didn't want promotion to the First Division. I certainly began to have grave doubts. He'd gone and screwed up the Sealy deal, and he wasn't daft. He hadn't made himself a multi-millionaire by being daft! He was certainly eccentric – at times you would even have had to describe him as barking mad – but this guy knew how to do a deal, he knew what the business was about, and I believed he had screwed it up on purpose.

The next time I spoke to Terry Venables, he told me his chairman, Jim Gregory, had been so fed up with the spate of phone calls he'd been getting from Ernie that he'd no longer felt willing to do a deal. Neither Venners nor I could make sense of it, but our loss was definitely QPR's gain. As it happened, just after Sealy would have signed for Fulham, somebody got injured in Venners' side and Tony stepped in to score some very important goals that ensured Rangers won the Second Division championship.

Unfortunately, as I had feared, it all began to slip away from us. We were eleven points clear in third place with nine games to go when we went to Cambridge United and got beaten 1–0. We were lacklustre up front without the fresh legs Sealy could have provided, and we won only three of our last eight games. From then until the end of the season, playing football stopped being a joy. It became a chore to the players, and there was very little I could do about it because the squad was so small I was limited numbers-wise. I shuffled the first team around as best I could, but Leicester were steadily eating away at the eleven-point difference between us. They took a really big bite out of it when they came to Craven Cottage at Easter and beat us 1–0. They came up for the battle and they outran and outfought us. That victory, I'm sure, gave them the final impetus to go for our jugular. It was still tight at the end, though: the third promotion place behind QPR and Wolves was not decided until the final day of the season, when we were level on 69 points with Leicester.

We had the more difficult final fixture, away to Derby, who were still in danger of relegation; Leicester, on the other hand, were at home to Barnsley, who were mid-table with nothing to play for. The old Baseball Ground was packed tight that afternoon, the atmosphere highly charged. It was 0–0 at half-time, then, with about twenty minutes to go, Derby scored. That was the signal for the crowd, believing the goal would keep them up, to start filtering on to the pitch. First they were on the track around the pitch, but then they started to encroach over the touchlines. And I'm not talking about just a few people, there were hundreds and hundreds of them. It was so bad that I had to stand several yards inside the touchline myself to see what was happening in the Derby half! The whole of their six-yard area was so full of people, I could barely see the goal. Yet the referee, for some reason, was letting the play go on. It was heartbreaking, because we were playing better than we had for about ten games. At one point, Robert Wilson went out towards the left wing to control the ball, and the next thing some youth had come out of the crowd milling on the sidelines and kicked Robert in the thigh. Down he went, Derby got the ball, and the referee waved play on! And that was how the final quarter of an hour of the game was played. We were trying to make shooting positions, but the players couldn't even see the Derby goal.

When the final whistle went, Derby the 1–0 winners, thousands of their fans invaded the pitch. Every blade of grass just disappeared and I was dreadfully concerned for the safety of my players. When I'd battled my own way to the dressing-room, thankfully it was pretty full, but Jeff Hopkins was missing. I went back out to find Jeff struggling in the midst of a swarm of people. He was fighting them off, literally fighting them off. That lad was usually as quiet as a dormouse, but when riled, by heavens, he had a temper! Anyway, he managed to escape the clutches of about a dozen people and literally fell down the tunnel. I picked him up and got him to the dressing-room, where he arrived wearing just his boots and socks. Those louts had stripped him of his shirt and shorts, and he was spluttering and crying with anger. This nineteen-year-old boy was so traumatised that he couldn't utter a word. When he tried to speak, only spit came out of his mouth. Then I looked at his body and saw a mass of welts and scratches on it; it seemed as though he'd been lashed with a cat o'nine tails.

In a fury now, I marched into the referee's dressing-room and demanded that he come and look at the state Jeff was in and put it in his report. He didn't want to do that, but I wasn't in the mood to take no for an answer. When the referee saw Jeff, he almost had a breakdown; he sort of collapsed in a heap and a linesman had to catch him. He kept saying, 'It's not over, the game's not over yet.' When I asked for an explanation, he said the whistle we had heard had not been his. There were still 90 seconds to play.

I made it clear my players could not be expected to go out again and play for another minute and a half. It was out of the question for Jeff Hopkins, and most of the others had suffered assaults of one kind or another. The referee himself was at a complete loss about what to do and left saying he needed to talk to the police about it. I went back to the referee's room, and there was a high-ranking police officer there telling him that there was no way he could get the pitch cleared for the game to continue. Still, the referee insisted. Even if it took an hour to clear the pitch, the game had to be completed.

During the state of limbo that existed over the next hour we heard that Leicester had drawn 0–0 with Barnsley, which put them a point ahead of us. Knowing this, I found myself walking out on to the pitch with Peter Taylor, the Derby manager and Brian Clough's old sidekick. He asked me what we were going to do, and I told him we would have to appeal to the Football League, subject to the referee's report. What I was hoping for, of course, was that the referee would abandon the game and it would have to be played again, but Peter poured cold water on that notion by saying, 'You've got no chance of getting this game played again. No chance at all. They will let the result stand.' When I asked him why he would say that, Taylor just tapped his nose with his index finger a couple of times and repeated, 'I'm telling you, you will not get it played again.'

It all sounded very conspiratorial to me, but the fact of the matter was that the game hadn't reached its conclusion and that had had nothing to do with us. We were the innocent party in all this. Ernie Clay hadn't travelled to the game, so I went into the Derby offices and phoned him to explain the situation. He said he'd been watching on television and asked what I thought we should do. When I told him that we had to appeal against the result through all the appropriate channels, he agreed to back me all the way. 'We've got plenty of legal brains to give you support,' said Ernie. 'You just let me know what you want, and I'll get it for you.'

He was as good as his word. When a Football League commission turned down our appeal for a replay without giving a reason, he told me to consult a senior QC and Privy Councillor, Tony Scrivener. I spent days in his office preparing a new appeal to take to the Football Association. The new evidence I'd unearthed included the claim, made to a journalist by a senior police officer in charge of security at Derby County, that there would be a pitch invasion before the end if Derby scored. It seemed the whole thing had been pre-planned. I also recruited the services of my solicitor brother Neil to prepare a case that was so complex legally that most of it was beyond me. But it was all so much wasted time and effort. The FA board, chaired by Sir Bert Millichip, gave us the impossible choice of presenting our old case without including any new evidence, or a new case that could not include any of the old evidence. In any event, as Neil pointed out, the appendices to FA rules gave them the scope to overrule the rules if they wanted to. It was a no-win situation. We opted to present the old case and tried to wangle in some of the new evidence, but it did little good. Again, our plea for a replay was denied.

Savagely disappointed at missing out on promotion to the First Division in this way, I couldn't help but remember a telephone conversation I'd had with Ernie Clay just before I'd set off for Football League headquarters, then at Lytham St Annes, with half a dozen Fulham players as witnesses to what had occurred at the Baseball Ground.

'You know you're not going to win, don't you?' Ernie had said.

'Well, thanks very much for the vote of confidence, Ernie!' I replied.

'No, you don't understand what I'm saying,' he added. 'They'll not let you win. They can't! They are having almighty pressure put on them by Leicester, who are now in limbo land. If our result stands, they are promoted and Derby are safe from relegation, so they won't let you win – they can't afford to. There would be too much of a mess at both ends of the table if they sanctioned a replay. Not only that, but Leicester have got a vital foothold in the League administration through the Shipman family.' Len Shipman, a former chairman of Leicester City, was also a former president of the Football League, and his son, Terry, was chairman of the club at the time we lodged our appeal.

I believe, though, that there was another reason for officialdom's refusal to give us a sympathetic hearing. Our promotion to the Second Division had granted Ernie Clay the opportunity he'd always wanted to have his say at chairmen's meetings, and he was so lacking in tact – often downright rude, in fact – that he'd put a lot of noses out of joint at other clubs. Certainly there wasn't a boardroom he'd visited where he hadn't left somebody very upset. So the rejection of our plea, I am convinced, was partly a case of football getting its own back on Ernie.

There was still another avenue open to us, however. Tony Scrivener had said all along that, while we were unlikely to win our appeals to the Football League and the FA, there was every chance we would be successful in a court of law. So, when I came out of Lancaster Gate, the FA's old headquarters in London, I told the media that Fulham Football Club would be seeking legal advice with a view to taking the matter further. At which point, the chairman, having promised to back me all the way, withdrew his backing! Back at Craven Cottage, I spoke to Ernie on the telephone and got the distinct impression that he was not prepared to go any further with the appeal. His manner had changed totally. I think the reason was partly a realisation that the rest of football was ganging up on him powerfully, and partly a question of having a hidden agenda that did not include promotion to the First Division for Fulham Football Club – of which more later. At all events, the question of using litigation to seek redress for what had happened to us at Derby was never raised between us again.

The fall-out from our narrow failure to go up was considerable. The players knew they had been cheated, that a great wrong had been done to them, and Ernie bollocked me for having wasted £3,000, as he put it, on another insurance policy. But that was not the reason I said no when Brian Dalton came to me at the start of the 1983/84 season and asked whether we should take out the policy again. I was convinced we would suffer a backlash from what had happened the previous season, knew there was no point in trying to recreate what we had had, and realised I had to start rebuilding the side. It was time to bring in promising youngsters like midfielder Peter Scott and striker Leroy Rosenior.

I didn't expect a lot from that season, and I was right. By March we were sitting just below halfway in the table and had never really had any involvement in the promotion chase right from the word go. Even so, we were well established in the Second Division. We underlined the fact by thrashing Manchester City 5–1 at Craven Cottage on 17 March. I remember that game vividly, not just because of our big win but because it was the day my first marriage broke up.

After the split, while driving back down to London with a back seat full of clothes from the home near Bedford I had shared with Julie and our five daughters, I knew that a story like this, involving – though not caused by – another woman, would be food and drink to the tabloids. I was no longer happy in my work either. Relations between Ernie and me had become very distant. He seemed to have lost all the good intentions that had made his general behaviour bearable, and I didn't think things were being shared with me any more. I decided to take the bull by the horns.

Knowing Ernie as I did, I knew I had to do whatever was necessary to retain control over my own destiny, so the following morning I got up very early and went round to his house at about eight o'clock.

Although his early-morning calls to me had now stopped, I knew he would be up. He was surprised to see me, but hid it well. Then he asked me what I was doing there.

'Well, Ernie,' I said, 'what I'm actually here to do is hand in my resignation, and I'll tell you why before you say anything.' Having explained my domestic situation, I added, 'I do not want that to bring any embarrassment to the football club, to you as chairman or to your family, so I feel it is only right and proper that I tender my resignation. It is verbal at the moment, but you can have it in writing tomorrow.'

To my surprise, he urged me not to be hasty. Not only that, he assured me that the problem could be sorted out and emphasised that Fulham Football Club did not want to lose me. I therefore left Ernie's house with a huge feeling of support that, almost touchingly, I had never experienced from him before. Sadly, though, it did not last.

The following morning, at the football club, I called the coaching staff together and made them aware of the situation. I told them about the meeting with the chairman the previous day and what had taken place during it. I also asked them for their support, because if the story broke, I knew we could face some unpleasant intrusion. I stressed, too, that nobody but them, the chairman and my wife and family was aware of events.

Over the next three weeks, we carried on business as usual. Ernie came in every day. He'd be there when I returned from the training ground and we'd go into my office and have a cup of tea. A month from the end of the season, of course, is the time when a manager is looking ahead to the next season and making plans for it, but Ernie didn't seem interested in discussing it. 'You know what you're doing,' he said dismissively. 'I'll leave that to you.'

Strange little things began to happen, too. George Noyce, the club secretary, had left to join the Kerry Packer organisation and been succeeded by Yvonne Haines, who had worked as secretary to both George and me. Dave Barnard, the ticket office manager, had been promoted to stadium manager, too. I had also better explain that I was Fulham's managing director as well as manager by now. The appointment had been made a couple of years earlier, when the Football League brought in a new rule that allowed each club one salaried director, which was me in Fulham's case. In that dual capacity, my instructions to Yvonne and Dave were basically to make their own decisions, but before implementing them they were to let me know what the decisions were in case the chairman came back to me about them. Yet time after time Ernie would come into my office and query things I knew nothing about. 'You really should be up on these things,' he'd say. 'Doesn't anybody ever tell you what's going on?'

One example was a letter we'd received from Ted Croker, the secretary of the FA at that time. 'I didn't want to bother you with it,' explained Yvonne when I asked her what it was all about, 'there was just a query on the registration form of a schoolboy.' She'd sorted it all out without any fuss, but I had to remind her of my instructions.

'OK, Yvonne,' I said, 'but you know what the rules are: make your own decisions, but let me know what they are.'

'Sorry about that!' she replied.

And that's all I seemed to be hearing from everybody as Ernie queried one little thing after another. 'You seem to be losing control a bit, don't you?' he would say. 'You don't know what's going on here, do you?' I just couldn't understand why people appeared to be blatantly refusing to follow my instructions. Ernie seemed to be aware of an awful lot of minor information there was no need for him, as chairman, to know, and I wondered what on earth was going on. In the end, I asked the coaching and office staff outright whether any of them was in regular contact with the chairman. 'Somebody has to be!' I said, but they all denied this and said that whenever Ernie approached them about me they said I wasn't around and avoided getting into a conversation with him. If it wasn't the staff, I thought, then the chairman must be getting his information some other way, so I stripped down both of the phones in my office to see if they were bugged. With the help of the youth development officer, Del Quigley, I even went so far as to take the wood-effect panelling off the walls of my office to see if there was a microphone hidden behind it! We drew a blank there, too.

Then, suddenly, I had a newspaper chasing me. A journalist friend in Fleet Street phoned one day and said, 'Watch out, the *Sun* have got the story about you and your marriage break-up and they're going to go for you big-time!' When I asked where the information had come from, he told me somebody had tipped the paper off. When I informed Ernie about this, I said the information the *Sun* had got had obviously come from somebody very close to me at my place of work.

'Now who could that be?' he said, turning the situation to his advantage again. 'Keep a close eye on your staff – you've got them against you now, haven't you?'

I gathered the staff together again that night and asked point-blank whether any of them had given the information to the *Sun*. They all said no and assured me they had treated the whole thing in absolute confidence.

The next Saturday, when we were due to play Carlisle at home, the situation really began to get out of hand. With all due respect to Carlisle, it wasn't the most attractive fixture in the world, yet Yvonne Haines told me we were getting an inordinate number of requests for tickets. Each paper seemed to be doubling up and sending a news reporter as well as a football writer to the game. Yvonne was struggling to find room for them all.

'There's a rabbit off somewhere, isn't there?' I said.

'Yes,' she said. 'It definitely looks like it.'

It looked even more like it when the game against Carlisle kicked off. The Fulham dugout was surrounded by photographers just taking pictures of me, and when the game finished all the attention was again on me, rather than on what had taken place on the field of play. At the press conference, I blanked all questions from faces I didn't know and talked only to the guys I did know.

I'd asked Reg Hayter to come and give me some advice, and he soon saw that something was up. When we went across to the boardroom on the other side of the ground, I told him and Ernie that it was mayhem over at the Cottage. 'There are news guys all over the place,' I said. 'The Sundays are at work here, so we can expect something in the papers tomorrow, but heaven knows what!'

'Oh, we'll sort it out,' Ernie said. 'We'll look after you.'

Even when, later that day, I was giving Reg a lift to Euston to catch his train back to Watford we were followed by a motorcyclist from the *People*. I know which paper he was from because I forced him off his bike, took his ignition keys and posted them back to his office.

The following day there were all sorts of stories about my marriage break-up in the Sunday papers. There were even pictures of the woman I was involved with, and the whole thing came flooding out with more innuendo than fact. It was then, after the story had been splashed across all the Sundays, that it became a vicious free-for-all. Over the years, I had had a lot of experience handling the press, but dealing with news desks is completely different from dealing with sports desks. I still don't know what the answer is, how best to play it, because no matter how hard you seek it, you can have no control over the situation. It becomes a sort of feeding frenzy, each paper competing with the other for an extra extraordinary angle to the story. It becomes complete mayhem.

It was all starting to get too much. All and sundry were coming at me, and what I found strange about it was that each journalist seemed to have a different, vital piece of information. It was as if they'd each been given a separate piece of a jigsaw puzzle, and not until they'd put them all together would they have the whole picture. I just wished I knew who had been feeding out those bits and pieces of information.

In the end, the whole thing became so intolerable that I again offered Ernie Clay my resignation. 'Right,' I said, 'do you want me out? I offered you my resignation four or five weeks ago – why didn't you accept it there and then?'

'Well,' he replied, 'I thought we could work it out. I didn't expect all of this to come flooding through the club. It's a very embarrassing situation.'

So I resigned as manager of Fulham for the second and last time. I had come to the conclusion that if quitting was the only way to quell the mass hysteria that had engulfed me and the club over my marriage break-up, then it had to be done. I thanked everybody – or nearly everybody – for their support, and there were a few tears at my leaving. Then I walked out of Craven Cottage and away I went.

Before I left, Ernie did have the decency to ask who I thought should take over from me, and I strongly recommended Ray Harford. I was pleased to see that he did get the job. I'm not sure Ray realised what he was taking on, though. He and I kept in contact, and he was soon saying to me, 'I don't know how you coped with the chairman. I've only been manager for a month and he's driving me insane!'

When I bumped into Yvonne Haines a little while later, I discovered how Ernie had been trying to drive me insane. Having asked how I was, and been told I was all right, Yvonne persisted. 'No, no,' she said, 'I really do mean "How are you?" Come on, you can talk to me!' It turned out that Ernie had told the staff that the club doctor had said I was in the process of having a nervous breakdown and that they were not to worry me with anything they could cope with themselves. So that was why so many little things had been kept from me, but not from the chairman! The staff thought they were trying to protect me when in fact they were enabling Ernie to undermine me. I was as near to having a nervous breakdown as the chairman was to outflying Concorde, but I suppose he needed to get rid of me in his own way, in his own time. If he'd accepted my resignation, he knew I would have had the sympathy of the press. They would have had to concede that here was a football manager doing the right and honourable thing in what could often be said to be a dirty business. He needed to turn that round and seek to appear the victim of it all. 'You see all the problems this guy is causing me?' he wanted to be able to say, when in actual fact it was he who was stoking the situation.

It was Ernie, I also discovered later, who had tipped off the *Sun* about the break-up of my marriage and then fed the press with the subsequent bits of information that kept the story going. As if that wasn't bad enough, he'd got into my personal life as well. Apparently, he'd been phoning my ex-wife and telling her, too, that I was having a nervous breakdown. It was all very dirty. And all the time he had been innocence itself. 'How can I help?' he'd say. 'What can I do? How shall we play this?'

Yvonne was horrified to learn what had happened and left a short while later to join Millwall. Dave Barnard got out, too; he joined Sam Hammam at Wimbledon. Eventually, Brian Dalton left as well. Then came the exodus of players. Ray Houghton was sold to Oxford, Tony Gale to West Ham and Paul Parker to QPR. Poor Ray Harford couldn't cope with the situation, and also escaped as soon as he could.

My belief is that, from the start, Ernie Clay was seeking to asset-strip Fulham and sell the club. That's why he didn't want to see us promoted to the First Division. Up there, the club would have been in the spotlight and he would have been found out in a lot of ways. He needed me and Brian Dalton out of the way before he could proceed with his secret plan, and once we'd gone he acted. I think he sold the club for close on £10 million, plus 2,500,000 shares in Marley Properties, the purchasers. Marley Properties had bought out Peachey Properties, whose chairman was Sir Eric Miller. It was what you might call a case of wheels within wheels.

# CHAPTER NINE
# THE WILDERNESS YEARS

When I walked away from Ernie Clay's machinations at Fulham and my first marriage in the late spring of 1984, I was confident I could get another managerial post in the game quite quickly. My record at Craven Cottage – promotion from the Third Division to the Second in my first full season, then a narrow, heartbreaking failure to go up into the First the following year – had surely marked me out as a young manager of promise. With Reg Hayter's help, I had also embarked on a huge clean-up operation with the media on my image. Not only that, but there were two jobs coming up I felt I had a very good chance of getting. One was at my old club, Newcastle, and the other was at Aston Villa. There was also a vacancy at Sunderland, to replace Alan Durban, but I wasn't going to get a job there, not in a month of Sundays!

What I understand happened at Newcastle was that the six-man board were split evenly over who should succeed Arthur Cox as manager for the 1984/85 season, me or Lawrie McMenemy. Then the chairman, Stan Seymour Jr, decided to throw in a third candidate,

Jack Charlton, as a compromise and got unanimous support for him. As for Villa, their chairman, Doug Ellis, telephoned me one day, and the conversation went something like this:

'It's Doug Ellis here, chairman of Aston Villa. As you know, I'm in the market for a new manager. What I'm looking for is a young tracksuited manager. Do you feel capable of being that?'

'That's definitely what I do, Mr Ellis.'

'Right. I expect you to be at the training ground five days a week and only to come into the club on a Friday afternoon to help me pick the team.'

'Mr Ellis, let me stop you there. That is a condition I could never accept. I'd have to have total control over playing affairs, in particular over who plays and who doesn't. You either accept that or this conversation is ended.'

'All right, we'll end the conversation, then. Thank you for your time. Goodbye!'

A couple of days later, Graham Turner was appointed to succeed Tony Barton, and I have often wondered whether Doug Ellis made the same outrageous demand of him and whether he was prepared to go along with it.

At this point, I had a chat with Ray Harford, who said something quite profound. 'You know,' he told me, 'football is a terribly old-fashioned and moralistic business. They seem to forgive almost anything but a split marriage. Football can't cope with that, and football will make you do a penance. You will not get a job offer for twelve months.' Unfortunately, Ray was well out in his estimate; it was three years before I got back into the game as a manager. At first, I made myself busy, put myself about, but I found I was unwelcome at most football clubs. Something was going on, and I discovered it was because Ernie was still stirring things up in the background. The information reached me that he was warning off other football chairmen by saying, 'Oh, no, no, no, you don't want to touch him! He's going through a very bad time.' He was, it seemed, souring my name, my reputation, with the people who were my potential employers.

Shunned by football, I decided to do what a lot of footballers have done and get myself a pub. The one I plumped for was the Wigmore

Arms in Worthing, Sussex, but I persuaded the brewery to change the name to the more appropriate – in my case – Far Post. I'd been there for nearly three years when, one day, a guy called Don Packham walked in and introduced himself. He was a financial services rep who had a friend in Brazil called Umberto Silva, and he showed me a letter he'd received from him. Umberto, the son of a São Paulo lawyer, had studied law himself in Brazil and England. He claimed to be very friendly with the players of Palmeiras, one of the great Brazilian clubs, and said that many of them were keen on a move to Europe at a time when the value of their currency was going through the floor. There was one player in particular, a free-scoring striker by the name of Mirandinha who was on the verge of breaking into the national team, he thought might attract a lot of interest at a fee of only a million pounds.

At first, I was completely sceptical about the whole thing. Don explained he had approached me because the world of football was a closed book to him and I was the only person he knew of who had access to it. All the same, this guy had just wandered in off the street and tried to convince me he had a brilliant Brazilian footballer for sale on the cheap. A likely story! I asked him to supply some proof of Mirandinha's ability by producing a video of the player in action, and I did some research myself. The story checked out, but I forgot all about it until about a month later, when in walked Don Packham with the video. Unfortunately, it wasn't compatible with my machine, but when I asked some friends at London Weekend Television if they could do anything with it, they lost the colour but managed to make it work in black and white. I regarded them as good judges of a player, and what they saw excited them so much that I could hardly wait to take a look myself. When I did, I realised I had been presented with the real thing. This guy was quick and could score goals. In other words, he was a man after my own heart.

First of all, I offered Mirandinha to Graeme Souness, who had been appointed the manager of Glasgow Rangers in April 1986. He was keen to sign him, but it didn't work out because the chairman, David Murray, suddenly put a block on Graeme's spending. I then approached Newcastle manager Willie McFaul, an old team-mate of mine, and got a favourable response. Newcastle became even keener to buy the Palmeiras striker when on 19 May 1987 he scored for Brazil at Wembley in a 1–1 draw with England.

The next step was to arrange for the president of Palmeiras to come over to England to negotiate the transfer. That first-class return ticket cost me £2,500, taking my initial outlay to well in excess of £10,000. It had already cost a fortune in lawyers' fees simply to cover me with regard to my appointment as one of the first football agents in the business, and to set up a limited company with Don Packham, Umberto Silva and me as directors. With phone bills on top of that, I was something like £12,000 out of pocket by then. I had also recruited the services of Bev Walker, a well-known sports agent at the time and a good friend. Being a new boy in the business, I felt I needed some experienced advice.

Bev and I went to meet the Palmeiras president at Heathrow, as arranged. The plan then was for us to drive up to Newcastle in Bev's Rolls-Royce. When we were approaching Newcastle, I was to call Willie McFaul to get the meeting organised. But when the Varig flight from São Paulo landed at Heathrow, there was no sign of the president at arrivals. Having verified, through Don and Umberto, that he had in fact boarded the flight in Brazil, there was only one conclusion to be drawn: he must have remained in transit and caught a plane to Newcastle. That meant it was more than likely Newcastle United had been doing a bit of plotting behind the scenes to cut us out of the deal. They must have made contact with the Palmeiras president directly and rerouted him to avoid us. Bev and I decided the only solution was to bomb up to Newcastle in his Roller as quickly as possible.

As we were racing up the M1, I made full use of Bev's car phone – a real luxury in those early days of telephone technology – to ring Newcastle United to try to find out what was going on. United, of course, denied any knowledge of the whereabouts of the president of Palmeiras, but I continued to smell a rat. The problem then was to try to work out where the Newcastle management and directors would be taking the president for talks. St James's Park was out of the question, because that's the first place we would look. It had to be in a hotel or restaurant in or near the city.

This is where my knowledge of the area came in handy. Having thought hard about it, I came to the conclusion that the perfect out-of-the-way place for a discreet meeting of the sort Newcastle would have had in mind was the Fisherman's Lodge. One of the best restaurants in the city, it's the only building you'll come across in the middle of a very pleasant walk through the Dene of Jesmond. There's a private road to the restaurant, but it's a devil of a job to find; and if you don't know it's there, you'll never find it.

A probable destination identified, we decided we would need the services of a lawyer, given the nasty turn the situation had taken. Bev recommended a guy he knew, an expert in contract law who was a partner in a very big law firm near the Quayside, and we used the car phone to arrange to meet him at the Fisherman's Lodge. We arrived there just after eight in the evening and sat at a place in the bar where we could see the front door of the establishment and keep a check on the restaurant itself. When we'd been there quite a while and had had a couple of pints of beer without seeing anybody from Newcastle, I went to take a leak.

The toilet was on the first floor, and when I went upstairs to use it, I saw a door marked PRIVATE. I had not been aware of the existence of this room, but I could hear muffled voices from within. On impulse, I decided to go for broke and just walked in without knocking, but ready to offer my apologies for upsetting somebody's dinner. No apologies were required, since I found myself staring at most of the Newcastle board, the manager Willie McFaul, the secretary Russell Cushing, and a foreign-looking gentleman I took to be the president of Palmeiras. 'Bingo!' I thought to myself, before saying, 'Good evening, everybody. My associates and I are sitting downstairs and I think you need to talk to us before anything gets concluded. See you in a while!' And, with that, I walked out.

When I told our lawyer what had happened, he said he would need to draft a legal document quickly. Fortunately, I had all the completed paperwork – in Portuguese and English – with me, so the lawyer was able to start on a handwritten agreement between Newcastle and our company right away. We were still sitting there after midnight. The restaurant was empty by his time, but nobody had come down from upstairs. The restaurant staff confirmed they were all still up there and assured us that the only way out was through the main door. So we just sat it out. I think Newcastle and company were hoping we would be kicked out, but I knew the people at the Fisherman's Lodge from years before – I'd been a very good customer when I was a player – and they were quite happy for us to wait downstairs at the bar. Finally, the party upstairs trooped downstairs, and we just let the lawyer get on with it. As a result, Newcastle United were persuaded to sign a deal that kept us in the transfer of Mirandinha.

What amazed me afterwards was the effrontery of the Newcastle board in continuing as normal afterwards without saying a word. They just carried on as if nothing had happened. Here I was, an ex-Newcastle player with no particular axe to grind; I was just trying to do a very complicated deal in as straightforward a manner as possible. It was a rare type of deal, too. Ossie Ardiles and Ricky Villa had of course gone to Tottenham, but there were precious few players from South America after that. Newcastle United knew I was several thousand pounds into it even before I made contact with them, yet they would quite happily have done that deal without me, leaving me heavily in debt. I didn't like doing business like that. Call me old-fashioned if you want, but I believe you can do a deal on a handshake, that somebody's word is their bond. I still prefer to believe that.

My costs were mounting all the time. The lawyer charged £150 an hour and had worked very productively for eight hours (7.30 p.m. to 3.30 a.m.). I was also paying for the use of Bev's Roller, and there were still hotel bills to be met for an overnight stop. I was now about £15,000 out of pocket. Worse still, I had to fork out for two more bloody plane tickets from Brazil to England for Mirandinha and Umberto Silva, without whom the player refused to travel, to come over for the actual signing. Newcastle didn't want to know about that.

When Mirandinha arrived with Umberto Silva, I introduced them to Bev, who laid out a whole list of things he'd set up for the player. One of them was a fantastic huge house on an exclusive estate that was to be sponsored for him throughout the duration of his stay in the north-east. I'd also negotiated a deal with Newcastle that would make the Brazilian the highest-paid footballer in the country and one of the highest paid in Europe. When all of this was done, Newcastle said they wanted the contracts signed at ten o'clock the following morning, followed by a press conference at eleven.

By then, Don Packham had turned up and joined us. That was bad news because he knew nothing about football transfers, and as a tied financial adviser he was not supposed to have a second job, which this transfer business could be interpreted as being. I had urged him to keep his head down, to keep out of the way, but there he was, all hyper and insisting he had to be in on it. Since I had to admit that without him and his approach to me none of this would be happening, I filled him in on the details.

Don spent that evening with Umberto Silva and Mirandinha while Bev and I went for a quiet meal together. We were back in the hotel bar at about one o'clock in the morning when Don walked in, a man transformed. Suddenly, from being this quiet, mild-mannered financial adviser earning £150 a week or whatever, he had become an expert on football transfers. Playing the big 'I am', he told us that he'd spoken to Mirandinha and thought that the player should be getting this and getting that. Moreover, he added, Umberto agreed with him.

'What the hell are you talking about?' I said. 'Are you telling us now that the player is dissatisfied?'

Don's reply suggested that he and Umberto had in fact been filling Mirandinha's head with nonsense, and Bev and I were becoming angrier by the minute.

'Look,' I said, 'you're not even supposed to be here! Leave us to do the business side of it. You know damn all about all of this, so don't start to put this deal in jeopardy now! I am the best part of £20,000 out of pocket, and I want it back. You've been to Brazil twice (I had sent him there to link up with Umberto Silva and Mirandinha); where do you think the money's been coming from? It's been coming from my bank account.'

But Don Packham was on a high, a complete ego trip. In fact, he said something to Bev that was such a professional slur that my agent friend lost his temper and grabbed him by the throat. 'If you ever talk to me like that again,' Bev said to Don, 'I will throw you out of this window, you ungrateful little shit!' Since the bar was on the sixth floor of the Swallow Hotel in Newcastle city centre, Don was rather shocked by Bev's reaction.

'Don,' I said, 'you asked for that. Don't come crawling to me for any sympathy. Keep your nose out of this business, it's delicate enough. We need it to go smoothly just until tomorrow when the whole deal will be signed and done.'

So Don went off with a flea in his ear and Bev and I sat chewing the fat. We were now aware we had to tread carefully and get Mirandinha to St James's Park for half past nine the following morning. But when Bev and I met down in the hotel lobby at about nine, there was no sign of the player, Don Packham or Umberto Silva. There was no reply from their rooms when we rang them, either, and they were not having breakfast, because we checked. In view of Don's attitude the previous evening, there could only be one explanation: they had gone up to St James's Park independently.

When we got there, it was too late. Don and Umberto had negotiated and Mirandinha had signed a new contract with Newcastle they all thought was superior to ours, but wasn't. Bev and I had got for him a basic wage of about £4,000 a week that could double if he scored a few goals, so he could have earned something over a quarter of a million from even a fairly poor season; under his new contract, the player was on £1,000 a week less than he would have been had he stuck with us. Part of the problem, I think, was that Umberto Silva was trying to get paid twice from the deal, once as an agent and once as an interpreter and companion to Mirandinha, something we had intended to include in our arrangement anyway. Bev and I had to just stand there on the sidelines at the press conference and watch as Don Packham and Umberto Silva presented themselves to the public as the men who had masterminded the first transfer to an English First Division club of a Brazilian footballer.

We did not lose out completely, of course. The deal we had struck with Newcastle United at the Fisherman's Lodge meant our company was still entitled to five per cent of the transfer fee, some £50,000. But by the time I had paid Bev, Don and Umberto what they were entitled to, and taken into account the money I had laid out in out-of-pocket expenses, I didn't make a penny from that historic transfer. Worse still, I discovered that the £10,000 I had put into a separate business account to settle income tax bills had been siphoned off in dribs and drabs by

Packham. Convinced he now knew everything about being a football agent, and still a director of the company, he had been withdrawing £200 a time to tout a Brazilian full-back called Nelsinho all over the place. Needless to say, he did not succeed in selling the player to any English club. He lost his job as a financial adviser, too, as I had warned him he would if he was seen to be doing anything that could be interpreted as another job. His employers could hardly miss him as a would-be football agent since the Mirandinha transfer was widely reported by both the newspapers and television. Eventually, his career disintegrated to such an extent that he was declared bankrupt. Nevertheless, he had to repay the missing £10,000 as best he could, so it was not as though Don Packham got away with anything in the end.

As for Mirandinha, I'm glad to say he did pretty well at Newcastle for a couple of seasons. At least the fact that he was one of United's leading scorers two years running supported my assessment of his ability. He did not stay for a third season. Newcastle let him go back to Palmeiras on loan before accepting a nominal fee for him. I think he'd made enough money by then to fulfil his real ambition, which was to become a pig farmer back in Brazil. Football was only a means to an end for Mirandinha.

All the hassle over the transfer put me right off any idea I might have had of becoming a football agent. Had it not worked out the way it did, I could have been nearly £30,000 worse off, if you include the tax bill. On the other hand, as I went back to my pub in Worthing, it did occur to me that the publicity I'd got from the deal might not be such a bad thing.

A few months later, in October 1987, my phone rang. It was Roger Fielding, the chairman of Huddersfield, offering me the manager's job. I'd first met Roger when I was commercial manager at Fulham. We'd become friends after I stood up at a Third and Fourth Division meeting in the north and suggested that clubs needed to look at the bigger picture and work together on major projects rather than be in opposition over small ones. It was a view Roger shared, and we got on like a house on fire. In the seven or eight years since then, he had become a very wealthy man. He and his partner had invented a lottery ticket counting machine that could differentiate between various types of tickets, and his company had been bought out by a French lottery ticket firm for a fortune. He had also become chairman of Huddersfield, and now he was asking me to take over as manager.

Even though I was itching to get back into the game and grateful to Roger for thinking of me, managing the famous old Yorkshire club was not the most inviting of prospects at that particular time. Huddersfield had been staving off relegation for about four or five seasons, and only a couple of months into the 1987/88 season they were rooted to the bottom of the old Second Division with only five points and no wins after eleven games. Steve Smith, the youth-team coach, had managed the club for a season, but had found it all a bit much and had stepped down. Nevertheless, I thought I owed it to Roger to go up and see what he had to say. I knew there was tremendous potential at the club, and Roger was infectiously enthusiastic about it all. He had quite a vision of where he wanted the club to go, too. He was not looking for instant results, he said; if Huddersfield went down that season, so be it. The plan would be to build for the future, the long term. 'The job you did at Fulham – that's the kind of thing this club needs!' he told me. So I accepted his offer, and we began the mammoth task of galvanising this old, historic club – champions of England three years running in the 1920s – and hauling it into the modern day.

Before we started, though, Roger gave me a warning. Huddersfield was a town of old wealth made from the wool trade, and it was old wealth that was on the board of directors in the main. He, not being a local and having gained a controlling interest in the club with new money, had not exactly been welcomed with open arms. 'They would prefer it if I wasn't there,' he said of his fellow directors. 'Whoever I appoint, you or anybody else, they will prefer him not to be there either. But don't worry. I have absolute control, so it'll just be a question of you and I working together.'

Reassured, I put the pub on the market, rolled up my sleeves and got down to my first football job for over three years. But nothing, it seemed, would go right. Take the case of Malcolm Brown, the right-back. When I was manager of Fulham, I thought Malcolm was one of the best players in the country. Having been at Newcastle for a while, he had re-signed for Huddersfield, and I was looking forward to working with him. But he was on the treatment table when I arrived, and I don't think he played a single game during the seven months I was at Leeds Road, the club's old ground. Nobody could tell me what was wrong with him other than that there was a problem with his thigh. Then there was Duncan Shearer, ex-Chelsea, up front. I had been rubbing my hands at the prospect of working with him, but he had the nightmare of nightmares while I was Huddersfield's manager. David Cork, Shearer's partner, was a hugely talented footballer who kept making chance after chance for the Scot, but Shearer just kept missing, missing, missing as the game went by. He could not get on the end of a chance for love nor money.

It didn't help, either, that Huddersfield did not own, or have use of, a proper training ground at the time. We used to run about a mile from Leeds Road to the foothills of the Pennines, where there was a bit of a level area. That was where we trained, but it was totally unsuitable, not least because it was nowhere near big enough. We couldn't do any full workouts on it; everything had to be done on a reduced scale. I complained about it constantly to club officials, but that didn't seem to do much good. I sensed a lot of hostility from them, partly because Roger had appointed me and partly because I was a southerner. As I mentioned at the start of the book, my mother had encountered the unfriendliness Yorkshire people can generate when she and my father moved to his home town of Hull, and now I was experiencing it myself.

Things went from bad to worse when we lost 10–1 – yes, 10–1 – to Manchester City at Maine Road in November. I'd signed the experienced Steve Walford on loan from West Ham in an attempt to stiffen the Huddersfield defence, but it didn't quite work out the way I'd hoped. I'd known Stevie from our playing days together at Arsenal, where he'd been cover for David O'Leary and Peter Simpson, then David and Paddy Howard. Although he was regularly a substitute at Highbury, Stevie was steeped in the discipline you have to have – or used to have to have – to play in an Arsenal back four. I told the three other members of my defence to take their cue from him. Unfortunately, Walford had spent so long at West Ham he seemed to have lost all his defensive nous. Time and again, we got caught by Manchester City, and every shot they had at goal went in. Shell-shocked, we were 4–0 down at half-time, left high and dry and playing just for pride in the second half. There wasn't much of that to be had, though, as another six goals flew into our net. David White, quick and skilful, and another brilliant player, Paul Stewart, caused us a right old problem that day, and our only consolation was a goal from the penalty spot. The crazy thing about it was, when I watched a video of the match a few days later, they had only had twelve attempts at goal to our seventeen!

That night, back in Huddersfield, I had agreed to go out for dinner with the chairman and his wife, but I was so upset and embarrassed by what had happened at Maine Road that when we got to the restaurant I offered Roger my resignation. Being a nice chap and somebody who knew something about the game, he told me not to be so silly and refused to accept it. He also offered words of encouragement. 'Come on,' he said, 'things can't get any worse, can they? I'm seeing all sorts of improvements in the team, and that's fine by me.' I decided to carry on trying.

I was quite happy with the coaching staff I'd inherited. Steve Smith, who'd stepped back down to youth level after managing the club for a time, was a good coach, and so was his former assistant manager, Jimmy Robson. They were two really nice lads who knew what they were doing with the youth team and the reserves; but I did need a good first-team coach. My search for one was concluded when I received a letter from an old friend of mine, Eoin Hand, who had gone out with me and Norman Piper to play for Lusitano in South Africa all those years earlier. Eoin's letter told me he was in the Middle East doing a job he hated, so I made contact with him and discovered he was returning home in a couple of days' time. We met up, and I asked him if he'd be interested in becoming my first-team coach. Eoin, of course, had been manager of the Republic of Ireland in the meantime, and I told him that he could use the appointment as a springboard for finding a manager's job in the Football League if he so wished. 'You can get yourself all around the place and talk to people,' I said. 'Use Huddersfield to find your own position. There are 92 League clubs, and you've got 91 to go for. Just leave my job alone!'

That is how we agreed it. Except, having agreed, Eoin then started kicking up a stink about his title. He said he wanted to be called assistant manager, not first-team coach. I was very reluctant to agree because I'd never had an assistant manager and didn't want one because it implied there was some sort of partnership involved. In the end, I relented, but not without pointing out to him that if he went touting for jobs as an assistant manager, prospective employers would be looking at him with suspicion as regards his loyalty. So, from the word go, I started to have my doubts about Eoin.

The next major development came after I'd been at Huddersfield for about three months. It came as a shock, too. One day, I got a phone call from Roger Fielding, who said, 'I've got some news, and I don't think it's going to be very good news for you.' He went on to tell me that he was no longer chairman of the club. He explained that he was planning to move to the tax haven of the Isle of Man, but had discovered he could not do that and keep any directorships on the mainland. He had to resign from the board, and from the chairmanship of Huddersfield Town.

'You mean, you're going altogether?' I said.

'I'm afraid so,' he replied. 'I'm sorry about that, and all I can do is advise you to watch out for yourself.'

No sooner had I put the phone down than my door opened and in walked the vice-chairman, Keith Longbottom, who announced he was now the chairman. I stood up, looked him straight in the eye and said, 'Congratulations, Mr Chairman. And when would you like my resignation?'

'We're not hirers and firers here,' he replied. 'Your job's safe, for the moment.'

'I bet it is!' I thought. 'I bet it is!'

That night, at home, I was undecided about whether to hand in my resignation or keep going. The trouble was, I'd just sold the pub and had nowhere else to go. Although I'd put it on the market straight away, I'd delayed selling the business during my first few months at Huddersfield, but in the end I was pushed to the point where I had to do the deal or lose it. Two weeks after selling, I received this bloody news! If I'd still had the bolthole of the Far Post, I'd have resigned there and then, but now I couldn't really afford to lose my salary.

It seemed a question of biting the bullet for the time being, but life was not made any easier by the bizarre demands the new chairman started to make. He insisted, for instance, that I be in my office at the ground at 12.30 every lunchtime so that I could phone him and discuss various matters, including transfer news. I protested that I did not get back from training – by now, I had persuaded the council to loan us a pitch once a week – until 1.30, and said I would always get on to him at once if there was anything to discuss, but he refused to listen to reason.

I was also continuing to have trouble with Eoin Hand. I tried to engage him socially outside the club, but I felt there had been a sea change in his personality from when I'd known him years before. There was a steeliness in his demeanour that made him very distant. To say he was difficult really is an understatement. Yet I felt I couldn't have been more generous in the way I had set out the position for him. All the time I implored him to use it as a springboard to other, better jobs in the game. I believed that I was winning the trust of the two other coaches, Steve Smith and Jim Robson, but all I sensed in Eoin was mistrust. He was certainly negative about anything and everything. All he did was moan, moan, moan. He complained, for instance, that I didn't give him his head in team meetings, so I told him to go ahead and do the meetings, as long as it was with a gusto and enthusiasm he'd failed to show up to then. I wanted him, in addition to setting out the coaching schedule, to suggest players we could afford who would improve the side, but all he could come up with was a couple of Irish lads he'd had under him when he was the Republic of Ireland manager. My feeling was that that smacked of nepotism, that we had to deal on a broader basis when it came to the recruitment of new players.

The sort of guy I was after was Mark Payne, an English lad I was tipped off about who at the time was playing in the Dutch Second Division for Leeuwarden but who had played in the Southern League in the early 1980s. He was a central midfield player who had never made it at League level here, but had then suddenly flourished after going abroad. Having heard his contract was coming to an end, and having received excellent reports on him, I flew over to Holland to watch him play. Mark impressed me a lot because he worked hard, had an awful lot of ability and wanted to get forward and get shots on goal. In fact, I thought he would make a hell of a difference to our side as the attacking midfielder. I arranged for this lad to come and see me after the game at my hotel. I explained who I was and that Huddersfield were about to be relegated from the Second Division, but that I wanted to rebuild the side completely for a promotion campaign with players like him. He, in turn, explained to me that he would be a free agent when his contract came to an end because there was no option clause in Holland as there was in English football. All he was looking for was a sizeable signing-on fee (by Huddersfield's standards) plus a contract. In other words, I was dealing with a Bosman-type transfer long before it became the norm all over Europe.

When I got back to Huddersfield and tried to explain the proposed deal to the chairman, I met with some resistance. The stumbling block, quite clearly, was the signing-on fee. The lad had asked for £50,000, so I told the chairman I thought I could knock him down to £35,000 and spread it over the three years of his contract. I also pointed out that if Leeuwarden had been asking a fee for the player, they would probably have wanted £100,000-plus, so even paying £50,000 we were getting him on the cheap. Even so, I could sense that same reluctance I had experienced with Lord Westwood, the Newcastle chairman. A mere footballer, picking up so much money for himself?

To my annoyance, because it suggested they did not value my assessment, the board then insisted on getting a second opinion on the player. And guess who they wanted it from? Yes, that's right – Eoin Hand. I called him in and told him to go out to Holland the following weekend to watch the lad and make a full report. Then I phoned the lad to find out where he would be playing with Leeuwarden, and he gave me very precise details. In addition, I got the flights booked and I typed out exactly where Eoin had to be and the time of the kick-off. In other words, I got the whole thing organised down to the last detail. It looked a perfectly straightforward trip, especially as Eoin, as a former international manager, had been all over the world and knew his way around foreign countries. After he'd left, I phoned Mark again to tell him Eoin was on his way and to ensure that he left a ticket for him at the gate. I also told him that I would ring him again on the Sunday night for a chat.

When I made the call, the lad told me the ticket had never been picked up. Finding that rather strange, I tried without success to contact Eoin. I had to wait until the Monday morning, when he came in late, to speak to him, and when I grabbed hold of him and demanded his report on the player he went bright red and just looked away, mumbling. Then, when I insisted on an explanation, he claimed he'd gone where I had told him to go but had found the stadium empty. I reminded him that I'd told him there were two stadiums in the town and had instructed him carefully as to which one to go to.

'Didn't you ask the taxi driver to take you to the other stadium?' I asked.

'Oh, I didn't think of that!' he replied.

'So what did you do?'

'I walked around and asked people, but everybody said there wasn't a game on that afternoon.'

'Funny, that,' I said. 'There were 12,000 people who knew about the game because they turned up and watched it!'

Eoin then started to plead with me. 'Look,' he said, 'please promise me you won't let anybody know that I never got there. I'll sort it out next week.'

Foolishly, I agreed. I say foolishly, because as I was getting ready for training I was told the chairman was coming into the ground and he wanted to see me. When I went to his office, I saw that it wasn't just the chairman waiting for me, but all the directors of the club. They wanted to discuss the player we were after in Holland, and asked after Eoin Hand's report on him. When I told them I hadn't got the report, they asked why, which rather put me on the spot. Not wanting to let Eoin down, I said that he hadn't yet made up his mind about the player and was planning to go out to Holland again to watch him. But they kept pressing me and, not unreasonably, suggested that Eoin must have given me some indication of his initial thoughts.

Finally, the chairman looked straight at me and said, 'Eoin Hand never did see him play, did he?'

Desperate for excuses now, I burbled on about not having had time to speak to him about the player, but I sensed the game was up.

'Right, thank you very much,' replied the chairman. 'That's all we wanted to know, because we can tell you quite categorically that Eoin Hand did not see the player!'

Suddenly, it hit me that I had been stitched up, really stitched up. I drove straight over to the training ground, told Steve and Jim to get on with the training, and ordered Eoin Hand to be at my house in exactly half an hour. When he got there, I gave him a hard time. Coldly and calmly, I accused him of many things, the thrust of which was that he had let me down badly, betrayed our friendship and, in effect, cost me my job. In response, he said nothing. All he did was look at the ground and go scarlet. I've never seen a man go so red in all my life. The colour was somewhere between a tomato and a beetroot. In the end, I ordered him out of the house and sent him on his way with utter contempt in my voice.

When he'd left, I got on the phone to the chairman and told him that I could see exactly what the situation was, that I'd been manoeuvred into a position where I had been forced to tell an untruth, and that I would be taking steps to correct it. I wrote a letter apologising for misleading the board in any way, and offered my resignation.

I arrived at the club the following morning to find the chairman already there. He called me into the boardroom and said, 'If you like, you can go.'

To which I replied, 'I just wish I'd gone right from the word go when you were appointed chairman!'

To make matters worse, he then accused me of having a drink problem and of other things. I told him I wouldn't deny there were occasions when I'd had a beer too many, but pointed out that I'd seen the vice-chairman drink us all under the table. 'What it actually boils down to, Mr Chairman,' I continued, 'is that you are happy for this club to be relegated as long as they maintain a nice middle-of-the-table position in Division Three. And that's where I expect to see you for a very long time to come!'

With that, I just walked away from the place. I didn't say goodbye to anybody. Needless to say, Eoin was appointed immediately as my successor, but his path and mine have never crossed from that day to this. I have done everything in my power to prevent that from happening.

As I walked away from Huddersfield's historic old ground that May morning in 1988, I knew in my heart of hearts I would never get another job in football. I was pretty well convinced the game had had it with me. I spent a long time at home thinking about what I was going to do, and it was during that time of contemplation, with my house in

Huddersfield on the market, that I got a message from somebody I knew telling me a fellow by the name of Alan Bowes was trying to contact me urgently about some business ideas. I thought I might as well phone the number I had been given.

Alan told me he was involved in the licensing trade and was based at Kingston in Surrey. He said he would like to meet me to talk about things that were happening within his company because he felt there would be something of interest for me in it. We met up in west London and talked at length. He told me that, essentially, he had bought licensed premises then tenanted them out. He also said he had a national account with Allied Breweries, which I knew, as a former pub landlord, was a major thing. It means you're buying your beer at rock bottom prices and it gives you huge standing with banks because you're deemed to be extremely good business and to have A1 ratings in every conceivable way. From what Alan said, it looked as though his was a small but quite substantial licensed property company. In fact, it was more like a group of companies, each one looking after its own section of the business.

I didn't get anything specific out of him at that first meeting, but during the second meeting we started to get down to brass tacks. Alan, who was from the north-east, spoke about the opportunities he foresaw up in that neck of the woods. Having achieved so much in west London, he felt he could do an awful lot more by expanding his interests up there, and without being specific he seemed to suggest that he wanted me to head the operation. He then took me on a bit of a grand tour around a whole host of licensed premises in the London area. We also met up with the Allied Breweries national account manager and talked in broad terms about what Alan Bowes' small company was doing and how rapidly it was expanding. And all the time he kept saying that the north-east was the place to be.

Everyone we met treated him with reverence, and everything he said seemed to stack up. He talked about his background in banking, and said he'd worked for the NatWest before being headhunted by a brewery firm in Dunbar on the north-east/Scottish border that had offices in London. It all seemed very, very sound, and each time I left the feller I was very impressed by what he'd shown me and by most of what he'd said. Even so, there was a question mark in my mind. I couldn't put my finger on the reason, but the question mark just wouldn't go away. Perhaps it was because the company was called ATG, which stood for the All Time Great group of companies, a grandiose name that ought to have been a warning in itself.

Finally, Alan introduced me to the directors of his company – a surveyor, an architect, an accountant and a bank manager. Their skills seemed to be exactly what a firm of property developers would need, and all of them talked about how well the business was doing and how everybody was convinced about the need to expand into the north-east. But still I didn't know exactly what it was they wanted me to do. When I pressed the point, they said they felt they needed a sort of satellite office up in the north-east and told me there were properties up there that had come to their attention.

At this stage I was getting into final negotiations on the sale of my house in Huddersfield and I didn't have anywhere else to go, but I was intrigued by these people. So Nicky, my second wife, and I travelled up to the north-east to meet them. We stayed in a hotel in Berwick, quite a large building overlooking the Tweed, and there was talk about buying it and running it as a hotel and restaurant business Alan Bowes' company could use as a sort of headquarters in the area. At last, we began talking about how I could become involved. In the end, we hammered out a deal whereby I would become a lessee of the hotel. It seemed ideal, because I had plenty of experience in the licensed trade and Nicky, having been brought up in the hotel business all her life, knew the game inside out. The building itself needed quite a lot of work doing to it to drag it into the twentieth century, but Nicky thought it had a lot of potential as a hotel. Not only that, but the deal was very favourable to us in that, though the rent was rather steep, we didn't have to pay anything for going in, other than buying initial stock. The ingoing fee is usually what cripples you, but I negotiated that out of the equation. Thus I found myself as part of Alan Bowes' company, and a customer as well. Everything seemed set fair. The hotel/restaurant was in a good tourist area, and Nicky was happy. The business was something she could get her teeth into, and she wanted to give it a go.

At about that time, too, I was approached by Capital Radio in London, and I started doing football commentaries alongside Jonathan

Pearce for their new station, Capital Gold. It was their pilot year, and they wanted to give football commentary a really big go, so although I was only on £100 per match plus expenses, it was more or less agreed that if I did it well for a year I'd receive a proper contract at the end of it. Since I was moving from Huddersfield to Berwick-on-Tweed, the travelling presented a bit of a problem, but there was a direct train straight into King's Cross and the weekend rates were pretty good, so I went ahead with that as well as the new business. I'd work in the hotel from Sunday to Friday, then leave Berwick on the seven o'clock train on Saturday morning for London, or wherever Capital Gold were covering the London club that would bring them the biggest audience. That could mean going to Blackburn or wherever, but in the main I was working down in London.

Back in Berwick, though, I had spotted this fabulous old building with a sort of Georgian façade near the centre of town. It had once been a hotel famed for its restaurant, but, having been closed down for three or four years, it had fallen into disrepair. It was going to need quite a lot of money spent on it, but it had more potential than our Tweed View Hotel in that it looked as though it could attract a more substantial trade than the tourist/company rep one we had at the other place. People from ATG would come up to the Tweed View Hotel occasionally and stay with us for three or four days, so I took the opportunity during one of these visits to tell them about the building I'd spotted in the town. They responded favourably, I set about costing the project, and suddenly it started to look realistic. It soon boiled down to the nitty-gritty of raising the initial purchase money. It could have been done through a brewery loan, but the brewery would not release the money until the building had been brought up to a reasonable standard, which meant taking out a bridging loan to meet the purchase price of £110,000. ATG said they were a bit stretched with other projects, so I offered to create the bridge myself.

I thought I had protected myself all the way, because I'd demanded a written guarantee from the brewery about the release of their loan and from ATG about the setting up of a fund to pay for the renovation of the building. It was also agreed that I would be in charge of the works. Then, when the project was completed, I would run this hotel as well as the Tweed View and pay the rent. But perhaps I should have smelt a rat when the account that was supposed to fund the works was always being promised by ATG but was never actually set up. Still, I was so anxious to get started on the project that I was prepared to take a risk. I felt I had to move the process on, and thereby force the hands of others.

We soon had the whole thing under way despite the non-appearance of the funding account. I actually knocked down a huge chimneybreast with a sledgehammer myself, helping to clear rubble and rapidly transforming this rundown building into a small, exclusive hotel with eight bedrooms, a bar and an à la carte restaurant. We also turned some storerooms into offices for ATG. They had been talking about expanding the company because the London office couldn't cope with all the business any more, and in any case they were spending so much time away from the capital they needed another base. At my suggestion, they set up shop in our second Berwick hotel, but that led to complications about the status of Nicky and me in the arrangement. Did the company own the hotel? Were we merely tenants? Could we be expected to pay rent when ATG were using the building as their north-east office? Were we being employed to run it? In the end, it was agreed that Nicky, as the hotel expert, would be paid a salary, but not as an employee. She would invoice a management fee instead.

Now there was a whole host of cross-payments with regard to both premises. Not only were we owed money by ATG for the refurbishment of the new hotel, but employees of the company had run up an unpaid bill of £7,000 for their stays at the Tweed View. By now, too, my involvement with Capital Gold was beginning to take over my life. From about Christmas 1988 we had started to cover midweek matches as well, so twice a week – Wednesday and Saturday – I was hauling myself down to London, or wherever they wanted me to be, from Berwick. As things got busier towards the end of the season, there were important games taking place on the Tuesday or the Friday, too. What with League Cup finals, FA Cup games and what have you, I was sometimes doing matches on a Saturday, Monday, Tuesday, Wednesday and Friday. The money was pretty good – at times in March and April 1989 I was invoicing for £500 a week plus expenses – but it was taking up an awful lot of my time at a stage when I had a major problem on my hands back in Berwick.

To cut a long and complicated story short, Nicky and I were conned completely out of the two hotels and all our money. The first step was taken when the brewery loan of £110,000 was finally paid into my trading account via ATG, but minus £3,000 claimed by their lawyers as a fee. When I complained that they had no right to a fee since I had set up the bridging loan myself, Alan Bowes told me to take the £3,000 off the rent I was due to pay ATG that particular month. I couldn't see how that would work, but Alan was quick to reassure me. 'Don't worry,' he said. 'The accountant will sort it all out.'

By then, the second hotel had opened with great success. The tills were clinking and everybody was very impressed with the renovation. But I was still pressing for repayment of the money owed to me without any success. Then came the real hammer-blow. I had assumed that the £110,000 from the brewery, minus £3,000, that had been paid into my account had squared the bank off for the bridging loan, but my latest set of accounts showed that I was being charged interest on the £110,000 – which meant, of course, that the loan had not been repaid. When I queried this with the bank, they told me they had been instructed to send the money to a lawyer in Scotland. When I asked who had instructed them to do this, they said I had. That was complete nonsense, I hadn't been anywhere near the bank to authorise any such thing, but the bank insisted I had given them the instructions in June, a month before the second hotel opened. Totally mystified, I went to see Alan Bowes at ATG, only to be told he was far too busy and wouldn't be able to see me for three days. Then I got a bailiff's letter telling me that, due to the non-payment of rent, I was going to be evicted.

I shot off immediately to my lawyers in Newcastle, who told me that technically I was in breach of the law and ATG had every right to evict me. When I protested that I had been told to offset the missing £3,000 against rent, I was told the arrangement had been made with the wrong company in the group. 'So that's how they do it,' I said to the lawyer, 'by fiddling and juggling things around the group of companies?'

'Yes,' he replied, 'you've got it.'

My only chance of getting the money back, the lawyer added, was to go to court, but he warned me it was likely to be a long, drawn-out process. As for the bailiff's letter, my lawyer advised me to get out of the hotel as soon as possible. I created a stalemate situation for a few weeks, but then I received a letter from ATG terminating any agreement with regard to the other hotel.

All of this did not come at the best of times because Nicky was pregnant, and the worst of the news arrived at exactly the time the baby was due. The day the bailiffs were due to come in Nicky was rushed into Ashington Hospital from the local hospital in Berwick because of complications and finished up having to have a Caesarean section. I had dashed down to Northumberland first thing in the morning, so I was missing from the Tweed View Hotel at the time the bailiffs came.

Having made sure mother and child were fine, I returned home not knowing what to expect. As it turned out, I got a pleasant surprise: our receptionist had given the bailiffs an absolute piece of her mind. Normally such a meek and mild woman, she'd sent them away in shame for having had the temerity to seek to evict people when the birth of their child was taking place. But it was only a temporary reprieve. With Alan Bowes now refusing point-blank to see me, I sought an interview with the chairman of the ATG group but got no satisfaction from him either. In the end, a second eviction date was set and my lawyers advised me to honour it. We took out everything we possibly could and bought a house in Berwick.

One of the worst parts, though, was explaining all this to the staff. When I asked ATG about their welfare, I was told, 'That's your problem. You sort it out!' At that moment, I thought, 'Right, you bastards, I'm going to hunt you down! I am not going to rest until I have my day of reckoning with you!' That was a long time coming, though. Before getting any sort of revenge, I had to endure the collapse of my proposed court case against ATG (the four companies in the group I had targeted conveniently went into liquidation), the unpleasant experience of going bankrupt and the break-up of my second marriage. All sorts of other factors were responsible for the latter, but I shall always remember what our first QC had said to us when we were putting together our lawsuit against ATG. 'Before you embark on this major step in your life,' he had advised us, 'you have to take into account one very important thing. I guarantee that, before it is finished, one of the following will happen: one or both of you will have a heart attack, one or both of you will have a nervous or mental breakdown, or you'll get divorced.' At least, I thought, both of us still had our health intact.

Having had the life sucked out of me for many months by the struggle with ATG, I suddenly found myself in a vacuum when the door to legal redress was closed. Therefore I didn't think twice when I was approached by some people to go to Switzerland to assist them in a financial transaction. I was offered a very sizeable fee, and I thought I might as well go for broke. Having ensured that it was all legal and above board, I decided I had nothing to lose. I also thought that, in the process, I might be able to get my head straight as to which was the best way to go after losing the two hotels in Berwick and all my money. Not only was I flat broke at this stage, my huge debts were continuing to mount because, hard as I tried, I couldn't stop companies supplying goods to the two hotels in my name. Every time I contested these bills I was told they had been authorised by ATG. I was on the phone constantly, pleading with the suppliers to stop, but still it continued. Every time I challenged them, they claimed they had the requisite authority. It was madness!

Switzerland wasn't exactly a great success either. Nothing came of it in terms of my earning money. You start dealing with banks over there and it's something else! I pulled as many strings as I could and tried to do my very best in the circumstances, but my partners in the venture left me somewhat stranded. Worse still, I made a surprise trip home during all of this, walked in unannounced and found somebody else with my wife.

I went to my Mum's in Sussex and spent a few days with her before flying back to Switzerland to attend to other business. From there, I took a train down to Italy because I felt it was all done and finished for me in England and I needed to take stock of my life. I stayed with a friend in Milan for a while and just enjoyed the lifestyle and the people there. The Italians have this wonderful ability to have fun at no cost whatsoever. Their pleasures in life come very, very cheaply, and it was wonderful to experience that. They work much longer hours than anybody in this country, yet they have a lot more fun as well.

When I finally managed to get my head sorted out, during the

1991/92 season, I started to do a weekly column for the *Daily Star*, who had contacted me over there. I also began working for Channel 4, who were covering Italian football at the time. Once again I had begun to generate an income, albeit nothing grand. At the end of that season, I went back to England resolved to sort everything out once and for all.

It soon became obvious to me, though, that I couldn't cope with the complexities of my financial situation, so I made an appointment to see somebody at the office of the Official Receiver in London. My case was far too complex for the first young lad I saw, and he referred me to a much more senior lady. And what a diamond she proved to be! Having grasped the situation completely, she reckoned there was obviously somebody in the background causing all this trouble and it was their job now to bring him to judgement. I could hardly believe what I was hearing. Then she added, 'We're not having things like that go on. Otherwise I'm going to have a stream of people following you into these offices.' I gave her every detail I could about ATG and arranged to meet her again the following week. What she discovered in the meantime was that the 26 companies in the group, having received the resignations of various directors, had been put in my name! She gave me a whole pile of photocopied documents and asked if the signature on them was mine. I proved they were not by signing my name about ten times on a blank sheet of paper. Having compared these with the photocopies, she came to the conclusion that somebody had quite obviously tried to forge my signature – hence, it seemed, the alleged disappearance of my £110,000 (less £3,000) to a lawyer in Scotland and the reluctance of companies to stop supplying the two Berwick hotels with goods. The whole thing was a major scam.

My female saviour advised me to go bankrupt, adding that after the statutory three years of not being able to run a business I would be able to get on with my life again. She also said that there were steps she could take against Alan Bowes about which she couldn't speak to me, which was intriguing. When I'd signed the bankruptcy forms she'd put in front of me, she said, 'What I can tell you is that I shall go after this fellow and I will have him. I have got powers that you will never understand.' And sure enough, it wasn't long before, by accident, I saw in the *Daily Mail* a list of people barred as company directors, and there was Alan Bowes' name. He'd been barred for between six and nine years; I can't remember the exact figure now, but it was a massive punishment. I thought, 'Right, there is my revenge!' I put the paper in the bin and decided to close the door on that episode of my life.

I have to say that going bankrupt in 1992 didn't make a great deal of difference to my life. That was largely because I went back to Italy, where our bankruptcy laws do not apply, and I lived there until 1996. In Italy, I was free to take the sort of opportunity that presented itself when I was introduced to a guy from a company in Hampshire called Telsis. He told me they were working with SIP, as Telecom Italia were known at that time, to set up a scheme for introducing premium phone lines in Italy. From what he said, it was a growing business around the world, and as it hadn't even reached the stage of birth, never mind infancy, in Italy, I thought perhaps I'd struck gold. I realised this chap from Telsis could give me all the information I needed about premium phone lines, and he was also kind enough to promise me the 'in' to the business.

Having drawn up a blueprint for a company based on all I could discover, I racked my brains to think of somebody back in England who understood this concept. After a lot of thought, it came to me that there was only one guy, and he was David Sullivan, the soft-porn mogul whose millions and business expertise were beginning to revitalise Birmingham City. A lot of his money, of course, came from premium phone lines, not all of them devoted to sex chat, which was banned in Italy anyway. I rang David about my idea.

'Well, what a small world this turns out to be!' he said. 'I have just spent a few days in Italy trying to get in on the premium phone lines over there and I can't. With all my pull, all my contacts, I couldn't do it. And you're telling me you can do what I can't do?'

Assuring him that I could, I warned him it would be a long-term proposition. Only nine companies, I explained, would be allowed to take part in the pilot stage of the operation, which was due to last for twelve to fifteen months; after that, the opportunity would be there for us to get into the business on the ground floor. But I urged him not to expect too much too soon. 'Please understand that they have totally different ways of doing things over here,' I said. 'It's not anywhere near as simple as it would be in Britain.'

Having seen my blueprint for the company, David authorised me to go and trailblaze for him in the Italian premium phone line business, and he sent over several thousand pounds to finance the fact-finding operation. The first thing I discovered was that SIP would only deal with the Italian equivalent of a limited company. But setting up a limited company in Italy is a much more complicated business than it is here in Britain, where you can take one off the shelf, pay your lawyer £150 and start trading. In the end, it took me nine months, and it involved lodging twelve million lire (more than £4,000) with the chamber of commerce in Milan.

Despite all my warnings about the slower pace of life in Italy, David was screaming and ranting at me because things weren't happening more quickly. He decided to introduce me to Darren Brady, the brother of Karren Brady, Birmingham City's high-profile managing director. The whole Brady family seemed to be linked to the Sullivan organisation because Darren and Karren's father was a printer who did an awful lot of the printing of Sullivan's magazines and things like that. Anyway, Darren's speciality was premium phone lines, and he came to Italy to see me and find out more about the operation. I showed him how it all worked, and what it meant in terms of costs and time. In fact, I went to a dinner party that weekend and met the owner of a technology company who told me it had taken him fifteen months to set one up. He was amazed to hear I'd done it in nine!

The next step was to open an office. In some countries – England and South Africa, for instance – you can run this kind of business from your home, but Italy wasn't having that at all. Their regulations were very strict, and they insisted on it being run from kosher premises. After viewing a number of properties with Darren Brady, we plumped for one close to Milan's Central Station. It was a relatively prestigious address, but our spacious first-floor suite was sorely in need of a coat of paint. I applied that myself, and got the whole place habitable. I even scrubbed the loo! After a German technician had installed all the equipment for the phone lines we were ready to go, but there was delay after delay after delay from SIP. The pilot scheme had started and was going very well, I understood, but it was a long time before SIP finally announced the terms for becoming a service provider, or SP. They sent me, as the all-powerful company secretary, all the bumf about it, and I – still struggling to master the language – did my level best to translate it and work out the charges.

It was no easy task, because the Italians had come up with a hugely complicated formula which involved a one-off payment of twenty million lire (about £6,000) followed by the renting of lines and numbers at a cost determined by things like how old or how memorable they were. You'd pay a lot more for a number like 118888, for instance. British Telecom, by comparison, made it much more straightforward by just attaching the lines and taking a big percentage of each call. In addition, SIP were demanding a deposit of three months' money on every number on every line. So, together with the upfront payment for being allowed into the scheme, it meant it was going to be very expensive to become involved. But, as I stressed to the Sullivan organisation, once the operation was up and running, the rewards would be far greater than under the BT method.

They supplied the finance, and I flew down to SIP's head office in Rome to pay all the money required up front. It was now almost twenty months after I had first made contact with David Sullivan, but we really were ready to go. A fortnight later, SIP came to install a line in our office in Milan, and then – nothing. The equipment didn't work! SIP sent a technician down, but he couldn't figure out what was wrong, and it wasn't until another technician, an American, came in that we discovered what the trouble was. It was quite simple: the £25,000 worth of equipment installed by the German was utterly useless. I discovered later it had been a bit of duff kit that had been going round the market, the price dropping all the time, and our people had been foolish enough to buy it.

In the meantime, thankfully, a company from Hong Kong had become involved in the venture, and they promised us the very latest kit, which was worth half a million quid. Sure enough, along came this ultra-modern piece of equipment one day. It was the size of a fridge-freezer and had wheels on it that actually enabled it to go up stairs. By now, I was feeling dead chuffed. I'd had this major piece of technology installed, I had this major Hong Kong player in the frame, and I was now convinced we could really make a go of the whole thing.

I had previously spent a lot of time giving prospective service providers from the UK the grand tour, but now the Hong Kong people told me that all the SPs would come through them. All they required me to do was make sure the services went out. I had made contacts of my own, though. One of them was the secretary of the Italian equivalent of our Football League, whose offices were not far from where I lived, opposite the San Siro stadium. Together, we put together all sorts of ideas for a daily football service from each club.

By the time Christmas rolled around in 1995, we were looking to go for broke. However, I had heard one or two whispers from contacts in the business that all was not well at SIP, and when I compared notes with the lass the Hong Kong punters had put in there, she told me she had heard rumblings too, but from a different quarter. Therefore, knowing the virtually unlimited powers of Italy's financial police to confiscate equipment, we decided to store our half a million quid's worth of technology in a bonded warehouse while we were away over the festive period. I went back to England and had a lovely Christmas with my mother and brothers.

I returned to Italy in January 1996 and phoned my assistant in Verona. She immediately informed me that the entire premium phone business had been closed down by the Italian government. A law had been passed to that effect on 28 December while everybody was away on holiday, and the financial police had gone into all the offices running the services and taken their equipment as collateral against any money owed to SIP. Fortunately, there was nothing to take in our case, but there were signs of entry. We weren't quite sure why the Italian government had taken such a drastic step, but we suspected it was because they had got their sums hopelessly wrong. It had taken a lot of money to set the service up, but they had got a lot of money up front from the service providers, so it had to be because the SPs – most of them foreigners – were clearing almost a pound a minute in profit on each call. Television game shows were being created around these phone numbers – you know, thousands of people ring in with answers to questions – and the Italians realised they had done themselves out of a lot of money. All we could think was that they had decided to scrap the original idea and start again at some future date – which they did.

Everyone goes nudge–nudge, wink–wink when you talk about premium phone lines, but there's a vast amount of money to be made from them through things other than sex. Did you know, for instance, that the extremely successful television programme *Who Wants to be a Millionaire?* is funded by a premium phone line? That's where they get their prize money. There was mention of one person having made as many as 8,000 calls trying to get on the show; at 50p a call or whatever, that's in the region of £4,000! And thousands of people are making those calls. And it's not just game shows and sex; there are dating lines, religious chat lines – all sorts of things.

Darren Brady and the guys from Hong Kong lost thousands on the enterprise because there was no compensation whatsoever from the Italian government. At least I had been able to save the Hong Kong company half a million pounds by putting their equipment in storage. I used it to my advantage in that I said I was prepared to release the kit subject to them allowing me to make a clean break. I wanted the rent on the offices paid up in full so that I didn't get into any trouble with the financial police, and I gave notice on my flat.

The company lawyer had warned me that it was not going to be easy to walk away from the whole thing if I stayed in Italy. He told me that, even though the plug had been well and truly pulled on the premium phone lines operation, the Italian government would keep coming at me for future payments on the SIP contract. It was no good complaining to Brussels, the EU or wherever, he added, because this was Italy, a law unto itself. His advice was to get out of the country as swiftly as possible.

Taking it, in May 1996 I threw a few suitcases into the back of my left-hand-drive car and, leaving behind loads of furniture in my flat, drove away from Italy. Not having made any real money from the premium phone line business, I returned to England with about £3,000 in my pocket and no obvious future prospects.

# CHAPTER TEN
# BACK IN TOON

When I returned to England in May 1996, I based myself at my mother's house in Sussex for a couple of weeks. I did a couple of little jobs for Sky and put myself about by getting on the phone to people I knew. Having been offered some work up in the north-east for three days, I was contacted by someone who worked for Century FM, or Century Radio as it was then. They asked me if I would pop into the studio and do some work for them while I was up there. They seemed to like what I did because John Simon, the programme controller, enquired whether I would be interested in fronting a completely new football phone-in programme they were thinking of launching. He said their major news programme between 5.45 and six o'clock finished with a sports bulletin, and they wanted to keep the theme going in the programme that followed. One of the aims was to catch people as they were listening to the radio driving home from work. The idea was to try the programme for a season and to see how it went, and that is how long my contract would be. I wasn't sure I wanted to do it because it meant moving from Sussex to the north-east lock, stock and barrel and removing myself from the London scene, which had been my initial target on returning from Italy, but after thinking about the offer overnight, I decided to give it a go. It was, after all, a major step into the broadcasting business, so I rented a flat on Tyneside and threw myself into this radio programme.

The only problem was the crippling pain I was now getting from my left knee – the one that had finished my playing career. I had been suffering quite badly with it during those last few months over in Italy, and it was getting worse, if not by the day then certainly by the week. I had been struggling to depress the clutch pedal in the car, and instead of climbing stairs I was having to wait for lifts. Now it had reached the stage where I'd look at a staircase and feel frightened! I'd be thinking to myself, 'It's going to be hard enough getting up there, but how the hell do I get down again?' I found myself getting back home after doing the radio programme, putting my leg up and being able to do very little else. The knee had become completely unstable, and I didn't trust it to support me. It was so bad that on more than one occasion I went to a football ground to watch a game and finished up turning round and going home because I couldn't get to where I needed to get to, namely up the stairs to my seat. And even if I did get up them, how was I to get down with thousands and thousands of people – on my backside? Tears would stream down my face as I tried to use that knee, and I wasn't even crying; they'd just come of their own volition.

The knee was causing another problem to develop too. While I was still in Italy, I'd found that drinking whisky, rather than a cold beer, would kill the pain a lot more and give me the opportunity to move, so before I had any task to do that required substantial movement, I'd started to have a drink. In those last few months in Milan, when I was closing down our premium phone business, my time had been more my own and I'd been drinking heavily. It was getting to the stage where I was seeing off a bottle of Scotch a day. I went to see a doctor and explained that I had a drink problem because there seemed to be little else I could do to ease the pain in my knee. It needed sorting out. Unfortunately, the doctors I consulted said there really wasn't anything they could do. I asked what would happen when I couldn't walk, full stop, and they talked about disability allowance. It felt as if I was being gradually backed into a wheelchair. They would talk about me having to cut down on the drink, but I pointed out to them that without it I couldn't get from A to B. The whole thing was an ever-increasing vicious circle in which I had to build myself up mentally just to go out in the afternoon to do the radio programme and return straight home.

Occasionally, there was a slightly comical aspect to my predicament. I was starting to get offers to do after-dinner speeches, but what I found was that I was doing them on one leg. With the tablecloth hiding my legs, I would stand there speaking, my left foot resting on the chair just behind me. Then, when I'd finished speaking, I'd find my foot was stuck on the chair and I didn't have the physical ability to remove it myself. I'd have to turn to somebody beside me and ask them to pull the chair out from underneath my foot! Understandably, they'd look at me as if I was a madman. My right knee, which was also giving me a bit of trouble, was suffering from the strain being put on it as well.

Then, in February 1997, two police cars followed me after I had finished doing the radio programme and was driving home from Century. When the officers stopped me after three miles, I asked them if there was something wrong with my driving or with the car. No, they said, there was nothing wrong with either; they would just like me to take a breathalyser test. When I did so and failed, I couldn't believe it. I hadn't had a drink since the previous night and I thought I'd be perfectly clear. The court case came soon afterwards, and I was banned from driving for eighteen months. The strange thing about the verdict was that I wasn't fined as well. Instead, they put me on probation for the first year of the eighteen months – a decision nobody could understand. So I had a monthly visit from a probation officer who would often arrive on my doorstep almost in tears because of the other people she was having to deal with. Without her breaking any confidences, I became almost like a father confessor figure to her, helping to solve the problems she was having with other people. It was good therapy for me as well as for her, I think.

I had pulled out of Century by then. Although the programme had been going well, it was agreed that I shouldn't continue there because of the scandal over the drink-driving charge. My case was splashed all over the country's newspapers and it seemed a very dark hour, not least because I suspected somebody had been very spiteful and pointed the police in my direction. I'm 99.9 per cent sure who it was who fingered me, but I'd rather not name names. Anyway, I'd broken the law and I had to take my punishment. What I found more difficult to take was the fact that everybody seemed to see me as a raging alcoholic; nobody bothered to find out the truth. The world and his brother were trying to get in on the act. I'd have people knocking on my door saying, 'Use our clinic!' That really was enough to drive somebody to drink!

Fortunately, I had somebody to help me through those bad times. One day, while I was still working for Century, a guy at the station asked if I was dashing off after the show. He was a renowned local comedian called Mike Elliott, and he did the next but one programme after mine. When I said I wasn't, he asked me to hang around for a bit because he had a bit of a surprise for me. As I came out of the studio at seven o'clock, Mike went, 'Da-daa!' and there was a lady called Carol Johnson standing in front of me. It was quite a shock, because I hadn't seen Carol in nearly 25 years. In fact, she didn't think I'd remember her, but I did. We'd first met back in 1973, when I was playing for Newcastle United and we were both married. Her husband was Brian Johnson, who later became lead singer with the rock group AC/DC but who was then fronting an up-and-coming Newcastle band called Geordie. I'd been asked to go along and help promote their first album at a press launch at the Imperial Hotel – now the Swallow Hotel – in Jesmond. There was the usual pandemonium at a do like that, but I found myself sitting down and talking quietly to Carol while it was all going on around us. I discovered her to be a person of immense character and personality, and I enjoyed her company very much. She was a lady, even then, who had her feet very firmly planted on terra firma, and she wasn't going to have her head swayed in any direction other than normality and acceptability. Carol was also experiencing a touch of post-natal depression after recovering from the birth of her second child, so the hullabaloo of that press launch was not really what she needed at that time, and I recognised the fact. I suppose, then, there was an empathy between us that neither of us had ever forgotten.

Anyway, after the shock of meeting again like that after all those years, we went to the pub across the road, sat there and talked and talked. We became very close very quickly and sort of picked up where we had left off about a quarter of a century earlier. In the meantime, both of us had been round the world over and over again, and both of us had got divorced. So, we decided to give it a whirl together. I gave up my flat and moved in with Carol, who was hugely supportive during the dark hour of the breathalyser.

Having rediscovered my soul mate, I was more determined than ever to sort out the problems with my knee and my drinking. What worried me was that I had been so far over the limit when I hadn't had a drink in nineteen hours, so I went to see a doctor who conducted a series of tests. He was surprised, given my drinking history, to find that all my vital organs were in perfect condition. When I explained to him that my body had always told me what it needed – cheese, sugar, meat or whatever – he came to the conclusion that it had been storing properties from the whisky and drip-feeding them to me so that I could retain some manoeuvrability in the knee. No wonder, then, that I had failed the breathalyser. But that theory, while reassuring in a way, didn't really solve anything, so I enquired about the possibility of having an artificial joint put into my knee. The doctor explained, however, that those joints had a limited lifespan, and they didn't like to install them until people were in their seventies.

Since I was only in my forties then, the future looked bleak. I was in despair, because this was a total reversal in life. My left leg had been responsible for making me my fame and fortune, as it were, and now it was having a completely opposite effect. Indeed, I was having to turn down engagements because there were too many flights of stairs involved, or because I couldn't get the car near enough to the venue.

What changed everything was the telephone call I got one day from an old mate of mine, Micky Burns. Micky, who used to be one of my team-mates at Newcastle and now works for the Professional Footballers' Association, said, 'I've seen a lot of bad publicity about you. You've got a problem, haven't you?'

'Yes, Micky, I have,' I said, 'but perhaps not the problem you think it is.'

'I know exactly what problem you have,' he replied. 'It's your knee, isn't it?'

For the first time in a long time, I felt a weight go off my shoulders. Somebody had actually recognised my real problem. I told Micky just how bad my knee was, and he promised to get something done about it. A couple of days later, he came up to Tyneside and talked about arranging an appointment with a specialist. When I reminded him that I hadn't been a player for donkey's years and wasn't a member of the PFA any more, he assured me they took care of all ex-members.

Soon afterwards, I got a letter from a Mr Weeber at Friarage Hospital in Northallerton, Yorkshire, giving me the date and time of an appointment with him. Carol drove me down there and I hobbled in to meet Mr Weeber. 'I'm an orthopaedic surgeon,' he said in a wonderful South African accent. 'I specialise in artificial joints, and from what I've seen already, you've got a problem, feller.' He put me straight into a wheelchair and whipped me down to the X-ray unit. When the pictures of my knee came back, Mr Weeber looked at them for no more than two seconds before deciding the existing joint had to come out. He explained the whole operation to me and added that I would have to spend ten days in hospital recuperating and beginning the exercise regime and physiotherapy that would last for a month to six weeks. After that, he predicted, I would be mobile again. 'You won't be running, but you'll be walking,' he said, 'and you'll be able to get up and down stairs as much as you want. You take care of the new joint, and it will take care of you. The lifespan is somewhere between ten and fifteen years, so don't twist it and you can make it last fifteen. You're 47 now, so if you take care of the new knee, you won't need another until you're 62. The second one goes in all right, it's the third that's the problem. How many times can you keep putting a screw back in the same hole? It's as simple as that.'

I was booked in for the following week, but I have to admit to wondering whether I'd made the right decision. I was certainly becoming increasingly nervous about the operation. There's an awful lot of agonising one goes through, because you are, after all, having a part of your body taken away and a bit of metal and plastic inserted in its place. I knew, too, that I was still going to be extremely limited afterwards in what I could do with the knee. But the staff at the hospital had seen my kind of nervousness many times before and knew exactly what to do about it. Not long after Carol had got me settled in my room, the ward sister came in and said, 'You're full of doubt about this, aren't you, Mr Macdonald? You're not sure you're doing the right thing?' When I asked her how she knew, she said, 'We've had professional footballers in before, and they're always the same. The joint's been part of their life, an integral part of their living. I know all about what you're going through.'

Then she said there was somebody she wanted me to meet. She took me into a general ward and introduced me to this lovely old boy in his sixties. 'You just have a chat with him for a few minutes,' said the ward sister. It turned out that this chap had had the same operation as mine a couple of days earlier. He told me the leg was marvellous, but I doubted he could make that sort of assessment after only two days, particularly when his leg was up on a machine that was doing the movement for him. With that, he whipped back the bed covers to reveal that he had had his other leg done six weeks earlier. 'I'm telling you,' he insisted, 'it's marvellous!' In other words, this game old fellow was going to be on two artificial limbs, in effect, for the rest of his life. 'Yes,' he said, 'but I'm going to be walking, and I haven't walked for twenty years!' What he told me had exactly the effect the ward sister had anticipated, of course. I thought that if he could do it, then by heavens I could do it too. I went confidently into the operating theatre, and I've never looked back since.

I did have to do a certain amount of readjusting physically afterwards, though. As most people interested in football will know, I was famed for being very bow-legged, but it was necessary, apparently, for Mr Weeber to straighten the knee during the operation. My left leg is now as straight as a snooker cue, which means that, with the right leg still bowed, I'm more of a D than an O these days! It caused a slight imbalance, but nature is a wonderful thing and I've worked that one out. It's a bit like walking on a short stilt, really. It's a small price to pay for being pain free and not having a drinking problem any longer.

Mr Weeber was certainly not surprised to hear that I'd been hitting the bottle. Every one of his patients suffering from an arthritic knee, he said, had had an accompanying drink problem. 'Why there is so much amazement about it I don't know,' he said. 'It's the only way people find they can move around. So don't think you're on your own here – you're not. It's just that the rest of the world doesn't want to accept it. They look at the one instead of the other. I will solve your knee problem, and you should be able to solve your drink problem.'

And he was right. I've not had a drink since the day of the operation in June 1997. Even though I used to enjoy social drinking before the knee problem flared up, I have to say that I don't miss it. I never even think about it. I never find myself at any stage of the day thinking, 'Cor, I couldn't half do with a drink!' I've revitalised my whole life, because my knee was debilitating, the drink was a way of easing that debilitation, and the drink is itself debilitating. You're on an ever-downward spiral. You think, 'Stop the spiral! I have to get off!' The only way to get off is for something extreme to happen, and in my case it was the operation. After that, it was totally mind over matter. It was a question of telling myself, 'From here on in, pal, don't let yourself down, don't let Weeber down, don't let the PFA down and don't let Carol down. In fact, don't let anybody down!' So, just by putting my mind to work, it never entertains the idea of drink at all. Even now, six years on from the time I gave up drinking, I see that people are a little embarrassed if they are with me at functions and they have a drink in their hands. When they ask me if they can get me a drink, the enquiry always has a double question mark at the end of it. I have to assure them that seeing them drinking is not a problem for me at all, and when somebody is ordering a round I simply ask for my usual tipple these days, a lime and soda.

One thing I must say is that when, after the operation, I did the remedial exercises, I found it gave me a new lease of life. I was never of a violent nature, but it certainly restored a calm in me I had not known for a long time. The exercises also got my muscles working again. In fact, I've got better muscles in my legs now than I had ten or fifteen years ago. I worked so hard on the remedials that when I went back to see Mr Weeber three months after the operation, he passed me A1. He also asked me how I was generally. 'Oh,' I said, 'it's such a relief. For one thing, I'm not having to think about the stairs that I have to face for the day, or where I'm going to park my car to avoid cobblestones and things like that. What is more, before doing something, I'm not constantly reaching for the bottle.'

It was during that consultation that Mr Weeber told me more about the operation, which had been filmed by Tyne Tees Television. What had happened was that, a few days before going under the knife, I'd been talking to a guy from Tyne Tees and he'd been absolutely fascinated by what I'd been told about the mechanics of it, so he'd got permission from Weeber to film the whole process. It was shown on the Mike Neville programme up in the north-east with a warning: anybody with a queasy disposition shouldn't watch for the next couple of minutes. No wonder. 'Oh, you've got hard bones!' Weeber told me. 'Bloody hell, you've got hard bones! Let me tell you, I'd opened up your knee, moved your kneecap out of the way and got the saw working. I was cutting away on the bone when the bloody saw broke. The blade pinged out of it and stuck itself in the ceiling! It was embedded in the ceiling with smoke coming off it! That bloody saw cost me over £10,000, and the bloody blades are breaking on me! So I had to put a new blade in it and had to shift the bloody camera out of the way because he was right in your knee joint with the bloody thing! When I started again, that blade broke, too. So now I've got two blades, both smoking, in my ceiling! Then I've looked over my shoulder and seen the sound man starting to keel over. "Oh, no," I thought, "a bloody fainter. That's all I need!" When the guy crashed to the floor, I just told them to leave him there. Hazard of the job! Finally, I got your knee/knuckle out and the other one in. And there it is – all on film.' And he proudly showed me the video of the operation Tyne Tees had sent him.

I shall always be as grateful to the PFA as I am to Mr Weeber for sorting out my knee. The players' union paid for the whole lot, including the remedials, and it cost them well in excess of £12,000. Many people were aware of how acute my problem was, but only the PFA sought to do something about it. Football's ruling bodies would have the general public believe that the PFA are a lot of greedy toe-rags because of the way they stuck to their guns during the last TV rights negotiations and held out for what was claimed to be an inordinate sum of money as their percentage. I think it was £25 million, when the whole deal was worth in excess of a billion. It was a bit rich when you think of all the money wasted by football's administrators over recent years. The PFA, on the other hand, use every penny to help all the ex-pros who find themselves incapacitated because of injuries sustained during their playing days to attain a reasonable living standard. I know I am one of many ex-pros who will be eternally grateful to the PFA for their kindness and generosity. I also know that, if there's another problem, all I have to do is pick up the phone and speak to them again.

Nor is it only ex-players they assist. They are the only people who will step in and seek to help clubs who are about to go to the wall. But nobody ever says thank you to them; instead, they are demeaned by all the other football bodies. Some people can't wait to castigate Gordon Taylor for the salary he's on, but he's worth every penny he earns. He's built the PFA up from being a one-man band, which was what it was when dear old Cliff Lloyd took on the powers-that-be, and turned it into a major professional outfit. He's given weight and substance to the union. Things don't happen now in football without the PFA being involved.

Having got back on my feet physically, psychologically and emotionally six years ago, I managed to do the same thing professionally about three years later. That happened when Capital Radio bought out the Century Group, and the north-east's commercial radio station became Century FM. The new managing director, Nick Davison, who is now managing director of the whole group, felt he had to bring a 'wow' factor to the station and took soundings from the profession locally. Time and again, he reported subsequently, two names were thrown at him: Mike Elliott, the guy who reintroduced me to Carol, and mine. So he brought us both back in.

Mike has since left Century FM to work for a competitor in the north-east, but I'm still there. I work on a phone-in programme called *The Three Legends* with Eric Gates, the former Sunderland and Ipswich striker, and Bernie Slaven, the extrovert Scottish forward who became an idol at Middlesbrough. It has been a great success because the chemistry between us is just right – and, of course, the three of us represent the north-east's major professional football clubs. What we're particularly proud of is that the programme is not just a place for serious football talk, it has become a recognised comedy show as well. In fact, we are congratulated more for our banter than we are for our football chat! It's gone from being a one-hour programme to a two-hour programme between six and eight every weekday evening, and the ratings have just soared. They are now better than those of the

Breakfast Show when that first started. The Breakfast Show has also improved its ratings, so that remains the number one programme – which is the case with every radio station – but we are still seeking to catch it up, and we won't rest until we have! There's plenty of time to do it because the three of us have just signed new contracts with the station for another few years.

I also work for Century FM at every one of Newcastle's home games, and even at one or two of their away fixtures. I went down to Fulham and West Brom during 2002/03, for instance. Then there is my weekly column in the *Newcastle Evening Chronicle*, which I do with my old mate John Gibson. This is the third time around for me, because I first did it when I was a player with Newcastle and was contracted to do it again while I was over in Italy. Invariably, I get a full page to air my views about football in general and the north-east in particular.

So, with a lot of after-dinner speaking as well, I live a pretty full and contented life now. My happiness was completed when Carol and I got married two years ago. Ironically, the marriage took place at the Fisherman's Lodge, the out-of-the-way restaurant where the Newcastle board had tried so hard to stitch me up over the Mirandinha transfer fourteen years earlier. The ceremony took place in the middle of June, but it absolutely chucked it down all day. All the wedding photographs were taken under a big Century FM umbrella, but we didn't give a damn. We had family and some special friends with us, and we just had a really super day.

Carol and I haven't looked back since. I earn a good living now and things are going well, but we lead a relatively simple life. People might imagine that we're out, gadding about here, there and everywhere, but nothing could be further from the truth. We have a nice house in the Co. Durham countryside and we just like to close the front door and leave the world behind. Our only companion is our dog, Ferdi. He's a little black terrier – a Patterdale, we think – who had been ill treated by his previous owners and was about to be put down until we took a liking to him. Now, the three of us are inseparable. Ferdi was certainly a huge boost to my recuperation after the operation in that he became my reason to get out and walk and walk without counting the miles. Within a matter of months, I was walking as near to normal as I ever had.

As for my past life, it is true that I was involved with Nicky, who became my second wife, before I left my first wife, Julie. Nicky wasn't the reason for the split, however, although that will never be accepted, so there's no point in my even discussing it. From one side it will always be that another woman broke up the relationship, but I know it was pretty much over and done with anyway. There's no point in discussing it in a book like this, I feel, because it's very much a one-sided conversation that opens itself up to opposing thoughts, feelings and memories. There's little doubt, though, that the pressures of life as a football manager had something to do with the breakdown of my first marriage. At Fulham, I was travelling anything up to six hours a day and working twelve-hour days. As for the other circumstances, I'm loath to get others involved out of respect for them. However this book was written, it would never be satisfactory to all the people who have been involved in my life. At times I have taken decisions from a selfish point of view. I gave my first marriage a long time, but there came a stage where I found myself saying, 'Enough is enough!' You find yourself in situations sometimes where a decision has to be made, and you have to make it selfishly. You'll never be right for being wrong, but you've got to make it.

I do admit, though, that it was an enormous emotional wrench to leave the five daughters, Claire, Jeanette, Louise, Emily and Lindsay, from my first marriage. Once the press got hold of the story, they made it doubly difficult – no, ten times more difficult. There was so much pressure from outside, you couldn't see the true picture for the cameras and notebooks. (Incidentally, I was told afterwards that the newspapers focused on my marriage split only after Terry Venables, who had broken up with his first wife, had given them the slip and gone to Barcelona.) But time got that sorted out to some extent, and I am in contact with all my daughters. To a degree, there is an understanding between them and me over the matter, but there will never be total understanding. The girls are grown up now with marriages and families of their own, and I would never dream of poking my nose into their affairs. They've got to get on with their own lives. If they ask me for a comment, I'll make it; if they don't ask me, I won't make it. It's their turn now, and good luck to them!

I also have a thirteen-year-old son, Matthew, from my second marriage and a ten-year-old daughter, Giorgia, from a relationship I had with an Italian lady called Vania while I lived in Milan. It was one of those things. Vania and I gave it a go, but it was not to be. At least something beautiful, Giorgia, was produced by what became a difficult relationship. These days, though, Vania and I have a very amicable relationship for Giorgia's sake. I see Matthew quite a lot, too. He often comes up to the north-east to stay with me and Carol. In fact, he has met, talked to and been charmed by Sir Bobby Robson.

Overall, I suppose, my life might be viewed more as a saga of hardships and unhappiness than as a tale of glamour and success, although there has been a fair amount of the latter, but I just see it as a number of challenges that had to be overcome. I know people get upset when life doesn't run smoothly, but I am philosophical enough to know that life is not there to run smoothly, that you just have to deal with things as they come along. Some you can deal with immediately, others take a lot longer, but in the long run you have to face everything with common sense. That's my advice, for what it's worth.

# EPILOGUE
# PAST, PRESENT
# AND FUTURE

I have my own little vision of football's not too distant future. I can see a beefed-up version of today's G14 group of clubs – a G20, if you like – getting themselves organised into a world league and buying an island somewhere. On it, they will build a couple of enclosed, air-conditioned arenas and twenty separate complexes. The complexes will be where the players of each club live and train, and the two arenas where the matches between them are staged. There will be no spectators, but the games will be televised around the world with crowd noise dubbed on to provide some atmosphere, just as they put a laughter track on comedy shows nowadays. And they will make a fortune, an absolute fortune. The league would comprise the likes of Santos, Real Madrid, River Plate, AC Milan, Bayern Munich, Ajax Amsterdam and Manchester United – the sort of clubs that could guarantee a worldwide television audience of a hundred million or so. In fact, that would be a condition of entry to this, the ultimate super league. That is what it'll come down to in the end, I'm sure, because the game is already beginning to move in that direction.

Over the past decade, Rupert Murdoch's Sky Television has revolutionised football in this country. Without any shadow of a doubt, the dramatic changes we have seen in players' salaries, the huge influx of top-class foreign footballers and the drift away from the traditional Saturday-afternoon programme are mainly down to him and the billions of pounds he has poured into the game. It has not been all one-way traffic, of course. He launched satellite television here on the back of Premiership football. How true it is, I don't know, but I understand that prior to Sky's launch in this country Murdoch was losing £50 million a day. It's all being reaped back now, though. If you want to see the best sides in the country play live, you have to have access to Sky, either in your house or in the pub. It's as simple as that. As a result, the television station has become a major player in all areas around the world, to the point where the likes of ITV and BBC just can't compete with them. And when they try, they go down the pan, as we saw with ITV Digital.

In staging his revolution, Murdoch has also shown the top clubs the way forward – you milk everything to the nth degree. When you think back to the time when I was playing, and, indeed, long afterwards, there was no sponsorship on shirts or around grounds because the BBC and ITV, the only television stations covering football then, didn't want it for one reason or another. That kind of thinking was financial suicide for the game, of course. English football had these events that could generate worldwide television audiences in excess of a hundred million, yet they refused – or were unable – to cash in on it until Sky came along. What Murdoch has done is shaken the apathy out of football and injected the life into it.

But Sky's domination is unlikely to continue indefinitely. Why do you think so many of our leading clubs are setting up their own television stations and seeking to extend their fan base in places like China and the USA? It's because, at some point, the higher echelons of the game will seek to break with Murdoch. Everybody in the game thinks that the internet and digital television, put together, are going to be the way forward. The intention, clearly, is for clubs to be able to broadcast their own games worldwide, via satellite and pay-per-view. Of course, this will lead to the rich getting richer. Where are the audiences going to flock? They are going to flock to see Manchester

United, Arsenal, Newcastle United, Liverpool, Chelsea and, maybe, Tottenham. And when you talk of getting richer, you are talking figures containing many, many noughts. That way, clubs can make much more money than they could from Sky and still have control over their own destinies. At that point, they may even start to usurp the authority of ruling bodies such as the Football Association and the Premier League. Then the clubs will start to pull the strings and set about establishing European and worldwide super leagues. What will also happen, once they start broadcasting on the internet, is that we can forget altogether about the traditional three o'clock kick-off on a Saturday afternoon. Every game will start at a different time over the weekend.

While we are waiting for Armageddon, I should like to pay tribute to the fantastic job Sir Bobby Robson has done at Newcastle United since he took over from Ruud Gullit in 1999. It was a crucial decision the Newcastle board had to make, having twice got it wrong with Kenny Dalglish and Gullit, and they got it absolutely right at the third time of asking, following the shock departure of the club's other 'messiah', Kevin Keegan. The city of Newcastle was absolutely galvanised by Bobby's appointment. Although, coming from Langley Park, he is not strictly a Geordie, he's as near as dammit to being one, and the fans welcomed him as such. He never played for Newcastle, but he had an instinctive understanding of what the club's supporters wanted from their team. Keegan, having played for Newcastle, knew it as well, whereas Dalglish and Gullit did not.

What Kevin achieved in the 1990s – taking Newcastle from the depths of the Second Division and transforming them into Premiership title contenders in the space of a few seasons – was little short of a miracle. And it was exactly the type of miracle Newcastle fans wanted, in that it came with exciting, exhilarating football. I think perhaps they would be happier to see the club finish second in the table playing attacking football than to watch them win the title with dull, dour stuff.

All of this put enormous pressure on Bobby, but he just took it and all the media interest in his stride. He was my first League manager, of course, and what I've watched him do is not dissimilar to what he tried to do at Fulham some 35 years ago. It was to get rid of the old guard, create a young side and let it develop under the guidance of the right influences within the team. And by right influences, I mean the Alan Shearer type of player.

Clearly, Bobby has forged a huge relationship with Shearer. You don't go making an enemy of your leading scorer – as Gullit did with Alan, and Gordon Lee did with me – and Bobby was far too sensible to fall into that trap. What he has done is put a lot of young legs around Shearer to do the running, and just asked Alan to make full use of his experience by holding the ball up, bringing others into the play and scoring whenever the opportunity presents itself. Basically, Bobby has given Shearer a situation where he can stay number one hero for as long as his body can keep him going. Mentally, he has got to that stage in a player's career where the pitch is twice the size it used to be, the defender a yard away isn't the problem he once was, and you feel you have twenty feet of space to spare.

Alan is the striker I most admire currently, but he took umbrage, I think, when I criticised him for the way he was playing during Kenny Dalglish's period in charge of the club. I'm one of those people who has to speak his mind, I'm afraid, and I felt he wasn't the player he'd once been. In fairness, Alan was getting little support from Andreas Andersson – the Swedish striker I suspect Dalglish, like AC Milan before him, might have mistaken for Kennet Andersson in the transfer market – and he could have been struggling with his knee injury as well. Essentially, though, I think Alan Shearer is a phenomenon. He is very clever, hugely intelligent when it comes to the game of football, and has adapted his play brilliantly to take account of his limitations. It is something a lot of people have got to learn, but Shearer knows implicitly what his limitations are. He plays purely and simply to his strengths, and he makes those strengths unbeatable. Basically, he is an all-round target man playing with his back to goal. Every midfield player would love him, I should imagine, because he always presents himself as a stationary target for their passes and acts as a sort of pinball machine, if you like. Having received the ball and played it off, he gets himself into the area for a scoring opportunity. And when he turns and faces goal, he becomes a different beast entirely, unleashing his killer instinct.

First and foremost, Alan Shearer is a man of exceptional determination – determination to get the very best out of himself, come what may. He will slog himself into the ground to make himself the very best in every way possible. His ball control now is so much better than it was ten years ago, it's untrue. He also writes the book on the tricks of the trade. For instance, he was the striker who introduced to this country the little ploy, as the ball is on its way, of grabbing hold of your marker's shirt and pulling him tight to you. The defender doesn't want to be there because, with the feller up against you, you can sense his balance, or lack of it, and turn him inside out if you want to. Shearer is a nightmare for centre-halves in so many ways. His decision-making is so good, it sticks out like a sore thumb when he does make a mistake – which is very rare.

Using Shearer as a peg to hang the whole thing on, Bobby Robson has put together a Newcastle team for the future. In the last two seasons, I've watched them finish fourth and third, and it's been an exhilarating experience. I know they weren't quite good enough to win the Premiership title, but at least they mounted a challenge. In the last two games of 2002/03, Bobby sent out the youngest teams in Premier League history. One of them was the youngest team he had ever picked during his long and distinguished career. There will be pitfalls ahead, but they will learn more from their mistakes than from getting it right in the first place.

In fact, this Newcastle team puts me in mind of the old advert for Turkish Delight. If that was full of eastern promise, Bobby's side is full of north-eastern promise. I've no doubt whatsoever that, if anyone is going to overtake Manchester United and Arsenal, it will be Newcastle United. What they have to do first, though, is win something. It is essential that the club's first trophy since 1969, when one of Joe Harvey's teams won the Fairs Cup, arrives soon on Tyneside. Bobby wants that so much, it hurts.

There are those who wonder whether, at 70, he has lost the plot because he gets names and places wrong. But he's always done that, throughout his career. Eric Gates played for him for fifteen years at Ipswich, yet he always called him Eric Sykes. Bobby may mistake Jermaine Jenas for Kieron Dyer, and vice versa, when he's talking to them, but he knows exactly who is doing what on the field of play, believe me. Not only that, but Bobby is still as fit as a fiddle. Last season,

I watched him take a training session in which they were practising moves inside one half of the pitch. The starting point for the whole thing, Bobby was running with the ball and pinging it 40 yards in a way I, at 53, could not have managed.

I've known Bobby throughout the whole of his managerial career, and I think he ranks very high in the list of all-time greats. Like no other, he has, time and again, taken each club he's gone to – Ipswich, PSV Eindhoven, Sporting Lisbon, Porto, Barcelona and, now, Newcastle – to European success. What is more, he was dreadfully unfortunate not to have won the World Cup with England in 1990. I thought he put together one hell of a side. I always felt that Bobby was a long-term sort of club manager who would build slowly from a youthful base, and I wasn't sure he'd be able to cope with the England job, where you're not involved on a day-to-day basis. Because that was what he thrived on – day-to-day involvement. For that reason, I thought the England job would be the ruination of him, but he took it on in brilliant style.

In the past three or four years, I have also watched the intriguing growth and development of a chairman, Newcastle's Freddie Shepherd. People in football will remember Freddie for being involved in that unsavoury *News of the World* sting about a Spanish brothel and what have you, but I think he was very unfortunate to be a tainted party in it all. At any rate, he's put that behind him and developed St James's Park into one of the most phenomenal football grounds around. Apart from being a wonderful arena to play in, it is a thriving business with six floors of conference facilities, meeting rooms, restaurants and so on that function 365 days of the year. He has set out a long-term plan that has fallen in line with Bobby Robson's. In fact, here you have a chairman and a manager working in absolute harmonious tandem. Unusually, too, the chairman is the younger man. It will be interesting to see just how far this partnership takes Newcastle United. It is my belief that Bobby engenders such feeling for him in his players that they will demand of themselves that they send this man off happily into retirement at some point in the future knowing that he's won a trophy.

I have to confess to a vested interest here, because it was Freddie Shepherd who enabled me to mend my broken relationship with Newcastle. I've no idea why the club turned against me, but there seemed to be some bad feeling from the time I left to join Arsenal. They probably didn't like the fact that I scored a hat-trick against them for the London club, then helped to tear them apart at St James's. It was almost as if they felt I held some sort of power over them. Whatever the reason, there seemed to be powers-that-be who railed against me, and it was made pretty plain that I wasn't welcome at the club.

I'll give you a couple of examples. On one occasion, when Radio Five Live had asked me to do some commentary for them at a Newcastle v. Chelsea match, I told them I would be interested to see whether they could get me a ticket for the press box. Sure enough, their application was refused on the grounds that the box was full. At the same time, I was approached by a Norwegian TV company to do a fifteen-minute programme on Newcastle's famous number nines. They took a live feed of Newcastle's games and the programme was designed to fill the half-time slot. I agreed to do it, and the Norwegians thought that the ideal location would be the statue of Jackie Milburn that used to stand at the entrance to the ground. The idea was for me to lean against the plinth as I talked about all the club's famous centre-forwards, then the camera would pan upwards to Jackie's face as I finished with a few words about him. 'Fine,' I said, 'but I think there could be a problem. Have you got permission to film there?' They dismissed that query by pointing out that, as they'd paid for the live feed, they automatically had permission to go anywhere they wanted in the ground.

So we walked over to the statue and the cameraman started filming me talking about Hughie Gallacher, Wyn Davies, myself, Kevin Keegan – though he wasn't a number nine, strictly speaking – Alan Shearer and, finally, Jackie Milburn. But I'd only just started, and was doing the hardest bit – about Hughie Gallacher, because he played a long time before I was born – when one of Newcastle's security guys came over and sort of banged the camera back into the cameraman's face. He ordered us to stop filming and told us to get off the property, even though it was all public access there because it was right by the club shop. The Norwegians protested that they were allowed to go anywhere they wanted at St James's Park, but it did no good.

Those two incidents were the final straw for me. The Norwegians asked if that was how my old club normally treated me, and I told them it happened all the time. They found it shocking, and Newcastle United plummeted in their estimation. I was becoming very anti-Newcastle United as a result, and it wasn't until my wife, Carol, suggested that I contact Freddie Shepherd about the problem that the situation began to change. When she was married to her first husband, the lead singer with AC/DC, they had lived for many years in a large house next door to Freddie's. Having built up a strong neighbourly friendship with him, she assured me he wasn't the sort of person who would be antagonistic towards me. Carol felt that he probably didn't even know what was going on, and that the hostility was coming from elsewhere.

But when I did write to him, the reply I got was the noncommittal sort that suggested he had never seen my letter in the first place. I wrote again, and I also got a message to him through a football writer. As a result, Freddie invited me to come and see him. When I listed my complaints about the club's attitude to me, he said, 'Right, I'm going to ask you one question. Do you feel you are treated the same as Bobby Moncur?' When I told him my treatment was quite the opposite, he raised his eyebrows and said, 'Really? Right, thank you very much for coming to see me. What I promise you is that it will change.' And, by heavens, it has. I am welcome at the club now, I do an awful lot for them, and they make use of me as I make use of them, as it were. It's a two-way street, and both parties come out winning. I'm now a great supporter of Newcastle United once again.

Another beneficial result of that meeting with Freddie Shepherd, I think, was the little club called Heroes that he set up. Its members are all Newcastle ex-players; if you are an ex-player, you are a member. I've no doubt some other ex-players were being treated like me, but now there's a camaraderie and it's all very much in support of the club we once played for. I think the greatest benefit of it is that supporters love it. They love to see the club and its ex-players all getting on, because everybody seems to be moving in the same direction, and they feel there's a greater support for the current players to do well.

So I take my hat off to Freddie Shepherd. He could have just gone through the motions, let me walk out the door and then moved on to the next problem. But he didn't, he did something about it, and I admire and respect him for that. Everybody who had found it difficult to talk to me can now talk to me. OK, I'm probably not the easiest person in the world to get on with, but I don't half pull in column inches and television and radio hours. In that sense, I can be a plus or a minus. I am no mouthpiece for the club – I do not stand to gain financially from promoting them in any shape or form, and I would stress that – but I am enjoying so much what they are doing and how it's going. They are giving me an immense amount of satisfaction.

Going back to Alan Shearer briefly, I think he was right to retire from international football when he did. By making that decision, and by bringing on the youngsters around him at Newcastle, he'll probably get two seasons out of himself that he might never had had otherwise. And I think Southampton's James Beattie is the player to replace him in the England team. He's got to keep working to improve his skills, but I think he's a major presence on the field of play wherever the ball is. It's a question of the other players in the side becoming aware of his presence and knowing how to use it, just as they learnt how to use Alan Shearer's presence. Had Beattie been playing for a more fashionable club than Southampton, I'm sure he would have been in the England side more often. He would certainly have got himself in the World Cup squad instead of Emile Heskey. The way Gérard Houllier and Sven-Goran Eriksson have stood by Heskey has amazed me. I am still waiting for somebody to tell me what the big Liverpool striker is really good at. All I know is that he tries hard and puts himself about, but I just see balls bouncing off his knees, in the main. I think there's only been one occasion when he's got into double figures with his scoring. I have nothing against the boy personally, but I can gauge a forward's qualities and there is a totally wrong message being sent out there.

Nor, I have to say, am I a great admirer of Heskey's Liverpool team-mate Michael Owen. Owen is a very good finisher, without question, but I think he has got to the stage now where he does what he does, and he's not going to enlarge on that. Michael has never improved his game by getting involved in the game further than ten yards from the opposing penalty area. You rarely see him showing himself on the halfway line for a full-back to knock the ball to him, as Wayne Rooney would do and Alan Shearer has always done. Rooney will be a long-standing success, I am sure, but not as a partner for Michael Owen. I think he will replace him in the England team.

I see Rooney and Beattie as England's attacking partnership of the future. If you watch Rooney, he much prefers to go left, so that he's coming in on to his right foot. Then watch Beattie, and you'll see that he much prefers to go right. The simple fact that they naturally split in opposite directions makes them an ideal pairing. People may laugh, but I think Beattie, potentially, is the nearest we have to a centre-forward like Real Madrid's Raul. He's got a lot of work to do over the next three or four years to get up to that level, but he has a presence on the field, makes himself available and doesn't just come to life when the ball is within ten yards of the penalty area. As for Rooney, the potential in the lad is truly astonishing. At seventeen, he seems to have grown very early into his adult shape by comparison to most players. Most get the body a couple of years before they get the body strength, but it's all come at once for Wayne. He certainly has a very acute eye for goal, too.

In fact, of all today's strikers he's the one who reminds me most of myself. I see the similarity in pace and physical strength, and, as it was with me, his immediate thought, as soon as he gets the ball, is, 'How can I score from here?' If the route to goal is closed off, then he'll start thinking of some way to get round, and that's exactly how I was. If I got the ball on the halfway line, my first thought was not how many defenders there were between me and the goal, it was how to beat them all and get a shot in. I didn't often lose the ball in that situation, but when you're up front you have the licence to lose it. You don't have that licence in defence or in midfield, but you do – or should do – up front. It is a striker's job to use that licence to create danger. The creation of danger puts doubt into defenders' minds. It makes them very aware of you, your pace, your strength, your power. And, having had fear instilled in their minds, they start to take up false positions, and a whole new set of possibilities is opened up. Get goalside of a defender, make it impossible for him to feel comfortable – that's what I used to do, and that's what Wayne Rooney does.

I envy him only one thing: the change in the offside law. Had it been possible, in my day, to be level with the last defender and still be onside, I have no doubt that Alec Stock would not have given me a target of 30 goals a season, it would have been more like 40. Now there's a thought.

# INDEX

# INDEX

## PHOTOGRAPHIC ACKNOWLDEGMENTS

*Plate section one*: Empics – page 2 bottom left: 4 top and bottom right, 6 bottom,
8 bottom; author's private collection – page 1, 3 top.
*Plate section two*: Empics – page 1 bottom, 2 top and bottom,
4 bottom; The People/Andrew Stenning – page 6 bottom left; Sporting Pictures –
page 7 top left; Daily Mirror – page 7 top right; Pro Pix/Tom Buist – page 8 top.

The Publishers have made every effort to find the source of all the photographs used
in this book. Please contact the Publishers if your picture has been used uncredited.